Stephen Crane, Journalism,

and the

Making of Modern American Literature

Stephen Crane, Journalism,

and the

Making of Modern American Literature

MICHAEL ROBERTSON

Columbia University Press • New York

Columbia University Press
Publishers Since 1893

New York   Chichester, West Sussex
Copyright © 1997 Michael Robertson

Library of Congress Cataloging-in-Publication Data
Robertson, Michael.
    Stephen Crane, journalism, and the making of modern American literature
    / Michael Robertson.
        p. cm.
    Includes index.
    ISBN 0–231–10968–7 (cloth). — ISBN 0–231–10969–5 (alk. paper)
    1. Crane, Stephen, 1871–1900—Knowledge—Communication.
    2. Journalism and literature—United States—History—19th century.
    3. Journalism and literature—United States—History—20th century.
    4. American literature—20th century—History and criticism.
    5. Crane, Stephen, 1871–1900—Influence. I. Title.
    PS1449.C85Z822 1997
    813'.4—dc21   97–15068
                                                              CIP

Casebound editions of Columbia University Press books
are printed on permanent and durable acid-free paper.
Printed in the United States of America
c 10 9 8 7 6 5 4 3 2 1
p 10 9 8 7 6 5 4 3 2 1

CONTENTS

ACKNOWLEDGMENTS

Over the years I have read many acknowledgments sections that use some variation of the phrase, "This book is the result of a collaborative effort." But it was not until I began this study that I realized how truly a collaboration any scholarly work is.

It is a collaboration, first of all, with scholars who have worked in the field previously. The introduction and my notes give some indication of how often I have relied on others' research and insights. However, the work of a few writers, not mentioned in the introduction, has been so critical in shaping my thinking that I want to acknowledge them here. In a variety of ways, I have been inspired by the work of Richard Brodhead, Philip Fisher, John Kasson, Lawrence Levine, Michael Schudson, Alan Trachtenberg, and Allon White.

I also owe a large debt to two institutions. A National Endowment for the Humanities Fellowship gave me the time to begin writing this book. Two FIRSL grants from The College of New Jersey enabled me to finish it.

Another institution, the American Journalism Historians Association, has been important to me in writing this book. I have not been a particularly good member of the AJHA—I'm probably behind in my dues right now—but the people I met through the organization came to represent my ideal readers: smart and sophisticated former journalists who are curious about my topic and impatient with jargon. I first tried out material from this study at an AJHA convention, and the AJHA's journal, *American Journalism*, published an early version of chapter 3. "Stephen Crane's New York City Journalism and the Oft-Told Tale" appeared in volume 9 (Winter–Spring 1992) and is used by permission. My thanks to John Pauly, from whom I learned much in his roles as both editor and scholar.

I received much help from many people at the libraries of The College of New Jersey, Columbia University, Princeton University, Syracuse University, and the New York Public Library. Special thanks to Diane Shaw at Lafayette College.

If I were to thank adequately all the friends and colleagues who have offered me encouragement and support over the years I have been writing, this acknowledgments section would become my longest chapter. Those who helped directly with researching, writing, and publishing include James Colvert, Emory Elliott, William Howarth, Lee Mitchell, Susan Osborn, Richard Preston, Melinda Roberts, and James West.

Michelle Parham Preston and Deborah Rosen played a major role in the writing of this book, reading early drafts of every chapter and kindly but firmly nudging me in the right direction. Kim Pearson and Donald Vanouse provided valuable comments on chapters. Shelley Fisher Fishkin and Lincoln Konkle generously commented on the completed manuscript. I also want to thank Thomas Connery and Paul Sorrentino, the readers for Columbia University Press, who offered a wealth of perceptive suggestions. Ann Miller at Columbia University Press has been a superbly helpful editor. Polly Kummel was the best copy editor I can imagine.

During the years I worked on this project, I have been blessed not only with generous friends and colleagues but with an equally generous family. My parents, Nancy Robertson and the late Leslie Robertson, were unfailingly supportive. My mother-in-law, Mildred Ladner Thompson, has been a model of a productive writer. Miranda Robertson has taken a keen, precocious interest in this project.

I have not included a dedication to this book because it doesn't seem mine to dedicate; it belongs at least as much to Stephen Crane and the scholars who preceded me as it does to me. But the writing of this book, like everything else I do, has been grounded in the love offered, so unstintingly, by Mary Pat Robertson.

Stephen Crane, Journalism,

and the

Making of Modern American Literature

INTRODUCTION

This book had its origins in my studies for my doctoral exams in American literature. Reading vast amounts of literature in a short time—Michael Wigglesworth cheek by jowl with William Faulkner, Toni Morrison one day and James Fenimore Cooper the next—one discovers new patterns, unexpected continuities. But I was particularly struck by a discontinuity that I encountered. As a former freelance journalist, I was alert to any mention of journalism in the novels and biographies I was reading, and in the course of my studies I kept encountering wildly contradictory references to journalism within a relatively brief period, from the 1880s to the 1920s.

On the one hand, reading novels of the 1880s, I found an unmistakable hostility toward journalism in works by William Dean Howells and Henry James. Howells's *A Modern Instance* (1882), for example, features a newspaper reporter as its central character—a weak, morally obtuse man whose writing functions as a countertext to the novel. The reporter's articles, as described by Howells, cover the same events that are narrated in the novel but take an exploitative, condescending view of their subjects. The articles are marked, in Howells's phrase, by an "essential cheapness."[1] Henry James's portrayal of journalists is even harsher than Howells's. In *The Bostonians* (1886), for instance, reporter Matthias Pardon is an odious character, a silly but dangerous man with no conception of privacy, who sees all of life—or, rather, all of other people's lives—as items to be printed in the newspaper.

On the other hand, Ernest Hemingway and Theodore Dreiser, both of whom began their careers as reporters, seemed to embrace journalism in their fiction, deliberately blurring the lines between the newspaper and the novel. Dreiser's *An American Tragedy* (1925), which is based on an actual murder case, calls attention to its newspaper origins. The name of protagonist Clyde Griffiths mimics that of the real-life Chester Gillette, and Dreiser incorporates in his novel large chunks from newspaper articles on the case, quoting verbatim from courtroom testimony and from the murdered woman's letters to her lover. Hemingway took similar delight throughout his career in blending journalistic and fictional discourses. For example, his first book of fiction, the Paris edition of *in our time* (1924), includes adaptations of some of Hemingway's newspaper dispatches.

The varying attitudes toward journalism displayed by novelists such as Howells, James, Dreiser, and Hemingway can be seen as part of the complex, evolving relationship between "high" and "low" realms of cultural production in the United States during the late nineteenth and early twentieth centuries. Whereas Dreiser and Hemingway set out to blur the boundaries between literature and journalism, Howells and James wished to sacralize the serious novel, establishing its superior position within a cultural hierarchy in which the newspaper was located firmly near the bottom.[2] The task seemed urgent to them because of the radical changes in both literature and journalism during the previous fifty years.

Early in the nineteenth century, journalism posed little threat to literature. The typical daily newspaper of the era was a four-page journal, sold only by subscription and aimed at a relatively small and almost exclusively male audience interested in business and politics. Newspapers existed to give financial and mercantile information and to promote the viewpoint of a political party or faction. Typically, two of a newspaper's four pages were devoted to business advertising, such as shipping notices and advertisements for wholesale goods and real estate. The news pages were filled with transcripts of the proceedings of national, state, and local government; editorials; and a miscellany of brief items reprinted from other newspapers. Even metropolitan dailies were produced by a staff consisting of the editor and one or two assistants.[3] The most popular literary forms of the era— poetry, romances, and domestic fiction—had little connection, in either form or subject matter, with the era's journalism.

The political-mercantile model of journalism was first challenged in New York City during the 1830s with the establishment of the mass-circulation "penny press." These newspapers, hawked in the streets for one cent, were aimed at a broad audience, including women and the working class. The penny press redefined the news. Broadening their attention beyond business and politics, the penny papers made room for "human interest" articles that covered everyday metropolitan life. The most successful of the penny papers, James Gordon Bennett's *New York Herald*, climbed toward a circulation of seventy-seven thousand during the 1850s (compared to an average circulation of twelve hundred for New York's traditional dailies in the 1830s) and employed a staff of twenty-four.[4]

During the years preceding the Civil War the penny press and the political-mercantile papers coexisted. After the war the mass-circulation press soon dominated. It became known as the "new journalism"—predating Tom Wolfe's use of the term by a century. Joseph Pulitzer's *New York World*, the most dazzling example of the new journalism, reached more than a quarter million readers in the 1880s and employed dozens of reporters.[5] At the same time, the literary movement known as "realism" gained ground in the United States.[6] Thanks in part to the tireless proselytizing of William Dean Howells, realist novels, such as those by Howells and his friends Mark Twain and Henry James, became the most prestigious literary form. Thus, just as many of America's most talented writers were turning to what they regarded as the realistic depiction of contemporary life, newspaper reporters were reaching a vast audience with human interest articles that in both form and content closely resembled the new realist fiction. Increasingly, the newspaper and the novel were covering the same terrain.

Howells and James responded with alarm and disdain to the convergence of journalism and fiction. They regarded the new journalism as a threat to literature and the reporter as a threat to the novelist. However, a younger generation of writers, born after the Civil War, came to regard the newspaper as a source of material for literature and reporting as valuable training. Stephen Crane was one of the first in an extraordinary succession of major American writers, from the 1890s to the present, who began their careers as newspaper reporters. The novelists born after 1865 who worked as journalists include not only Stephen Crane, Theodore Dreiser, and Ernest Hemingway but also Richard Harding Davis, Frank Norris, Abraham Cahan, Willa Cather, Katherine Anne Porter, Sinclair Lewis, James M. Cain, John O'Hara, John Steinbeck, Eudora Welty, and William Kennedy, among many others. In this dazzling array of writers none illustrates more clearly than Stephen Crane the shift from an antagonistic to a symbiotic relationship between journalistic and literary careers.

This book focuses on Stephen Crane for a variety of reasons. Aside from Richard Harding Davis, Crane was the first of the post–Civil War reporter-novelists to win fame. His career, along with that of the popular Davis, set a pattern for other writers. H. L. Mencken testified to Crane's influence on an entire generation of young people who learned that the immensely popular and critically esteemed *Red Badge of Courage* had been written by a newspaper reporter: "The miracle lifted newspaper reporting to the level of a romantic craft, alongside counterfeiting and mining in the Klondike."[7] Just as Bob Woodward and Carl Bernstein, the *Washington Post* reporters of Watergate fame, inspired droves of would-be investigative reporters to apply to journalism schools in the 1970s, Crane helped to draw young people with literary ambitions into newspaper work at the turn of the century.

Moreover, Crane did not abandon journalism once he had published a successful novel, as so many writers since have done. He continued to write for newspapers throughout his career. During the few years between the publication of *The Red Badge of Courage* and his early death Crane produced a prodigious amount of journalism: feature articles on New York City, travel journalism, war correspondence, even sports reporting. Borrowing Richard Brodhead's useful term, we can say that for his entire writing life Crane was immersed in the "culture of letters" associated with mass-circulation newspapers.[8]

Part of the attraction of the journalistic culture of letters for a young male artist in the 1890s was its reinforcement of his masculine identity. Exploring the journalistic careers of Willa Cather or Katherine Anne Porter or Eudora Welty would offer a valuable perspective on late nineteenth- and early twentieth-century journalism—and those explorations are ripe to be made—but the experiences of these women writers were atypical. Few women worked for newspapers before World War II, and the meaning of newspaper work for most journalists of the era—including Stephen Crane—was tied to issues of male identity.

Michael Davitt Bell has argued persuasively that a primary function of Howells's program of literary realism was to reassure novelists that they were "real men" in a culture that regarded artists as feminized. Bell sees Crane as less driven by gender anxieties than Howells, but this may be only because Crane was less given to unbuttoned autobiographical musing.[9] Crane sought out homosocial, aggressively masculine pursuits and institutions throughout his life, beginning with his transfer at age sixteen from a Methodist secondary school to a military academy. In college he joined both a fraternity and the baseball team. The world of urban newspaper reporting, which Crane entered after he dropped out of college, was equally masculine. Ben Hecht and Charles MacArthur's *The Front Page* (1928), although written thirty years after Crane's experience, offers a vivid, disturbing portrayal of a big-city reporters' culture marked by male bonding, misogyny, and homophobia. Almost immediately after the publication of *Red Badge* Crane sought a position as a war correspondent; numerous reminiscences of the Spanish-American War show how completely he fit into the intensely masculine, militarized culture of war reporters. During the 1890s Crane's two preferred modes of journalism—urban reporting and war correspondence—could serve an artist as a certificate of authentic masculinity.

Most Crane critics have viewed his journalism largely as an adjunct to his fiction.[10] I argue that much of his newspaper writing deserves to be studied on its own as literary journalism. Crane fits into a rich tradition of American literary journalism, stretching from Mark Twain to Michael Herr.[11] Critics who have dismissed Crane's journalism as dealing with "bare facts" have misread both his career and 1890s journalism.[12] Except during his teenage years, Crane seldom worked as a conventional reporter. He was a freelance writer of "specials," or feature articles, which formed part of the fact-fiction discourse of 1890s journalism.

I have adapted the term "fact-fiction discourse" from Lennard Davis, who traces the origins of the English novel to what he calls a "news/novels discourse" that existed in England from the late sixteenth to the early eighteenth centuries. During this era before the appearance of either newspapers or novels, printed ballads served as a source of both news and entertainment.[13] Davis argues that readers of the era knew perfectly well the distinction between facts and fiction, but they were relatively unconcerned with making those distinctions in their reading material. Readers' acceptance of textual ambiguity provided a hospitable discursive ground for some writers of genius in the eighteenth century—among them Daniel Defoe, Samuel Richardson, and Henry Fielding—who produced a new genre of text, the novel, that proved vastly entertaining while also insisting on its truthfulness.

The new journalism of the late nineteenth century proved similarly hospitable for Stephen Crane, providing a discursive terrain that was as fruitfully ambiguous in genre and truth status as the news/novels discourse of two hundred years earlier. Before the Civil War political and financial news dominated U.S. newspapers. During the 1920s the ideology of objectivity gained a stranglehold on American journalism.[14] In between, during the era of Joseph Pulitzer's new journalism, a fact-fiction discourse existed in much of U.S. journalism. Newspapers of the 1890s—particularly the Sunday editions in which Crane published most of his writing—indiscriminately mixed news, fiction, and feature articles that had an indeterminate truth status. The strict departmentalization of contemporary newspapers—which places news, opinion, and feature articles in separate sections—was much less rigid in the nineteenth century. A single newspaper page in the 1890s might include an article on Washington politics that was clearly factual, a serial installment of a clearly fictional novel, and several sketches of the urban scene that might, or might not, prove to be verifiable.

Modern readers' unfamiliarity with the fact-fiction discourse of late nineteenth-century journalism and our rigid generic categorizations have distorted our readings of many of Crane's works. Some superb pieces have been classified as journalism and ignored by most students of American literature. In the pages that follow I try to retrieve these works from the generic basement to which they have been relegated and offer them for renewed inspection. Alternatively, some works solidly in the Crane canon, such as "An Experiment in Misery" and "The Open Boat," have been removed from their journalistic context and treated as fiction; I re-situate these texts in the fact-fiction discourse and examine how they functioned when they originally appeared.

Although my chapters on Crane read his journalism closely, this book as a whole is a work of literary history that narrates the change from Howells's and James's hostility toward journalism to Dreiser's and Hemingway's embrace of it. As my title suggests, this narrative is crucial for understanding modern American literature. I do not want to imply that it is *the* story of the making of modern literature, but it is one thread in a complex tapestry.

In writing this study I have benefited greatly from previous works on turn-of-the-century journalism and literature. In the 1960s Ellen Moers and Larzer Ziff published books containing groundbreaking discussions of 1890s journalism and literature. More recently, Christopher Wilson, Amy Kaplan, and Thomas Strychacz have written extremely perceptive, sophis-

ticated analyses that broadly consider the relationship among professionalism, the mass media, and literature in the late nineteenth and early twentieth centuries.[15]

In addition, two recent books analyze at length the interaction of journalism and literature in the United States. Shelley Fisher Fishkin's *From
Fact to Fiction: Journalism and Imaginative Writing in America* offers
detailed analyses of five major writers who began their careers as journalists: Walt Whitman, Mark Twain, Theodore Dreiser, Ernest Hemingway,
and John Dos Passos.[16] She argues that each began his career by writing
journalism along with uninspired poetry or fiction and achieved success
only when he fused the reporter's realistic observation with the poet's
imaginative vision and linguistic daring. Although my work builds on
Fishkin's, it differs in three major ways. First, I regard Stephen Crane,
whose career does not fit Fishkin's paradigm, as a crucial figure in the study
of journalism and imaginative writing in the United States. Next, I am less
willing than Fishkin to draw sharp generic distinctions between fact and
fiction. It was Crane's immersion in the ambiguous fact-fiction discourse
of 1890s journalism that gives his work much of its power, I argue. Finally,
my study differs from Fishkin's in the attention given to historical change.
Fishkin sees the same journalism-fiction dynamic operating in the careers
of all the writers she treats, from Walt Whitman in the early nineteenth
century to John Dos Passos in the early twentieth. I argue that the years
between 1880 and 1925 were a crucial transition period during which
journalism, fiction, and literary careers changed decisively.

The second work, Phyllis Frus's *Politics and Poetics of Journalistic
Narrative*, rejects the premises on which Fishkin and most of the other
critics I have mentioned base their work. Frus argues against "the usual
view . . . that realism in fiction . . . developed out of the major realists'
experience as journalists," and she refuses terms that have proved indis-
pensable to others, such as "literature," "journalism," and "literary nonfiction." Frus wishes to "collapse all discourse back into one category."[17]
Although I have not followed Frus's deconstructive methodology, I am in
sympathy with her challenge to conventional generic classifications. Frus's
poststructuralist analysis and my historical approach lead to similar conclusions: contemporary distinctions between literature and journalism
obscure as much as they reveal. Stripping away generic preconceptions
offers new insights into work by Crane and other reporter-novelists.

This book begins by exploring the relation between journalism and fiction in the work of two writers a generation older than Crane, whose careers overlapped his and who served, to varying degrees, as his mentors. Chapter 1 opens with biographical accounts of the journalistic experiences of William Dean Howells and Henry James. Early in their careers both writers had brief and disastrous stints as reporters for metropolitan newspapers. Both made use of these experiences in their fiction, depicting journalism as a vulgar threat to literature and reporters as rivals of novelists. I view Howells's and James's hostility to the new journalism of the era as a response not only to their journalistic experiences but, more broadly, to the dramatic changes in the late nineteenth-century literary marketplace, the rise of commercial mass culture, and the attendant anxieties of Gilded Age authorship.

Chapter 2 examines Stephen Crane's precociously stylish early journalism, written before he was twenty-one. These early pieces—reports from New Jersey shore resorts and sketches about rural Sullivan County, New York—reveal how Crane flourished within the fact-fiction discourse of 1890s journalism. They also show Crane developing the pervasive irony that would be a hallmark of his work, and they reveal the metafictional concerns with narrative conventions that have made Crane a popular subject of postmodern critics.

Chapter 3 examines Crane's New York City journalism. Between 1892 and 1896 Crane wrote two dozen feature articles on New York City street life, articles that still maintain their power to shock with their vivid depictions of poverty, violence, and crime. Although Crane's novel *Maggie* (1893) remains the best known of his works about New York, much of his newspaper journalism is as powerful and subversive as his more famous novel.

Chapter 4 explores Crane's travel writing. Crane first tried to wrangle an assignment to write travel journalism when he was twenty years old. He finally succeeded in 1895, and during the next two years he wrote pieces from Mexico and the American West, England and Ireland, and Florida. Examining Crane's travel journalism reveals the brilliance of some previously neglected pieces and throws new light on such celebrated works as "The Blue Hotel," "The Bride Comes to Yellow Sky," and "The Open Boat."

Chapter 5 covers Crane's extensive war correspondence and examines his changing attitudes toward war, the soldier, and the representation of battle. When *The Red Badge of Courage* was published in 1895, its twenty-three-year-old author had never seen battle. Almost immediately upon its appearance Crane began casting about for ways to make up for that lack. After covering the brief Greco-Turkish War of 1897 Crane rushed eagerly into the Spanish-American War of 1898. He spent eight months in the Caribbean covering the war and its aftermath, gained a reputation as the best of the war's correspondents, and produced work that rivals—and challenges—*The Red Badge of Courage.*

The final chapter discusses two authors, Theodore Dreiser and Ernest Hemingway, directly influenced by Crane's life and work. I consider how Crane's example shaped their careers and explore the ways in which the two authors' work altered the relation between American journalism and fiction. These two shapers of modern literature brought the newspaper and the novel closer together, with Dreiser claiming the newspaper's most sordid and sensationalistic subject matter as appropriate material for fiction and Hemingway appropriating the terse "objective" style of the modern newspaper for his own ends. Crane, Dreiser, and Hemingway—along with other reporter-artists of the early twentieth century—used journalism and their experience as reporters as crucial elements in the making of a modern American literature.

CHAPTER 1

~~~~~

Journalism as Threat

WILLIAM DEAN HOWELLS AND HENRY JAMES

To understand how Stephen Crane and the reporter-novelists who followed him used newspaper journalism as one element in the making of
modern American literature, we need to know how earlier nineteenth-century writers regarded the newspaper. To be brief: they detested it.

Not all writers, of course, and not throughout the century. Early in the
century, before the advent of the penny press, William Cullen Bryant comfortably filled dual roles as editor of the staid, small-circulation *New York
Evening Post* and as beloved fireside poet. Bryant experienced little conflict
between his duties as editor of a four-page journal intended for New York's
business elite and his production of poetry for the educated classes.
However, the advent of the mass-circulation penny papers in the 1830s
began to alter the relationship between journalism and literature. The
penny press was one of the forms of cultural production that helped to initiate the distinction between elite and mass culture that developed during
the nineteenth century.[1] As early as 1838, only five years after the first
penny newspaper appeared, Ralph Waldo Emerson confided to his journal
his disgust with the penny press. When he learned that the *Boston Globe*
had reached a circulation of thirty thousand, he wrote, "3,000,000 such
people as can read the Globe with any interest are as yet in too crude a state
of nonage to deserve any regard."[2] In a well-known passage in *Walden*
(1854) Henry David Thoreau satirized the triviality of the information
conveyed with great celerity to a widespread audience through the news-

paper: "We are eager to tunnel under the Atlantic and bring the old world some weeks nearer to the new; but perchance the first news that will leak through into the broad, flapping American ear will be that the Princess Adelaide has the whooping cough."[3] In an 1854 speech Thoreau was even blunter. The newspaper is "the only book which America has printed, and which America reads," he said. "The people who read [it] are in the condition of the dog that returns to his vomit."[4]

Emerson and Thoreau, disdainful of the wide readership and sensational style of the penny press, implicitly contrasted the newspaper with their production of complex poetry and densely allusive essays. However, as the most talented U.S. writers turned to prose fiction after the Civil War, the line between low and high culture that had seemed so easily fixed to Emerson and Thoreau became blurred. Elite, small-circulation newspapers like Bryant's *Evening Post* virtually disappeared, replaced by the "new journalism"—the postwar term for a mass-circulation press that appealed across class lines with lively human-interest stories.[5] At the same time, serious novelists were producing realistic fiction about contemporary urban life, thus sharing subject matter with the newspaper.

William Dean Howells and Henry James both reacted with hostility to the convergence of journalism and literature. Howells's *A Modern Instance* (1882), for example, skewers its journalist hero with a vigor that has struck many readers as disproportionate. James's attacks were even more militant. His campaign against journalism began with *The Bostonians* (1886), which features a newspaper reporter who can most kindly be described as an odious snoop; it reached its zenith in a 1905 speech in which James declared newspapers to be a primary threat to American civilization.[6]

Howells's and James's hostility to journalism had its origins in part in personal experience. Early in their careers both writers worked briefly as reporters for mass-circulation metropolitan newspapers. Howells spent one month as city editor and local news reporter for a Cincinnati daily in 1857, when he was twenty. James's first encounter with newspaper journalism came after he decided to settle in Europe in 1875, at age thirty-two, and to supplement his income from fiction writing by producing a biweekly letter from Paris for the *New-York Tribune*. Despite the differences in their working conditions—Howells walked the streets and observed the police courts of a midwestern city, whereas James strolled through the art exhibitions of Paris—both writers' experiences in newspaper journalism ended disastrously. Both would later write pained autobiographical accounts of their work as reporters, still licking their wounds after the passage of decades. And both put their familiarity with newspaper journalism to use in their fiction's acid portrayals of reporters and reporting.

Howells's and James's disdain for journalism reveals as much about the changing status of literature and the attendant anxieties of Gilded Age authors as about the new journalism of the era. Faced with the need to earn a living in the mass marketplace, authors such as Howells and James saw their role as uncomfortably close to that of the hired reporter. In their fictional portrayals of journalists Howells and James frequently cast their criticism in moral and aesthetic terms; however, it is possible to see their works as an attempt to defend literature's privileged status and the author's prestige in an era when both were threatened by mass-circulation journalism's commodification of writing. Understanding Howells's and James's complex reaction to the new journalism of their era throws light on the different responses of the next generation, as revealed in the career of Stephen Crane.

William Dean Howells hated his one month's work as a metropolitan reporter in Cincinnati, an episode all the more distasteful to him because of his boyhood experiences in country journalism. Howells's father was the peripatetic editor of a string of small-town Ohio weekly newspapers, and Howells literally grew up in a newspaper office. "I know when I could not read," he writes in one of his volumes of memoirs, "but I do not know when I could not set type."[7] By age ten Howells's formal education had ended, and he assisted his father full time.

If that life sounds hard, Howells, looking back on his childhood, did not emphasize the difficulties. "The Country Printer," an 1893 essay about one of the family newspapers, is saturated with nostalgia. This autobiographical essay describes the *Ashtabula County Sentinel*, a newspaper that his family took over during the 1850s, when Howells was a teenager. In his essay Howells portrays the *Sentinel* as an integral part of Jefferson, Ohio, the village where the newspaper was published. In Howells's recollection Jefferson appears as a harmoniously democratic town where the conversation of the yeomen who loitered about the printing office alternated between the merits of Shakespeare and the evils of slavery. The Howells family newspaper was as decorous and high-minded as the Ohio villagers and farmers who were its subscribers. As Howells describes it, the newspaper's front page was invariably given over to poetry and fiction. The insides contained more literature, correspondence on Washington politics and New York City art, and editorials dealing with the pressing concerns of sectionalism and slavery. Illustrations, blaring headlines, and sensational accounts of murders and crimes did not appear in the paper.[8] In Howells's account the country newspaper and its office serve as synecdoche for an idyllic antebellum culture—a world of villages and farms where artisans and farmers met on a basis of equality, a time when people spoke with easy familiarity about the works of Poe and Shakespeare and debated the great, morally charged political issues of the day.[9]

Howells left Jefferson when he was nineteen and soon after was invited to serve as city editor and reporter on the *Cincinnati Gazette*. The transition took him from decorous country journalism to the routines of metropolitan reporting in one of the Midwest's largest cities. The change proved devastating to this sensitive young man who aspired to be a lyric poet. Howells had to cover the police courts, an assignment that brought him into daily contact with urban crime and vice. During a single week he reported on wife beatings, assaults, brawls, robberies, confidence schemes, prostitution, an attempted suicide, and a murder.[10] Howells lasted just one month in his new job. In a memoir he mentions two decisive episodes. One involved a man, prominent in the city, who came to the newspaper office late one night to plead with Howells and the other staffers not to print the news of his adulterous affair. Much worse for Howells were the ravings of a drunken woman one night in the police station, where his "abhorred duties took [him] for the detestable news of the place." It was this latter episode that made Howells decide to give up his job. The young literary-minded Howells detested his forced contact with sordid realities, and he gladly left behind the urban journalist's daily encounters with "patrolmen and ward politicians and saloon-keepers."[11]

⁓

Henry James's career as a newspaper journalist began in 1875, when he arrived in Paris for what he intended to be a lengthy settlement. Before his departure from New York James had arranged to send regular correspondence to the *New-York Tribune*. The *Tribune* already had two Parisian correspondents who supplied it with political news; James proposed a miscellaneous letter on manners, habits, people, and art. The *Tribune*, founded as a penny paper in 1841, was regarded as the most prestigious mass-circulation newspaper in the United States in the 1870s. James told his friend John Hay, an editor on the staff, that he regarded the *Tribune* as "the only paper where business could be combined with literary ambition."[12]

Arriving in Paris in mid-November 1875, James sent his first letter to the *Tribune* a few days later. He packed the lengthy piece with a variety of topics: an American's impressions on returning to Paris for a second visit, the decline in tourism, a new play by Alexandre Dumas, the architecture of the new opera house, and a successful Italian actor.[13] The piece promised well for James's journalistic success, yet ten days later he was complaining in a letter to his brother William that he had exhausted the Parisian scene in only one letter. "I can think of nothing in life to put in the *Tribune*," he wrote; "it is quite appalling."[14]

James met the difficulty by devoting his second letter to art criticism, reviewing three exhibitions. From this point on James frequently filled his letters with detailed reviews of art, theater, and books; an alternative was to journey outside Paris and write the sort of descriptive travel essays that he had published at the beginning of his career. All the while he kept up his complaints that he could find little to write about. "Subjects are woefully scarce," he wrote to his mother in January 1876. Three months later he wrote his father that "there has been a painful dearth of topics to write about." James biographer Leon Edel has commented on the peculiarity of these complaints: "We have thus the spectacle of a man of James's large imagination unable to imagine subjects for a newspaper—and in a city teeming with them."[15]

Part of James's difficulty in completing his letters may have been a psychological block resulting from his deep-seated hostility to U.S. newspaper journalism and the burgeoning mass culture of which it was a part. Although he had assured the *Tribune*'s editors that he regarded it as the one outlet suitable for a writer with literary ambitions, he wrote to his father from Paris that "the vulgarity and repulsiveness of the *Tribune*, whenever I see it, strikes me so violently that I feel tempted to stop my letter."[16] Soon after this outburst he evidently decided to assuage his distaste for the *Tribune* by asking editor Whitelaw Reid for a 50 percent increase in his payment for each letter.

The exchange that followed between editor and author is worth quoting extensively. Reid replied to James's request for a raise on August 10, 1876:

Dear Mr. James:

I am in receipt of your favor of the 25th July suggesting an advance of one-half the payment for your letters.

I have been on the point of writing you making a suggestion of a quite different nature. It was to the effect that the letters should be made rather more "newsy" in character, and somewhat shorter, and that they should be sent somewhat less frequently. . . . We have feared that your letters were sometimes on topics too remote from popular interests to please more than a select few of our readers. . . . If you can adopt this suggestion, I think you will agree with me that there would then be less occasion for a change in the rate of payment.

You must not imagine that any of us have failed to appreciate the admirable work you have done for us. The difficulty has sometimes been not that it was too good, but that it was magazine rather than newspaper work.

James replied on August 30:

Dear Mr. Reid:

I have just received your letter of August 10th. I quite appreciate what you say about the character of my letters, and about their not being the right sort of thing for a newspaper. I have been half expecting to hear from you to that effect. . . . But I am afraid I can't assent to your proposal that I should try and write otherwise. I know the sort of letter you mean—it is doubtless the proper sort of thing for the Tribune *to have. But I can't produce it—I don't know how and I couldn't learn how. . . . It would be poor economy for me to try and become "newsy" and gossipy. I am too finical a writer and I should be constantly becoming more "literary" than is desirable. . . . If my letters have been "too good" I am honestly afraid that they are the poorest I can do, especially for the money! I had better, therefore, suspend them altogether.*[17]

James's witty penultimate sentence contains a crucial misreading of Reid's letter. Ignoring Reid's negative, James quotes him as saying that the letters had been "too good" for the newspaper. With this creative misreading James begins the process of constructing a myth about the artist and the newspaper. James would draw upon his letter to Reid and the myth he constructed there numerous times in the years to come, in both his autobiographical writings and his fiction. The myth has both aesthetic and social elements. Aesthetically, James establishes a hierarchy of discourse, with the "literary" firmly fixed above the "newsy." Socially, he constructs a narrative about the artist, his audience, and the marketplace. In the letter's terms the artist is helpless to control his level of discourse; he does not know and cannot learn how to adjust his language in order to descend to the level of the mass audience. Try as he might, he is unable to shake his language loose from the elevated level of the "literary." And the only motive for descending to the popular level is financial. Money may tempt the artist to cheapen his discourse, to make it the poorest he can. But his failure is inevitable. As James was to write in one of his later stories of literary artists, "You can't make a sow's ear out of a silk purse!"[18]

If the hostility to metropolitan journalism that characterizes numerous works by Howells and James from the 1880s on has its origins at least partly in their unhappy experiences as reporters, it is rooted even more firmly in their responses to the dramatic changes in Gilded Age journalism. U.S. newspapers grew explosively between the Civil War and the end of the century. During the 1870s, the decade in which both Howells and James came to artistic maturity, the number of daily newspapers published in the country almost doubled.[19] The rapid increase continued during the remainder of the century. Between 1870 and 1900 the number of daily newspapers multiplied four times, and overall circulation increased six times. Circulation figures for individual papers during the period are just as striking. The *New York World*, which had a circulation of fifteen thousand when Joseph Pulitzer purchased it in 1883, reached nearly one million readers during the late 1890s.[20]

In addition to serving as testament to journalism's growing influence in American culture, the fiction of Howells and James records their recognition that the newspaper and the novel were becoming more alike, whereas the roles of the novelist and the reporter were converging. Their fictions from the 1880s on record their reactions to the new parallels between newspaper and novel, reporter and artist.

The rise of the new journalism after the Civil War meant that human-interest journalism became widespread during the same period that literary realism gained force in the United States. Such overlapping between journalism and fiction was not unknown in the antebellum era. For example, *Uncle Tom's Cabin* (1852) owed its immense popularity to the way it translated newspaper accounts of runaway slaves and congressional debates on slavery into vivid narrative. However, most novelists in the sentimental tradition from which Stowe came dealt with domestic concerns foreign to antebellum journalism. In contrast, postwar literary realists frequently shared both subject matter and technique with the newspaper. For instance, Howells's first novel, *Their Wedding Journey* (1871), grafts a narrative of a newlywed couple onto the form of the journalistic travel sketch, and most of James's early and middle work is firmly grounded in contemporary social reality.

Post–Civil War literary realists like Howells and James faced a situation unknown to antebellum writers: the novel and the newspaper shared both subject matter and narrative technique. At the same time, the institutions of journalism and literature and the roles of reporter and novelist were drawing closer. During the early years of the American republic the distinction between journalism and belles lettres had seemed straightforward. Newspapers were associated with politics and commerce; belles lettres were considered the realm of the gentleman amateur. Historians of the early republican period have pointed out that the conception of the gentleman-author reflected an idealized notion of the European past as much as it referred to contemporary reality; still, even as myth the idea had much power.[21] Moreover, authors who may have wanted to escape the old system—in which writers either wrote for their own pleasure without expecting monetary reward or sought their living from a wealthy patron—were checked by the lack of an adequately developed system of book publishing and marketing.

The role of newspaper reporter was as undeveloped during the antebellum period as the profession of author. Small-town weekly newspapers were essentially one-person operations, produced by an individual who served as writer, editor, and press operator, with the aid of family members and apprentices. On metropolitan dailies the editorial and mechanical functions were separate, but most antebellum dailies, only four pages in length, were put together by a single editor with one or two assistants. Reporting—the sine qua non of modern journalism—had little importance in antebellum journalism. Reporting was limited to transcripts and summaries of the proceedings of legislative bodies and police courts. Aside from that nod to newsgathering, journalists stayed in their offices, wrote editorials, clipped news from other newspapers, and depended on public officials, interested parties, and personal friends to stop by their offices with news of the day.[22]

After the Civil War the newspaper and book publishing industries both grew dramatically. The consolidation of the publishing industry in New York and a variety of technological innovations—such as typesetting machines, faster presses, and wood-pulp paper—enabled publishers to produce books more quickly and less expensively. Improvements in transportation and communication, such as the vast expansion of the railroads and the telegraph, united regional markets into a single national market. A rapidly growing population, increases in literacy, a shortened work week, a rise in real income—all these factors combined to increase the size of the book-buying public.[23]

By the 1880s, if "literature" still signified monuments of unaging intellect, it also denoted a commercial institution devoted to selling its products to a mass public. Similarly, "author" signified both creative artist and producer of commodities. Although antebellum American novelists were unable to support themselves by their writing, large numbers of postwar writers conceived of themselves as professional authors and depended on sales of their work for a living. Their situation as professional writers was close to that of postwar newspaper reporters. After the Civil War, as metropolitan newspapers expanded from four to sixteen or more pages, newspapers found it necessary to hire staffs of reporters. Two new occupational groups, the professional fiction writer and the newspaper reporter, arose virtually simultaneously.

Howells and James were highly conscious of similarities between novelists and reporters. Realist literary practice was, as many observers of the era pointed out, remarkably similar to reporting. A writer in the prestigious *Century* magazine, reviewing Howells's *A Modern Instance*, began by observing that America's "most artistic novelists"—he reveals later that he is referring to Howells and James—"seem to have cut quite loose from the old-fashioned story . . . and to have settled down to steady observation and reportorial reproduction"; throughout the review he refers to Howells as a "reporter."[24] In fact, in the course of writing *A Modern Instance*, which has its climax in an Indiana courtroom, Howells had traveled to Indiana to observe a trial. Later in the decade James would visit London's Millbank prison and write about it in *The Princess Casamassima* (1886). Moreover, like reporters, both Howells and James earned their livings as producers of prose. When the system of the gentleman author held sway as myth and partial reality, it had been possible to regard a written text as a work of art and an offering of individual expression—and only incidentally as a marketplace commodity. However, the late nineteenth-century novelists who depended on their writing for income were forced to acknowledge the commodity status of their work. Novels, like newspapers, were consumer items in a crowded marketplace; novelists, like reporters, were workers paid for producing prose.

Writers' responses to the professionalization of literature were various. When the Authors Club of New York was founded in 1882, journalists were expressly barred from membership.[25] The club can be seen as a rearguard action intended to protect the special status of the artist and hold off the hordes of commercially motivated writers. On the other hand, only a few years later a new journal, the *Writer*, was founded, subtitled *A Magazine for Literary Workers*. Both it and the *Author*, also founded during the 1880s, were trade magazines dedicated to helping writers advance their careers and maximize their income in the increasingly large literary market.[26]

The responses of individual writers were similarly conflicted. On the one hand, Howells and James resisted the commodification of literature and fought to maintain its status as an elite production removed from the sordid marketplace. James professed to detest the mass audience and to desire a return to the small homogeneous coterie that characterized earlier readers of American belles lettres. When early in James's career his brother William criticized Henry's travel letters to the *Nation* as being too refined, he replied that he "must give up the ambition of ever being a free-going and light-paced enough writer to please the multitude. The multitude, I am more and more convinced, has absolutely no taste—none at least that a thinking man is bound to defer to. To write for the few who have is doubtless to lose money—but I am not afraid of starving."[27] A decade later, writing to Howells, James professed an indifference even to an audience of the like-minded few and suggested that the artist should write only for himself: "The vulgar-mindedness of the public to which one offers the fruits of one's brain would chill the artist's breast if those fruits were not so sweet to his own palate! One mustn't think of the public *at all*, I find."[28]

Although Howells did not share James's disdain for the mass audience, he was equally dismayed by literature's commodity status in Gilded Age America. Howells's 1893 essay "The Man of Letters as a Man of Business" begins by arguing that the two roles cited in his title are contradictory, that literature should have nothing to do with business. "I do not think any man ought to live by an art," he writes.[29] Howells believed it humiliating for an artist to have to haggle over terms. He thought that art should be offered freely to the public, as the outpouring of a soul speaking its truth to others. Broadly democratic in his sympathies, Howells wanted to reach a large audience; his objection to Gilded Age publishing was that the interaction between writer and public had become commercialized.

Yet for all their attacks on the commercialization of literature, Howells and James both proved to be shrewd negotiators in the literary marketplace. Howells was a hard bargainer who in the 1880s signed an innovative long-term contract with Harper & Brothers that made him one of the best-paid writers in the United States.[30] For the first three decades of his career James was a writer of "ferocious ambition"—the term is his own—who bargained skillfully to get the best possible terms from publishers.[31] James's expatriation to Europe, frequently interpreted as a rejection of American crassness in favor of European culture and as a sign of James's paramount devotion to his art, was motivated at least in part by economic considerations. By establishing residence in England while maintaining his U.S. citizenship, James was one of the only writers in the era before the 1891 international copyright act who was able to negotiate contracts with both U.S. and British publishers. The strategy enabled him to "doubl[e his] profits," he wrote.[32] Actually, James received four sets of payments for virtually every novel he wrote before his major phase: he made contracts for serial publication of his novels in both a U.S. and a British periodical, then signed with a publishing house in each country.

Howells and James had a complex and conflicted relationship to the Gilded Age literary marketplace. Although they denounced commercialism as the enemy of art, they shrewdly bargained to assure their works the widest circulation possible. Their reactions to the unabashedly commercial newspaper were equally complex. They attacked journalism for its close connections to a vulgar commercial culture, portrayed reporters as panderers to the mass audience, and depicted the newspaper as a corrupted discourse. Yet Howells, who wrote that literary realism could be defined as "democracy in literature," also recognized that the newspaper was thoroughly democratic in its commodity form, available for pennies to a readership of all classes.[33] As we shall see, even James, uncommitted to egalitarian values, acknowledged the newspaper's democratic possibilities.

～

Howells was in the expansive mood of an author whose current project is going well when he wrote to a friend in 1881, "I'm making the hero of my divorce story a newspaper man. Why has no one struck journalism before?"[34] Howells perhaps intended to invoke a mining metaphor, with journalism as a rich lode of material just waiting to be struck by a literary miner. But there is another way to read the verb—as a reference to combat, a subtle declaration of war on journalism. *A Modern Instance* (1882), Howells's "divorce story," is as much about the battle between competing modes of representation—the newspaper and the realist novel—as it is about the antagonism between a husband and wife. *A Modern Instance* is the first of a number of Howells's novels that contain portrayals of newspaper journalists. An examination of these novels reveals Howells's uneasy recognition of the similarities between newspaper journalism and realist fiction. It also reveals Howells's efforts to highlight the differences between them and to establish the superiority of his program of literary realism.

A Modern Instance is Howells's first work to record the parallels between newspaper and novel in post–Civil War America, but David G. Croly, a perspicacious journalist, had made similar observations a decade earlier. He wrote in 1875,

> The modern novel and the newspaper are beginning to assimilate, and are becoming very much alike. The popular novel of two hundred years ago [sic] dealt with the ideal world, with fairies, ghosts, etc. Mrs. Radcliff's and Monk Lewis' romances were among that list. The popular novels, in their characters and plots, were remote from human interests. But the progress of fiction-writing has brought the novelist down to the affairs of everyday life. The popular novels of the day . . . are intensely realistic. . . . On the other hand, the newspaper in times past thought it beneath its dignity to discuss anything of a domestic or social character. The topics treated were abstract, and remote from men's daily lives. But now journalism is taking greater hold of social questions.

Croly went on, in a boosterish tone, to predict that the illustrated newspaper of the future "will occupy the field that the novel . . . now does."[35]

Croly's fond hope was Howells's nightmare. *A Modern Instance* illustrates Croly's observation that the realist novel and the postwar newspaper had come to share subject matter, but Howells emphasizes journalism's shortcomings, dismissing it as an inferior form. The newspaper functions in *A Modern Instance* as a vulgar countertext; journalist Bartley Hubbard, the novel's protagonist, serves as a "demonic realist," to use Amy Kaplan's appropriately melodramatic phrase.[36]

Throughout *A Modern Instance* Howells sets up a structure of parallel texts: his narrative and Bartley's "human interest" feature articles that cover the same incidents. The novel offers a subplot of textual battle, with the realist novel pitted against the newspaper. The first and most extended of these discursive battles occurs in the logging camp episode in chapters 9 through 11, when Bartley visits a logging operation in the Maine woods at the invitation of Kinney, the camp's cook. Howells not only describes Bartley's visit in detail but prints extracts from an article about the camp that Bartley publishes in a Boston newspaper. The episode offers the novel's most vivid example of the differences Howells perceived between his literary method and journalistic discourse.

The logging camp episode serves as a classic example of Howellsian realism; three characteristic elements of Howells's art are particularly evident. First is the concern with delineating individual character. With lavish attention to details of dress, action, and speech the episode brings to life Kinney—self-educated, voluble, warm-hearted; Bartley—ambitious, fastidious, self-absorbed; and several minor characters. Next, the episode draws fine distinctions of class, tracing the complex interactions among characters of varying socioeconomic levels: Kinney and his fellow lumbermen; Bartley, college-educated but from a modest background; and the camp owner and a party of wealthy friends from Boston and Montreal. Last, Howells engages his characters in a subtle moral drama. Reduced to a plot summary, the episode seems slight: the visitors stay a few hours; they leave; Bartley quarrels with Kinney and departs abruptly. However, the real action goes on within Bartley's consciousness as he flirts with one visitor, a pretty married woman from Montreal. The novel subtly analyzes Bartley's motives, showing how the flirtation both flatters his ego and serves as displaced revenge on Marcia Gaylord, a beautiful and proud young woman who has just broken off her engagement to Bartley. In addition, Bartley's temporary infatuation with the willful married woman alienates him from the loyal and generous Kinney, when Bartley subtly pokes fun at the eccentric cook in order to display his wit to the attractive visitor. The novel challenges the reader to follow its extremely subtle delineation of character, social class, and moral action; *A Modern Instance* is a pedagogy of serious reading, in Alan Trachtenberg's phrase.[37]

In contrast to the novel's concern with delineating moral drama, Bartley is interested in selling melodrama. When Bartley settles down to talk with Kinney before the visitors arrive, he encourages the cook to recount exciting incidents that Bartley can use for a newspaper article:

> I'll tell you what I think I'll do, Kinney: I'll get my outlines, and then you post me with a lot of facts,—queer characters, accidents, romantic incidents, snowings-up, threatened starvation, adventures with wild animals,—and I can make something worth while; get out two or three columns, so that they can print it in their Sunday edition. And then I'll take it up to Boston with me, and seek my fortune with it.[38]

Bartley succeeds in selling his article to a Boston newspaper, and the novel reprints the subheadings that he uses for his article:

THE PINE-TREE STATE'S STORIED STAPLE
MORE THAN A MILLION OF MONEY
UNBROKEN WILDERNESS
WILD-CATS, LYNXES, AND BEARS
BITTEN OFF
BOTH LEGS FROZEN TO THE KNEES
CANADIAN SONGS
JOY UNCONFINED
THE LAMPLIGHT ON THEIR SWARTHY FACES (127)

The headings reflect the cagey journalistic strategy of Bartley's article, which moves from decorous information on economic aspects of the lumber industry—spiced with a euphonious reference to "more than a million of money"—to accounts of gruesome disasters, to sentimental treatment of the human angle. In contrast, Howells's novel completely ignores lumber industry economics and adventure tales of the northern woods. The two texts overlap only in their discussion of the Canadian lumber workers. While Bartley offers sentimental and condescending tributes to the French

Canadians, typing them as joyous "swarthy" men, the novel records subtle class conflicts absent from the newspaper article. When the ebullient
married woman from Montreal asks the lumbermen to sing and dance for
her, some men "hung gloomily back; they clearly did not like these liber-
ties, this patronage" (94).

The lumber camp episode is the first in a series of events that are
inscribed both in Howells's narrative and in Bartley's newspaper articles.
None of the subsequent episodes includes extracts from Bartley's articles,
but Howells continues to distinguish strongly between his text and
Bartley's vulgar countertexts. For instance, after a chapter in which Bartley
and Marcia, now married, hunt for lodgings in Boston, Bartley decides to
write a newspaper article about the experience. "He had the true newspaper instinct," the narrator observes, "and went to work with a motive that
was as different as possible from the literary motive" (135). The narrator
then describes—by enumerating what is missing from Bartley's article—
the literary motive that animated the preceding chapter: "[Bartley] did not
attempt to give it form,—to imagine a young couple like himself and
Marcia coming down from the country to place themselves in the city; he
made no effort to throw about it the poetry of their ignorance and their
poverty, or the pathetic humor of their dismay at the disproportion of the
prices to their means" (135–36). Howells is here thumping his own drum,
distinguishing the form, poetry, and pathos of *A Modern Instance* from
Bartley's newspaper article, which he describes as a spicy exposé marked by
an "essential cheapness" (136).

The textual battle between journalism and realist fiction that is enacted
within the pages of *A Modern Instance* is one-sided; Bartley's articles are
invariably cheap and meretricious. The battle concludes with the death of
Bartley, who falls victim to poetic—or, rather, journalistic—justice. After
abandoning Marcia and their child, Bartley eventually wanders to Whited
Sepulchre, Arizona, where he establishes a gossipy weekly newspaper. It
is so successful that he lays plans to publish a daily edition, plans interrupted "when he chanced to comment upon the domestic relations of
'one of Whited Sepulchre's leading citizens.'" Howells summarizes what
ensues:

> The leading citizen promptly took the war-path, as an esteemed con-
> temporary expressed it in reporting the difficulty with the cynical light-

ness and the profusion of felicitous head-lines with which our journalism
often alleviates the history of tragic occurrences: the parenthetical touch
in the closing statement, that "Mr. Hubbard leaves a (divorced) wife and
child somewhere at the East," was quite in Bartley's own manner. (360)

In Howells's strict moral economy sensational journalism leads not only to
Bartley's death at the hands of an outraged reader but to his reduction to
subject matter for another reporter's sensational scoop.

Bartley's death seems to bring *A Modern Instance*'s novel-versus-news-
paper subplot to a clear and happy (at least for Howells) conclusion.
Journalism has been exposed as a debased and vulgar form; the journalist has
been silenced. Yet Howells undercuts his triumphant conclusion; for, after
all, we learn about Bartley's death through the words of another reporter.
Whatever the fate of the journalist within Howells's novels, in Gilded Age
America the newspaper was winning the contest for a mass audience.

As if in acknowledgment of the newspaper's power to resist his efforts
to silence it, Howells resurrected Bartley Hubbard for the opening chapter of *The Rise of Silas Lapham* (1885). The novel begins with Bartley, soon
after his arrival in Boston, interviewing the wealthy paint manufacturer
Silas Lapham for a newspaper article. Like the logging camp episode in *A
Modern Instance*, the opening chapter of *Silas Lapham* moves back and
forth between Howells's narrative voice and excerpts from Bartley's published article. A sample excerpt from Bartley's journalism, describing the
discovery of a paint mine on the Lapham family farm, reads:

> Deep in the heart of the virgin forests of Vermont, far up toward the line
> of the Canadian snows, on a desolate mountain-side, where an autum-
> nal storm had done its wild work, and the great trees, strewn hither and
> thither, bore witness to its violence, Nehemiah Lapham discovered just
> forty years ago, the mineral which the alchemy of his son's enterprise and
> energy has transmuted into solid ingots of the most precious of metals.[39]

Bartley's flattering tone and orotund periphrastic style scarcely conceal his
cynicism. In contrast, Howells offers readers moral earnestness and a
"plain" prose style.[40]

Yet if *Silas Lapham* draws attention to the differences between journalism and literary realism, the juxtaposition of the two forms may also
remind readers of their similarities. Howells's technique of including both

discourses in his text emphasizes that in the 1880s newspapers and novels treated the same subject matter. The story of a businessman's financial success could attract both reporters looking for a celebrity interview and novelists searching for material. And although Howells emphasizes the two discourses' differing appeals—Bartley offers melodrama, Howells moral drama—even the most serious of Howells's original readers must have been drawn to his fiction by its ability to satisfy one's curiosity about the dramatic changes in individual fortunes, business practices, and urban life during the Gilded Age—the same topics that formed much of the daily newspaper's fare.[41]

Howells's most extended fictional study of journalism occurs in his 1891 novel *The Quality of Mercy*. *The Quality of Mercy* not only draws a parallel between literary realism and journalism, as do *A Modern Instance* and *The Rise of Silas Lapham*, but also compares the different modes of reporting produced by two journalist characters, Lorenzo Pinney and Brice Maxwell. The two reporters enter the novel when John Milton Northwick, a larcenous businessman, flees to Canada with his company's funds. Pinney is an enthusiastic reporter on the *Boston Events*, a newspaper that, we learn, was formerly edited by Bartley Hubbard. Pinney's article for the *Events* on Northwick's crime is a sensationalistic "masterpiece" worthy of Bartley himself. The narrator calls the article "flashy and vulgar and unscrupulous."[42] Howells writes that "it appealed to every nerve in the reader's body, with its sensations repeated through many columns, and continued from page to page with a recurrent efflorescence of scare-heads and catch-lines" (149).

Maxwell's article is the direct opposite of Pinney's, just as the two reporters are opposed character types. Whereas Pinney is small, energetic, and unreflective, Maxwell is tall, consumptive, and artistic, a would-be poet and playwright temporarily making a living in journalism. He writes for the *Abstract*, whose idealistic editor, Ricker, clashed with Bartley Hubbard in *A Modern Instance*. Maxwell's interest in the Northwick case comes from an unproduced play he has written about a similar crime. He turns in to Ricker both a brief unsensational summary of the Northwick case and a long editorial about the social causes of such everyday business peculations. Ricker has him combine the two pieces, and the *Abstract* prints the resulting article as its only report of the event. Maxwell's article takes "a very high philosophical ground in [its] view of the matter," according to the narrator, and accuses "the structure of society." His arti-

cle is "humane," "forbearing," and "enlightened," "so dignified and dispassionate that it had the grace of something remote in time and place."
That is, Maxwell's article is scarcely journalism at all but more like the
work of one of the great reflective nineteenth-century historians; the narrator compares him to Hippolyte Taine (157–59).

Maxwell's article points the way to a transformed journalism in which
all sensationalism has been eradicated, replaced with a lofty and dispassionate blend of fact and reflection. However, this model of refined journalism never moved beyond the pages of Howells's novel. *The Quality of
Mercy* seems to record Howells's recognition that Maxwell's blend of news
article and editorial could not serve as a blueprint for change. Although
Ricker is eager to print similar pieces, Maxwell is unable to repeat his initial success. In the course of the novel he leaves the *Abstract*; he reappears
in a later Howells novel as a playwright.

The Quality of Mercy reveals a paradox in its treatment of journalism.
Maxwell's article for the appropriately named *Abstract*, which focuses on
social institutions rather than on individuals, depends for its production on
the inspired individual and withers away after a single instance. Yet
Pinney's article, which is "helplessly and thoroughly personal," can be
explained by reference to institutions (151). In an important passage the
narrator describes the *Events*:

> [It was] a journal without principles and without convictions, but with
> interests only; a map of busy life, indeed, but glaringly colored, with
> crude endeavors at picturesqueness, and with no more truth to life than
> those railroad maps where the important centres converge upon the
> broad black level of the line advertised, and leave rival roads wriggling
> faintly about in uninhabited solitudes. (152)

The comparison is telling. The railroad map is a false representation of reality, the passage asserts, because the sponsoring company's economic interests are furthered by distorting geography. Similarly, the *Events*'s lurid sensationalism distorts reality but inflates circulation figures. Just as Maxwell's
article links Northwick's crime to the U.S. economic structure, *The
Quality of Mercy* links newspaper sensationalism to the capitalistic drive for
profits. Howells used both the larcenous businessman and the sensationalistic newspaper as synecdoches of American capitalism.[43]

As his 1893 essay "The Man of Letters as a Man of Business" reveals,

Howells feared that literature might become as fully determined by economic factors as was Lorenzo Pinney's journalism. Moreover, he recognized that literature's importance in U.S. society was diminishing. In Howells's recollection antebellum America was marked by a more prominent social role for literature and a greater respect for authors. Howells's memoirs of his first trip to New England, when he called on Lowell, Holmes, Emerson, and other writers, have a hagiographic tone, marked by the reverence of a pilgrim approaching Mecca. Antebellum Boston held "a group of authors as we shall hardly see here again for hundreds of years," he wrote. "There was such regard for them and their calling, not only in good society, but among the extremely well-read people of the whole intelligent city, as hardly another community has shown."[44]

The New England writers were highly respected not only in Boston but nationwide. Howells once recalled a visit he paid to James Garfield, later president of the United States but then a member of Congress from Ohio. One summer evening Howells called at Garfield's home in Hiram, where they sat outside on the veranda and Howells began telling about his encounters with famous writers. Garfield stopped him, then ran toward the nearby houses where the neighbors were gathered on their porches. "Come over here! He's telling about Holmes, and Longfellow, and Lowell, and Whittier!" the congressman yelled excitedly, and through the darkness Howells could soon perceive figures climbing the fences and running into the Garfield yard in order to hear the young writer's tales.[45]

The small-town Ohioans' eagerness to hear about the great antebellum poets testifies to these writers' cultural importance. Of course, Howells's remark that the "whole . . . city" of Boston esteemed its poets is an exaggeration. Aside from the large numbers of antebellum Americans who did not, or could not, read literature at all, good-sized reading publics ignored the standard authors in favor of sentimental fiction or "dime novels"— inexpensively produced adventure fiction. Yet Howells's reminiscences of antebellum poets' importance give a sense of the prestige and authority of the genteel literary establishment. Before the Civil War a genteel elite dominated American literature and held great importance within the national culture. During the Gilded Age the literary culture of the United States became increasingly fragmented, literature held a much diminished importance in national life, and authors were no longer seen as important national figures.[46] Howells, whose career straddled the Civil War, was highly conscious of the change. He was not alone. In Alan Trachtenberg's phrase Howells was one among the "legions of nervous intellectuals seeking a role for themselves and a sense of control" in Gilded Age society.[47]

Howells believed the diminishing importance of literature to be directly linked to the growth of journalism. Everyone among the "well-read people" of antebellum Boston was interested in literature, he recalled. But in Gilded Age America, he said repeatedly during the 1880s and '90s, only women read books; men read nothing but newspapers.[48] Howells's reaction to this gender division in the textual marketplace was conflicted. On the one hand, he accepted the feminization of the literary audience, writing with a stoic air, "The man of letters must make up his mind that in the United States the fate of a book is in the hands of the women" and declaring, more positively, that a novelist's greatness depended on his ability to portray women.[49] On the other hand, he worried about the manliness of his profession of authorship. Howells's critical writings and memoirs repeatedly emphasize a dichotomy between literature and life, categories that for Howells have gender associations, with literature inherently feminine, life inherently masculine. Literature, Howells wrote, "gives one no . . . certain station in the world of men's activities," and the artist is regarded as "a kind of mental and moral woman."[50] Michael Davitt Bell has argued that Howells's creed of literary realism, elaborated over dozens of "Editor's Study" essays in *Harper's* magazine and collected in *Criticism and Fiction* (1891), is unconvincing and incoherent when regarded as literary theory but perfectly reasonable if viewed as an effort to locate literature within the world of "men's activities."[51]

In Howells's view newspapers were inherently part of the masculine world; they effortlessly captured the male readership that literature had lost. In addition, reporters' daily work brought them into contact with reality in a way that a literary realist could envy. In his memoirs Howells more than once regretted that he had abandoned his work as a metropolitan reporter after only a few weeks, sordid and disgusting though the work may have seemed at the time. Looking back at his younger self, Howells saw a dreamy youth too interested in literature, too little concerned with life. Speaking of his missed chances as a reporter, Howells wrote, "I have often been sorry since, for [reporting] would have made known to me many phases of life that I have always remained ignorant of, but I did not know then that life was supremely interesting and important. I fancied that literature, that poetry was so." Had he only realized it, the newspaper could have been a "school of reality."[52]

Not only did the newspaper describe the commonplace reality that the mature Howells wished to capture in his fiction, it reached the democratic audience he longed for, appealing to readers across class and gender lines, available for pennies to an audience of millions. In his critical essays on literature Howells imagined a central social role for realist fiction as a text that would not only describe American reality but unite all classes as readers. However, his novels record a world in which the newspaper not only encroaches on the subject matter of serious fiction but bests it in the contest for a broad readership.

~

Throughout much of his career Henry James attacked journalism with a zest that the more temperate Howells never mustered. Writing in 1889, James declared the "most distinctive sign" of his era to be its "colossal, deafening newspaperism."[53] A 1905 speech contains an even livelier attack; there, he declares newspapers to be a threat to American civilization. James describes the newspaper's "ubiquitous page" as

> bristling with rude effigies and images, with vociferous "headings," with letterings, with black eruptions of print, that we seem to measure by feet rather than by inches, and that affect us positively as the roar of some myriad-faced monster—as the grimaces, the shouts, shrieks and yells, ranging over the whole gamut of ugliness, irrelevance, dissonance, of a mighty maniac who has broken loose and who is running amuck through the spheres alike of sense and of sound.[54]

In this melodramatic passage newspapers become a raging demonic force, their victim nothing less than both sense and sound—that is, both ideas and expression, both civilization and its literature. James's image of the monster suggests a corresponding image of the victim—culture itself—cowering in a corner as the mighty maniac approaches, intent on violation.

The monster/victim imagery of this passage is literalized in *The Bostonians* (1886), which serves as James's *A Modern Instance*—that is, the first of a series of works that feature journalists as characters and illustrate the author's fear and loathing of journalism. In *The Bostonians* journalism's victim is embodied by Verena Tarrant, whereas the maniac takes the unprepossessing form of Matthias Pardon, a slight, effeminate Boston newspaper reporter who threatens Verena not from any personal monstrousness but because of the vast system of publicity that he represents.

Critics of *The Bostonians* have generally treated the book's structure as triangular, with two strong personalities—the wealthy Boston feminist Olive Chancellor and the ambitious southern lawyer Basil Ransom—engaged in a struggle over the young, beautiful, and still unformed Verena Tarrant. A widely circulated paperback edition of the novel, released at the same time as the 1980 film version, gives the triangle graphic form. Its cover depicts Vanessa Redgrave, portraying Olive Chancellor, and Christopher Reeve as Basil Ransom looming over Madeleine Potter's Verena, who is seated between them.[55] Yet if this triangle of characters accurately represents the film, which necessarily simplified James's lengthy book, the novel could be better represented by a quadrangle, with Verena, Olive, and Ransom joined by journalist Matthias Pardon, who serves as a third competitor for Verena.[56]

Although Pardon considers himself, at least for a time, to be a potential suitor for Verena, he does not pose a serious sexual threat to either Ransom or Olive. Rather, his aim is to turn Verena into a celebrated speaker for women's rights, fodder for the machinery of publicity with which he is infatuated. James depicts Pardon as a sort of journalist-monster, insatiable in his desires to publish the personal and the trivial. The physical peculiarities that James gives to the character—his long white hair at twenty-eight, his "small, fair features" and "pretty eyes" surmounting a white moustache—make him a freak, poised disconcertingly between male and female, youth and age (100). Writing in his notebook about his desire to make *The Bostonians* "as American as possible," James added, "There must, indispensably, be a type of newspaper man—the man whose ideal is the energetic reporter. I should like to *bafouer* [ridicule] the vulgarity and hideousness of this—the impudent invasion of privacy—the extinction of all conception of privacy, etc."[57]

The uncharacteristic awkwardness of James's prose as he thumps on the theme of privacy signals the intensity of his hatred of publicity and his contempt for reporters. That intensity is carried over to the novel, where the narrator introduces Pardon in a curious passage:

> For this ingenuous son of his age all distinction between the person and the artist had ceased to exist; the writer was personal, the person food for newsboys, and everything and every one were every one's business. All

things, with him, referred themselves to print, and print meant simply infinite reporting, a promptitude of announcement, abusive when necessary, or even when not, about his fellow-citizens. He poured contumely on their private life, on their personal appearance, with the best conscience in the world. His faith . . . was . . . that being in the newspapers is a condition of bliss, and that it would be fastidious to question the terms of the privilege. (100)

The passage may seem straightforward enough, a denunciation of the snooping reporter. However, the first sentence reveals a loss of artistic control on James's part. Its references to the artist-writer have no relevance to anything in *The Bostonians*, in which no fiction writer appears. The only citizen whom Pardon is stalking is Verena Tarrant, not a writer at this point in the novel and certainly not an artist. James was evidently so determined to *bafouer* the energetic reporter that he abandoned his narrative for a personal outburst.

James's disgust with reporters was a response to new developments in post–Civil War journalism. Before the war, reporting about individuals was limited because the interview was virtually unknown as a journalistic form. Although antebellum newspapers occasionally printed a question-and-answer session with some public figure, newspapers favored transcription of public addresses over interviews. When Ralph Waldo Emerson went on a lecture tour, newspapers in the cities where he stopped were likely to print an announcement of his arrival accompanied by a transcript of his lecture; it would not have occurred to a newspaper editor to approach the author himself. It was not until after the Civil War that interviews became common.[58] By the 1870s—the period in which *The Bostonians* is set—the interviewing reporter had become a familiar enough figure to merit a cartoon in *Puck*, a series of drawings that show the mishaps of "The Great American Interviewer" as he peers into keyholes, sewers, and active chimneys in search of news.

Matthias Pardon, who is described as "the most brilliant young interviewer on the Boston press" (100), occasionally serves as James's counterpart to the cartoon reporter, seeking out trivial personal facts. Yet in the novel as a whole Pardon represents massive forces of modern publicity that serve as a genuine threat to both Ransom's and Olive's plans for Verena. Ransom and Olive, competitors for Verena's affection from the moment they meet her, are alike in their distaste for Pardon. Ransom, infatuated

FIGURE 1.1 "The Great American Interviewer" from *Puck*, March 1877.

with Verena, has nothing but contempt for both her ability as a speaker for the rights of women and for the publicity that Pardon wishes to use to abet her career. "If [women] would only be private and passive, and have no feeling but for that," he reflects early in the novel, "and leave publicity to the sex of tougher hide!" (7). Olive, in contrast, is committed to women's political emancipation and intends to use Verena's speaking gift in the cause. Yet at the same time she wants to draw Verena to herself in an intense friendship, a private relationship that Pardon threatens.

However, by the end of the novel the struggle for Verena has become a two-part contest. Olive joins forces with Pardon, and Ransom is left to fight alone against them. Olive capitulates to Pardon and decides to propel Verena into public life in order to separate her from Ransom. Witnessing Ransom's determined campaign to win Verena, and aware of Verena's increasing attraction to the handsome southerner, Olive makes plans for Verena to speak in Boston's largest auditorium, the Music Hall, and enlists Pardon's aid. The Music Hall speech was originally Pardon's idea, and he says with satisfaction on the day of Verena's address that "Miss Chancellor came round—came round considerably, there's no doubt of that; because a year or two ago she was terribly unapproachable" (350). If Olive comes 'round to the side of Pardon, the newspapers, and publicity, Ransom does not. Shortly before the Music Hall speech it becomes clear to him that Verena "would become 'widely popular.'" The idea, we learn, "simply sickened him. He felt as differently as possible about it from Mr. Matthias Pardon" (323).

Ransom's struggle to win Verena is a battle against the strong-willed Olive; in the novel's final chapters it becomes a battle against journalism, publicity, and the mass audience as well. Early in the novel Pardon remarks that he wants "to see [Verena's] name in the biggest kind of bills and her portrait in the windows of the stores" (103). The phrase is, for Ransom, a fearsome trope of publicity; the image recurs in the novel and becomes a reality before the Music Hall speech. When Ransom enters the sold-out auditorium, where he finds swarms of boys hawking Verena's portrait, he is determined to prevent her from speaking. Minutes before Verena is scheduled to appear, Ransom makes his way backstage to convince her to abandon the auditorium along with her plans for a public career and to marry him. This backstage scene is one of the most vivid in James's work, almost cinematic in quality, accompanied throughout by the dull roar of the Music Hall audience in the background, their stamps and shouts swelling and ebbing as the starting time of the lecture passes and Verena does not appear. Ransom dismisses the crowd as a "raving rabble" and "senseless brutes" (366, 368). The narrative never enters the auditorium to offer us a view of the audience; they remain a faceless, noisy, inarticulate mass. As they roar their hostility, Ransom convinces Verena to flee with him, escaping Olive Chancellor, feminism, publicity, and the mass audience—signifiers of the modern culture that Ransom detests.

Yet Ransom's victory is clearly Pyrrhic. The novel's famous concluding sentence undercuts Ransom's ambitions for a blissful private life with Verena. When Ransom discovers, as they leave the Music Hall, that Verena is in tears, the narrator adds, "It is to be feared that with the union, so far from brilliant, into which she was about to enter, these were not the last she was destined to shed" (370). More broadly, the novel as a whole undercuts Ransom's political and cultural ambitions to promote a domestic privacy in opposition to the forces of publicity and mass culture. James portrays the victory of mass culture as inevitable. At the novel's end Ransom is fighting a lonely battle, the sole resister to Matthias Pardon and the enormous Music Hall audience. Along with Olive, every other character in the novel—except for Mrs. Luna, Olive's shallow and Europeanized sister—accepts the publicity surrounding Verena's address and supports her appearance in the Music Hall. Ransom may have won his private battle, but the new mass culture has won the war.

So far, I have analyzed *The Bostonians* largely on its own terms, showing the text's opposition between Ransom's—and to some extent Olive's—desire for privacy and love and the mania for publicity associated with Pardon and the newspapers. Without going outside the text we can see how the novel reveals its author's anxiety about the growth of journalism, publicity, and the mass audience. However, if we view *The Bostonians* in light of its era and Henry James's career, we can see how other anxieties shape the text: anxieties about gender, literary realism, and the literary marketplace.

Although *The Bostonians'* sexual politics has become a major concern of the novel's recent critics, they have given surprisingly little attention to a passage in which Ransom describes for Verena his quarrel with his age. He has a mission to "save" the male sex, he tells her, and when she asks, "To save it from what?" he delivers a tirade:

From the most damnable feminisation! I am so far from thinking, as you set forth the other night, that there is not enough woman in our general life, that it has long been pressed home to me that there is a great deal too much. The whole generation is womanised; the masculine tone is passing out of the world; it's a feminine, a nervous, hysterical, chattering, canting age, an age of hollow phrases and false delicacy and exaggerated solicitudes and coddled sensibilities, which, if we don't soon look out, will usher in the reign of mediocrity, of the feeblest and flattest and most pretentious that has ever been. (275)

The Bostonians depicts Ransom as the sole, embattled defender of this masculine faith. Editors reject his efforts to get his ideas into print, and Ransom confirms Verena's conjecture that he is "the only person in this country" who expresses such ideas (271). To my knowledge, Alfred Habegger is the only critic who has pointed out that the portrait of Ransom as the lone iconoclast willing to challenge the feminization of the United States reverses the actual power relations of men and women in that era. "Such is James's authority," Habegger writes, "that many readers have innocently accepted the notion that American culture and history had in some way become women's work, thus managing to forget that law, politics, industry, commerce, and finance were run almost exclusively by some men."[59] We can add journalism to Habegger's list. James offers Matthias Pardon as the sole representative of journalism: a near-hermaphrodite in James's depiction of him, whose goal as a journalist is "to help the ladies. . . . I want to work for their emancipation" (117). *The Bostonians* would have us believe late nineteenth-century journalism to be a thoroughly "womanised" institution.

The reality was that nineteenth-century newspapers were owned, edited, and written almost entirely by men. In both reporting and editorial policy metropolitan daily newspapers were overwhelmingly hostile to women's suffrage. Why, then, did James in his portrayal of Matthias Pardon offer such a distorted picture of his era's journalism? One reason may have been his anxieties—similar to Howells's—about his gender role. As Habegger says, James's personal sense of his masculinity "was problematic in the extreme."[60] More than that, in their social role as writers of novels Howells and James were "sissies," to use a slang term that became popular after the Civil War.[61] The majority of novelists and novel readers of the time were women, whereas journalism, a rival field of writing, was both produced and read predominantly by men. In *The Bostonians* James not only reverses the power relations between men and women, as

Habegger points out, but also reverses the gender orientation of journalism and fiction. Journalism becomes a feminized realm, a subservient branch of the women's movement, whereas the novel—that is, the text of *The Bostonians*—provides a forum for Basil Ransom's patriarchal views.

Although the negative portrait of journalist Matthias Pardon derives from James's anxiety about journalism's hold on the male audience, it also reveals his uneasiness about the practice of literary realism. Throughout his career James regarded authorship as a calling, a quasi-sacred role akin to a religious vocation. However, as he commenced writing *The Bostonians* in the 1880s, James made an alteration in his literary career that brought this high priest of literary art into an uncomfortably parallel course with the newspaper reporters he despised. As every student of James's career has observed, with *The Bostonians* and *The Princess Casamassima* (1886) James deliberately turned to the mode of writing that we now term literary realism and that James thought of as "naturalism." As numerous critics have remarked, *The Bostonians* and *The Princess Casamassima* fit, better than any of James's other works, the definitions we now use to describe the body of late nineteenth-century fiction known as realism. Both novels describe with great fidelity the material conditions of everyday life; both include people drawn from a wide range of social classes; both include accurate descriptions of specific public sites—in the case of *The Bostonians* Harvard's Memorial Hall and the Boston Music Hall; and both deal with contemporary social and political movements. All these characteristics of realistic fiction are also, not coincidentally, features of late nineteenth-century journalism. In their content of current social-political movements and in their mimetic form James's novels of the 1880s had much in common with the newspaper, a resemblance that may well have caused James considerable anxiety.

Moreover, James's practice as a realistic novelist in the 1880s resembled the work habits of reporters. We know from a letter to Thomas Sargeant Perry that James visited London's Millbank Prison to collect notes for a scene in *The Princess Casamassima*. "You see, I am quite the Naturalist" he wrote to Perry.[62] "Quite the Journalist," he could have written with equal truth, although the acknowledgment would have revealed his kinship to the odious Matthias Pardon. *The Bostonians* is journalistic in ways beyond James's fidelity to the physical scenes of Boston, Cambridge, and New York. When the novel's initial installment appeared in *Century* magazine, many readers assumed that James had, Matthias Pardon–like, violated privacy and decorum by writing about the well-known Boston reformer Elizabeth Palmer Peabody under the name of Miss Birdseye. Although James protested in a lengthy letter to his brother William that his character was not directly modeled on Peabody, he acknowledged the striking resemblances. It seems possible that James's vigor in attacking Pardon for violating privacy by describing prominent Bostonians in print may have come from his uneasy realization that in his depiction of Miss Birdseye he was doing the same thing.[63]

James may also have felt an uncomfortable link to his journalist character's canny commercialism. When Verena speaks at Miss Birdseye's—the occasion when Olive and Ransom first meet Verena and become, in their varying ways, infatuated with her beauty and her power as a speaker—Pardon reacts only to her financial potential: "There's money for some one in that girl . . . !" he exclaims (51). Thereafter, Olive remains suspicious of Pardon and implies that his interest in her is mercenary—a suspicion that Pardon cheerfully acknowledges to be at least partially true. Just as the narrator's attacks on Pardon's violation of privacy may arise in part from James's uneasiness about his practice in the novel, Pardon's commercialism may reflect James's concern about his relation to the marketplace.

James's negotiations with magazine and book publishers over *The Bostonians* reveal a shrewd, aggressive bargainer, as obsessed with the commercial prospects of his novel as Pardon is with Verena's potential earnings. In the course of writing *The Bostonians* James abandoned long-standing relations with the *Atlantic Monthly* magazine and Houghton Mifflin publishers in order to win better terms. The agreement that James negotiated with his new publisher, James R. Osgood, was so unusual that the Osgood firm was unable to use its preprinted contract. The contract for *The Bostonians* was a handwritten four-page document that combined elements of British and U.S. publishing practices and ensured James a substantial amount of money on completion of the manuscript, without the customary delay. As Michael Anesko points out, James's innovative contract anticipated the advance payment against royalties that is now standard in U.S. publishing.[64]

When James signed his contract with Osgood in April 1883, he promised to furnish "a substantial part of [*The Bostonians*] during the first two months of the year 1884."[65] As it turned out, the novel began serialization a full year later, in part because James delayed starting the book in order to take up a more lucrative offer: he intended to write for the newspapers. The publisher of the *New York Sun* had invited James to write a series of short stories for the Sunday edition, with syndication to other newspapers. James won an extension from Osgood, then wrote to friends and family informing them what he had done. "Lately I have been doing some short things, which you will see in due time in the Century, & eke three or four in (horresco referens!) the New York Sunday *Sun!*" he wrote to one friend. "That journal has bribed me with gold—it is a case of gold pure & simple."[66] James decried the horror of appearing in a Sunday newspaper, yet he found the prospect of reaching a mass audience appealing. "The die is cast," he wrote to another correspondent, "but I don't in the least repent of it—as I see no shame in offering my productions to the widest public, & in their being 'brought home,' as it were, to the great American people."[67] The contrasting attitudes of embarrassment and pride—or at least lack of shame—in these two letters are combined in an intriguing letter to *Atlantic* editor Thomas Bailey Aldrich:

> Three or four short tales, from my turning hand, are to appear (this is a profound secret)—have been, in a word, secured, *à prix d'or* in—*je vous en donne en mille*—the New York Sunday *Sun!!* This last fact, I repeat, is really as yet *a complete and sacred secret.* Please bury it in oblivion and burn my letter. I mention it . . . simply to denote that by July 18[8]5 I expect to be in the enjoyment of a popularity which will require me to ask $500 a number for the successive instalments of *The Princess Casamassima.*[68]

The letter's succession of tones is remarkable. The passage begins with James as the blushing upper-class maiden revealing to a friend that she has fallen in love with a farmhand. He wants to reveal his secret, yet he can scarcely force it out; a series of interrupting phrases issues from his pen before he can write the name of the newspaper. Coyly, he underlines the clandestine nature of this news and asks Aldrich to burn the letter—a peculiar request considering that the *Sun*'s 150,000 subscribers are about to learn the "sacred secret." But the tone changes abruptly from coy maiden to hard-nosed businessman as James tells Aldrich that his anticipated popularity will "require" him to ask double the *Atlantic*'s usual price for serialization. If James's willingness to publish his work in the newspapers links him to Matthias Pardon, he is perhaps even closer to Olive Chancellor, who "for the sake of the largest hearing," as Ransom reflects, "conform[ed] herself to a great popular system" (354). Like his characters in

The Bostonians, James was inextricably involved in the journalism, commercialism, and publicity of his era.

James's high commercial hopes for *The Bostonians* and *The Princess Casamassima* were destroyed by the two novels' stunning lack of success. James wrote to Howells after *Princess* was published that the two novels had "reduced the desire, and the demand, for my productions to zero."[69] He dramatized his despondency in a series of tales, written during the 1890s, that deal with the literary life. All feature an artist of exquisite subtlety—a writer not unlike Henry James—who faces threats from journalism and the mass market. Journalism threatens James's artists in two ways. First, as an outlet for publication the newspaper serves as a monetary temptation, but in its preference for "trash" (James's term) over art it inevitably frustrates the writer of talent. Second, as an organ of publicity the newspaper destroys the writer's privacy and turns him from artist into celebrity. The literary mass market serves as journalism's equally evil twin. The marketplace inevitably rejects the serious writer, because marketplace success is dependent upon a vulgar public that unerringly prefers the second rate.

In response to the perceived threats from journalism and the mass market James created two central myths in his 1890s tales of the literary life: the myth of the artist incapable—no matter how strong the motivation—of producing the hack work needed for journalistic and mass-market success, and the myth of the artist besieged by publicity. I use the term "myth" not to imply that James's tales have no basis in fact—James insisted on the stories' autobiographical origins[70]—but to draw attention to their status as narratives that provide coherent and satisfying ways of understanding the world.[71] James's notebook entries for these stories reveal how they served to assuage slights and to exorcise the author's personal demons. The stories have also influenced the way in which generations of loyal James readers have viewed the role of literature and the literary artist in the modern era.

The myth of the literary artist incapable of descending to journalistic hack work had its origins, as James's notebook entries make clear, in personal experience. In part, James drew on his brief stint as a writer for the *New-York Tribune,* an episode James repeatedly probed like a sore tooth. He referred to it in two separate notebook entries for "The Next Time," his 1895 tale of a "poor man of letters," in the words of one entry, "who squanders his life in trying for a vulgar success which his talent is too fine to achieve." According to James's somewhat self-serving notebook recollection of his exchange with *Tribune* editor Whitelaw Reid, Reid had demanded that the newspaper letters be "baser and paltrier," more "vulgar." With the satisfaction of a wit savoring one of his best bons mots James more accurately recalled his reply to Reid that the letters were the worst he could do for the money. In his notebook entries we can see James turning the *Tribune* affair into a paradigmatic tale of the artist incapable of meeting the marketplace's vulgar demands.[72]

"The Next Time" is about Ralph Limbert, a writer desperate for financial success. Early in his career Limbert needs money to marry; later he must support his wife, a large brood of children, and a demanding mother-in-law. Limbert gains a small circle of admirers who regard him as an exquisite talent, but he is unable to produce a popular success. He studies popular fiction formulas and regularly assumes, optimistically, that the next time his work will sell. However, his would-be potboilers turn out to be masterpieces appreciated by only a select few. Limbert lacks the vulgarity that, according to James, is necessary to make a popular success. Every bit an artist, Limbert is unable to descend to the level required to reach beyond the small circle of sympathetic souls able to appreciate his genius.

James makes Limbert's career parallel his; at one point Limbert writes letters from London for a provincial newspaper, the *Blackport Beacon*. His fate is the same as James's at the *Tribune*. Although Limbert tries mightily to stoop to the journalistic level, he is fired. The reason, Limbert's fiancée explains to the narrator, is that the newspapers want "something more chatty. . . . More gossipy, more personal. They want 'journalism.' They want tremendous trash."[73] In defining journalism as simply "tremendous trash," she articulates James's view of the newspaper. Limbert is given James's own words to Whitelaw Reid, writing to the newspaper that "such work as he has done is the very worst he can do for the money" (252).

Just as James rewrote his letter to Whitelaw Reid for "The Next Time," he was to rewrite "The Next Time" later in his career, in the 1900 short story "Broken Wings." Mrs. Harvey, one of the story's two artist-protagonists, is a novelist reduced to writing London letters for a provincial newspaper—this time called the *Blackport Banner*. She has as little success as Ralph Limbert. Like him, she is incapable of producing the "trash" that newspaper readers—"the people"—want.[74] In the artistic hierarchy of James's tales the only true success is popular failure. Ralph Limbert's sister-in-law, a best-selling novelist, is positively envious of Limbert's lack of success; she yearns to be, at least once, "an exquisite failure." The best-selling sister-in-law agrees with the narrator that it is "the age of trash triumphant"; in such an era a failure in the marketplace is a sign of artistic success (245).

"The Next Time" and "Broken Wings" transform James's personal failures in journalism and the literary mass market into mythic tales about unrecognized artists casting their pearls before swine. Of course, James was scarcely unrecognized; despite his disappointing sales figures in the decades following the success of *Daisy Miller* (1879) he remained one of the era's best-known artists. Yet in James's view such recognition had its perils, which he explored in stories of artists besieged by journalistic publicity. "The Death of the Lion" (1894) is the first of these tales. Neil Paraday, the story's protagonist, has for years been an exquisite failure as a writer, living in obscurity in the countryside. However, as the story opens and Paraday's fifth novel is published, an eminent London newspaper praises Paraday in an editorial. The story's narrator—an admiring journalist who throws over his profession in order to devote himself to protecting Paraday—is aghast. "The big blundering newspaper had discovered him," the narrator muses, "and now . . . the poor man was to be squeezed into his horrible age."[75] Within hours of the newspaper's appearance the narrator's fears are confirmed; a journalist who writes for the "Smatter and Chatter" column of the *Tatler* appears at Paraday's house to write a chatty personal article about the author at home.

The rest of "The Death of the Lion" describes how Paraday is transformed from obscure artist to national celebrity, besieged by interviewers and sought by society hostesses—none of whom has the least interest in his work. Paraday's novels remain unread, and he becomes famous—to use one definition of a celebrity—for being well known. As with "The Next Time," James based "The Death of the Lion" on his experience. He began his notebook sketch for the story:

> Could not something be done with the idea of the great (the distinguished, the celebrated) artist who is tremendously made up to, *fêted*, written to for his autograph, portrait, etc., and yet with whose work, in this age of advertisement and newspaperism, this age of interviewing, not one of the persons concerned has the smallest acquaintance? It would have the merit, at least, of corresponding to an immense reality—a reality that strikes me every day of my life.[76]

According to his notebook, James was regularly pestered by "ravenous autograph-hunters" and "exploiters of publicity."[77] In "The Death of the Lion" James ups the stakes, and Paraday, in ill health, is literally driven to his death by publicity-maddened hunters on the trail of a literary lion. At the same time, the flighty aristocrats who make Paraday a part of their whirling round of country-house gatherings manage to lose the manuscript of his most recent and greatest novel.

"The Death of the Lion" was the first of a series of tales about artists, publicity, and the invasion of privacy. All the tales feature an artist whose work is appreciated only by a small select group but who is sought by journalists bent on delving into his personal life. In "John Delavoy" (1898) the editor of a mass-circulation magazine absolutely refuses to have anything to do with the title character's work, because it deals frankly with "the relation of the sexes." Instead, he attempts to persuade the author's sister to write a personal article full of "anecdotes, glimpses, gossip, chat"; failing in that attempt, he publishes the author's portrait, to great acclaim from a public uninterested in actually reading what John Delavoy wrote.[78] In "The Real Right Thing" (1899) a novelist's ghost appears to warn a young journalist not to write his biography. Ashton Doyne, the writer who is the subject of "The Real Right Thing," is the only artist in James's tales who escapes intrusive publicity. In the world according to James's imagination it takes supernatural intervention to halt the publicity machine.

Both "The Death of the Lion" and "The Next Time," tales about writers appreciated only by a small coterie of readers, appeared, appropriately, in the *Yellow Book*, a London journal founded in 1894 that was intended for an equally small audience of the self-declared avant-garde. James's tales and the journal in which they appeared mark a new development in nineteenth-century publishing. Stories and magazine alike reveal the increasing fragmentation of the era's literary marketplace into distinct cultures of letters.

When James began his career in the 1860s, he published most of his work in the *Atlantic Monthly*, one of a small group of magazines that dominated the market for serious fiction. The *Atlantic Monthly* and its peers—notably *Harper's*, *Scribner's*, and the *Century*—held enormous cultural authority; they defined literature for the educated middle and upper classes who held cultural and political power in the United States. During the course of his career James saw that publishing system and its audience fracture. On the one hand, newspapers, with their stunning post–Civil War increases in circulation, helped to define a new mass audience in contrast to the genteel public of the magazines. On the other hand, the *Yellow Book* and similar ventures that arose in the 1890s turned away from the genteel magazines' effort to reach a relatively broad audience and instead aimed themselves at a small group of aesthetic elites. The *Yellow Book* and its American avant-garde equivalents, the *Chap-Book* and the *Philistine*, were the precursors of the "little magazines" of the early twentieth century that published the deliberately difficult work of the modernists, including James Joyce, Ezra Pound, and T. S. Eliot. The appearance of "The Death of the Lion" and "The Next Time" in the *Yellow Book* is an enactment of the tales' themes: at century's end the true artist is doomed to failure in the marketplace and is appreciated by only a handful of admirers.[79]

However, as Anne Margolis has pointed out, the Henry James of the 1890s can be described as schizophrenic.[80] For at the same time that he was publishing, in a small-circulation avant-garde journal, tales about the artist's inability to create a popular success, he was energetically attempting to strike it rich in the theater. James's tales of the 1890s oppose art to journalism, yet in 1896 he serialized a melodramatic novel, *The Other House*, in the *Illustrated London News*. James's desire for popular success in the theater and even (*horresco referens!*) in the newspaper reflects a reluctance to accept the logic of his tales, which suggest that the artist should be content to address a small appreciative band of aesthetes. During much of the 1890s James was torn between a contempt for journalism and the mass audience and a willingness to attain popular success by whatever means necessary.

If, during the decade of the 1890s, James attempted to seduce the mass audience and even cohabited with the newspaper, by the turn of the century the romance was over. James's notoriously difficult late style, generally studied as an aesthetic achievement, can also be seen as a social action, a rejection of the mass audience and a conscious counter to journalism.[81] James's late works are difficult enough to prove daunting to all but an interpretive elite, readers who enjoy the challenge of threading their way through densely entangled syntactical thickets. As Allon White writes, James's "cultivated obscurity" serves as "a stylistic barricade against the mob, a disdainful rejection of the common reader."[82] With his late style James rejected both the common reader and the common person's most frequent reading, the newspaper. "The *faculty of attention* has utterly vanished from the general anglo-saxon mind, extinguished at its source by the big blatant *Bayadère* of Journalism," he wrote to Howells in 1902. One could read a newspaper or picture magazine, he wrote, "without . . . having to attend *one minute* of the time."[83] In contrast, James's late works remain impervious to skimming; they require a constant vigilant attention on the reader's part.

James's late novels challenge the big blatant bayadere of journalism not just in style but in subject matter. As an increasingly sensationalistic press was turning to reports of sexual scandals as a means of increasing circulation, James turned with greater frequency to stories of sexual intrigue. However, in place of the newspapers' blatant and titillating headlines James wrote stories that are not directly about sexual behavior but about the process by which a finely conscious individual uses the subtlest of clues to piece together the story of others' sexual actions. This drama of comprehension forms the plot of most of the novels of James's late phase, from *What Maisie Knew* (1897) to *The Golden Bowl* (1904).

All of James's late novels implicitly challenge journalism; the challenge is explicit in *The American Scene* (1907), a nonfiction account of his visit to the United States in 1903–1904. A reader who picked up *The American Scene* could be forgiven for expecting a "journalistic" book, a factual account of James's travels. The table of contents reveals chapters titled straightforwardly with the names of the cities and regions that James visited. However, what readers actually encounter is a book that can best be characterized as antijournalism.

The American Scene may well be the most maddening travel book ever written. It deliberately upsets all one's preconceptions about travel literature, leaving unsatisfied one's curiosity about the material facts of places and people. *The American Scene* has little description of landscape or buildings, and it does not name or describe a single person James met on his trip. It purports to describe eleven different regions of the eastern United States, ranging from New England to Florida, but in James's account there is little to distinguish one place from another. In the witty phrase of W. H. Auden *The American Scene* "is no more a guidebook than the 'Ode to a Nightingale' is an ornithological essay."[84]

In the first chapter of his book James acknowledges his lack of interest in the standard people-and-places subject matter of travel journalism. It is "the human, the social question" that concerns him. "The *manners*, the manners: where and what are they, and what have they to tell?"—that question is the "haunting curiosity" that always buzzes about his head,

James writes.[85] Yet as an essay on American culture *The American Scene* is disappointingly thin. In essence, the book only repeats at stultifying length the insights James recorded more concisely and concretely in his 1879 book on Nathaniel Hawthorne: American life is dominated by the quest for business success; compared to Europe, the United States lacks tradition and history, the forms that give texture and meaning to social life. Moreover, James's consideration of manners accounts for only portions of the book. *The American Scene* contains long stretches that, although they are certainly not journalistic description, cannot be classified as social or cultural inquiry. These sections are instead a record of the growth of insight, an epistemological diary. Henry James turns himself into a Jamesian protagonist and makes the action of *The American Scene* the same as in the late novels: the protagonist's enlargement of perception.[86]

A key to the method of *The American Scene* lies in one of James's chapters on New York City. There he acknowledges, "almost blush[ing]," that the only adventures he has to offer are those of "the critical spirit." However, he counters, "I draw courage from the remembrance that history is never, in any rich sense, the immediate crudity of what 'happens,' but the much finer complexity of what we read into it and think of in connection with it" (182). James here dismisses the journalistic enterprise of reporting what happens as mere crudity; yet note that his concern is not with some substratum of final truth. What is important, James's two final verbs suggest, is the individual's play of consciousness, the process of reading and thinking about the text of events.

This process of perception forms the real plot of *The American Scene*, as we can see in any of dozens of passages. I have chosen one to illustrate the process. This single, typically dense paragraph typifies the book's action; it also demonstrates how eager James is to distinguish his approach to his subject—an American city frequently featured in newspaper articles—from that of a journalist writing on the same subject. The passage appears near the beginning of the chapter on Baltimore:

> I arrived late in the day, and the day had been lovely; I alighted at a large fresh peaceful hostelry, imposingly modern yet quietly affable, and, having recognized the deep, soft general note, even from my windows, as that of a kind of mollified vivacity, I sought the streets with as many tacit questions as I judged they would tolerate, or as the waning day would allow me to put. It took but that hour, as I strolled in the early eventide,

to give me the sense of the predicament I have glanced at; that of find-ing myself committed to the view of Baltimore as quite insidiously "sym-pathetic," quite inordinately amiable—which amounted, in other words, to the momentous proposition that she was interesting—and still of wondering, by the same stroke, how I was to make any such statement plausible. Character is founded on elements and features, so many par-ticular parts which conduce to an expression. So I walked about the dear little city looking for the particular parts—all with the singular effect of rather failing to find them and with my impression of felicity at the same time persistently growing. The felicity was certainly not that of a mere blank; there must accordingly have been items and objects, signs and tokens, there must have been causes of so charming a consequence; there must have been the little numbers (not necessarily big, if only a tall enough column) for the careful sum on my slate. What happened then, remarkably, was that while I mechanically so argued my impression was fixing itself by a wild logic of its own, and that I was presently to see how it would, when once settled to a certain intensity, snap its fingers at war-rants and documents. If it was a question of a slate the slate was used, at school, I remembered, for more than one purpose; so that mine, by my walk's end, instead of a show of neat ciphering, exhibited simply a bold drawn image—which had the merit moreover of not being in the least a caricature. The moral of this was precious—that of the fine impunity with which, if one but had sensibility, the ciphering could be neglected and in fact almost contemned: always, that is (and only) *with* one's finer wits about one. Without them one was at best, really, nowhere—even with "items" by the thousand; so that the place became, quite adorably, a lesson in the use of that resource. It would be "no good" to a journal-ist—for *he* is nowhere, ever, without his items; but it would be every-thing, always, to the mere restless analyst. He might by its aid stand against all comers; and this alike in pleasure and in pain, in the bruised or in the soothed condition. That was the real way to work things out, and to feel it so brought home would by itself sufficiently crown this par-ticular small pilgrimage. (308–309)

The passage begins with a snippet of journalistic travelogue: after arriving in Baltimore on a lovely day James went to a hotel and took a walk. But after a single sentence that deals with the immediate crudity of what hap-pened, James shifts his procedure. First, he records his impression of the city: it is "sympathetic," "amiable," "interesting." Next, he moves from adjectives of classification to verbs of process: he "wonder[s] . . . how I was to make any such statement [that Baltimore is interesting] plausible." For the rest of the paragraph James elaborates on his mental process, using a characteristically extended metaphor of a schoolboy's slate. James is careful to emphasize that he does not use his mental slate to accumulate facts, as a journalist would; instead, he uses his sensibility to draw a single bold image.

The paragraph ends in a mood of triumph, couched in a monarchic metaphor of crowning. Yet what James is celebrating is not the impression of Baltimore that he has formed—that is, after all, only the embarrassingly banal conclusion that the city is "interesting," scarcely an insight worth any regal ceremony. Rather, James's triumph is his recognition of the validity of his process of perception, the artist's reliance on personal impressions as opposed to the journalist's collection of facts. James proudly proclaims his failure as a reporter, his inability to gather any specific "items" about Baltimore to convey to his readers. *The American Scene* does not attempt to be a guidebook; it is a disappointment as an essay on American culture; but it is a success as antijournalism, a work that deliberately rejects the specificity of reporting in order to defend and celebrate James's artistic method.

Although James may have been willing to publish his work in the *New York Sun* and the *Illustrated London News,* all the fiction, essays, notebook entries, and letters that I have discussed so far have been unrelievedly hostile to journalism. Yet James's mind, in Lionel Trilling's phrase, is nothing if not dialectical.[87] During the 1880s, in his "international phase," James offered in his fiction an alternative view of the new journalism, presenting it as the inevitable adjunct of American democracy.

The short story "The Point of View" (1882) is dialectical in its structure. A collection of letters from passengers on a transatlantic ship, written as they approach the United States and in the weeks following, the story is an extended debate on democratic manners. Frequently, the newspaper serves as representative of American manners, as in a letter from Gustave Lejaune, an eminent French writer making his first visit to the United States. Lejaune, appalled at the absence of distinction, finds the United States to be marked by a "colossal mediocrity" except in technology. America's mass newspapers, a physical product of new technology, he finds a horror:

Such a tone, *grand Dieu!* The amenities, the personalities, the recrimi-
nations, are like so many *coups de revolver*. Headings six inches tall; correspondences from places one never heard of; telegrams from Europe
about Sarah Bernhardt; little paragraphs about nothing at all; the *menu*
of the neighbour's dinner; articles on the European situation *à pouffer
de rire*; all the *tripotage* of local politics. The *reportage* is incredible; I'm
chased up and down by the interviewers. The matrimonial infelicities of
M. and Madame X. (they give the name), *tout au long*, with every
detail—not in six lines, discreetly veiled, with an art of insinuation, as
with us; but with all the facts (or the fictions), the letters, the dates, the
places, the hours.

Lejaune's attack on newspapers is immediately followed by a letter from
Marcellus Cockerel, a forthright young American lawyer, grateful to be
home after an extended stay in Europe. Like Lejaune, Cockerel takes the
newspapers to be representative of the United States:

Delightful country, where one sees everything in the papers—the big,
familiar, vulgar, good-natured, delightful papers, none of which has any
reputation to keep up for anything but getting the news! . . . In Europe
[the tone of the press is] too dreary. . . . Here the newspapers are like the
railroad trains, which carry everything that comes to the station, and
have only the religion of punctuality.[88]

Cockerel cheerfully acknowledges the newspapers' vulgarity, but he also
insists on their journalistic democracy: they carry "everything" in their
pages, refusing to discriminate. The patriotic Cockerel sees newspapers as
the embodiment of basic American values, and he finds them "delightful."
    The divergent attitudes toward Europe and America, distinction and
democracy, privacy and publicity that James assigned to different characters in "The Point of View" are combined within a single character in *The
Reverberator* (1888), a novel in which journalism plays a central role. The
dialectical structure of "The Point of View" is reproduced in the dilemma
facing protagonist Gaston Probert, a young man who must choose
between a Europe that treasures privacy and a United States linked to the
new journalism. Gaston is the French-born son of an American family long
settled in Paris. Gaston's grandfather left his South Carolina plantation
early in the nineteenth century and made a place among the French aris-

tocracy. After three generations the Probert family has become thoroughly assimilated into French society. Gaston's father is a familiar figure in the most exclusive salons of the Faubourg Saint-Germain. Gaston's three sisters are married to a marquis, a count, and a baron. Gaston shares the Proberts' values: a devotion to family and "the worship of privacy and good manners."[89]

When Gaston falls in love with Francie Dosson, a young American traveling in Europe with her father and sister, he finds himself among a family as quintessentially American as the Proberts are European. Whereas the Proberts worship privacy, the Dossons live a public life, staying at hotels, eating in restaurants, and reading U.S. newspapers. Their first acquaintance in Paris is George M. Flack, European correspondent for a U.S. newspaper whose name gives the novel its title. Flack is a more virile but equally brash Matthias Pardon; like his counterpart in *The Bostonians*, he regards "everything and every one [as] every one's business." Early in the novel Flack confesses his journalistic ambitions to Francie Dosson. He dreams of taking over the *Reverberator* and giving it a fresh new slant:

> There are ten thousand things to do that haven't been done, and I'm going to do them. The society news of every quarter of the globe, furnished by the prominent members themselves (oh, *they* can be fixed—you'll see!) from day to day and from hour to hour and served up at every breakfast-table in the United States—that's what the American people want and that's what the American people are going to have. . . . I'm going for the secrets, the *chronique intime*, as they say here; what the people want is just what isn't told, and I'm going to tell it. . . . That's about played out, any way, the idea of sticking up a sign of "private" and thinking you can keep the place to yourself. You can't do it—you can't keep out the light of the Press. Now what I am going to do is to set up the biggest lamp yet made and to make it shine all over the place. We'll see who's private then! (60–61)

While first planning *The Reverberator*, James wrote in his notebook, "One sketches one's age but imperfectly if one doesn't touch on that particular matter: the invasion, the impudence and shamelessness, of the newspaper and the interviewer, the devouring *publicity* of life, the extinction of all sense between public and private."[90] George Flack is the embodiment of impudence and shamelessness, a whirlwind of publicity. Yet

Francie likes the young journalist, who introduces her to Gaston Probert. After she and Gaston become engaged (the thought of the Dossons' money reconciles Gaston's family to his alliance with a vulgar American), Francie repays Flack for his introduction by sitting down for a long talk about the amusing history of the fascinating Probert family. Soon afterward an article on the Proberts appears in the *Reverberator*. It leaves out nothing that Francie has told Flack. All the Proberts' most intimate secrets are there: the many love affairs of Gaston's sisters and their titled husbands, the long-buried scandal of a kleptomaniac sister-in-law. The Proberts are horrified, and they attempt to break off Gaston's engagement to Francie.

James poses Gaston squarely between Europe and America. On the one side are the Proberts, with their allegiance to family, discretion, and privacy. On the other are the Dossons, with all their naive pleasure in publicity. The Dossons cannot comprehend why the Proberts resent Flack's article. It appears to them to be "lively, 'chatty,' even brilliant" (157). To Mr. Dosson, the narrator explains, it was much more definite that "the soreness of the Proberts was a kind of unexpected insanity . . . than that a newspaper-man had misbehaved in trying to turn out an attractive article" (168).

The odds seem in favor of the Proberts and privacy and against the vulgar Dossons. Yet Gaston's choice is not so simple. The Proberts' discretion, after all, hides a long history of adultery, whereas Francie's friendship with Flack is the natural result of her candor and innocence. In his preface to the revised edition of *The Reverberator* James writes of "the extraordinary . . . native innocence" of the Americans he encountered in Europe in the 1870s and '80s. Their most general appearance, he goes on to say, was "that of being almost incredibly *unaware of life*—as the European order expressed life." Yet James acknowledges that in the case of certain young women, possessed of "the grace of youth and innocence and freshness . . . , their negatives were converted and became in certain relations lively positives and values."[91] Francie Dosson is inextricably linked with the American world of journalism and mass publicity, yet in her youth and innocence and freshness she represents for Gaston Probert his chance for moral freedom.

Until he meets Francie the deracinated Gaston, not wholly French yet not American, finds his identity solely through his family. His love for Francie becomes a way of establishing his independent selfhood. After

Flack's article is published, Gaston hovers between his attraction to Francie and his devotion to his family, who demand that he end the engagement. Gaston's sole American friend interprets his dilemma as a choice between European rigidity and American freedom. The Proberts, he tells Gaston, are "doing their best to kill you morally—to render you incapable of individual life" (196). Gaston eventually turns his back on Europe and his family. In marrying Francie—and thus accepting the publicity and journalism with which she is linked—Gaston makes a declaration of moral independence. American journalism, as represented in *The Reverberator*, is no less vulgar and intrusive than in any of James's other works. Yet the novel links the newspaper to fundamental American values of honesty and independence.[92]

Journalism also plays a role in James's greatest international novel, *The Portrait of a Lady* (1881). Henrietta Stackpole, Isabel Archer's comic confidante, is a correspondent for the *New York Interviewer*. With typical journalistic intrusiveness Henrietta writes an article about her hosts on the morning after her arrival in England. Isabel, with difficulty, dissuades her from sending it. "My poor Henrietta," she says wonderingly, "you've no sense of privacy."[93] If Isabel is amazed principally by her friend's brashness, the reader is also aware of the journalist's naïveté: she imagines that she can describe a complex society on twenty-four hours' acquaintance. Yet the narrator of *Portrait* never attacks Henrietta in the way that the narrators of *The Bostonians* and *The Reverberator* attack Matthias Pardon and George Flack. Henrietta is a likable and even admirable character; one of the first facts we learn about her is that she uses her income from journalism to support the three children of an infirm widowed sister.

Henrietta serves as a moral touchstone in the novel: other characters reveal their true nature by their reaction to her. Like Isabel, the novel's admirable characters are fond of Henrietta, although they are careful to ensure that she does not describe them in print. In contrast, Gilbert Osmond dislikes the young journalist. And it is Osmond's objections to Henrietta, when she visits the Osmond household shortly after Isabel's marriage, that first lead Isabel to view her husband in a critical light. Osmond's grim protests against Henrietta are Isabel's first hints of his narrowness of character. Isabel, the narrator tells us, was "disappointed at her husband's not seeing his way simply to take the poor girl for funny. She even wondered if his sense of fun, or of the funny—which would be his sense of humour, wouldn't it?—were by chance defective" (2:138–39).

Whereas the humorless, morally corrupt Osmond detests Henrietta, Isabel's cousin Ralph Touchett confirms his sense of humor by becoming good friends with her. Yet along with his humorous acceptance of Henrietta, Ralph has an uneasy recognition of the threat that this representative of the new journalism poses to the cultural and artistic values he cherishes. In a symbolically laden gesture the dying Ralph leaves his extensive library to Henrietta. Ralph has no illusions about her fondness for literature; he intends her to sell his books and use the money to start a newspaper. Henrietta "smell[s] of the Future—it almost knocks one down!" Ralph exclaims upon meeting her (1:131). His bequest is a sly comment on the future of literature and journalism. In *The Portrait of a Lady* James offers a witty, uneasy glimpse of a future in which the big blatant bayadere of journalism supplants literature.

James's and Howells's fiction records with varying degrees of fear and resignation their recognition of the growing importance of journalism in American culture and the increasing links between novel and newspaper, artist and reporter. Generally hostile to journalism, they used their fiction as a bulwark, shoring up the high culture's defenses against the encroachments of mass journalism. However, they were fighting a rearguard action. The defenses they erected were undermined during the 1890s by a young writer, friend to both novelists, who moved easily between journalism and fiction, ignoring the distinctions between low and high culture that they had worked so assiduously to maintain. The young writer's name was Stephen Crane.

CHAPTER 2

The Launching of Stephen Crane

EARLY JOURNALISM

Howells and James filled their stories and novels with unflattering portraits of newspaper journalists. However, none of their fictional characters better illustrates the two writers' hostility to reporters than the odious Matthias Pardon of *The Bostonians*. James writes of his prying reporter, "[Pardon] had begun his career, at the age of fourteen, by going the rounds of the hotels, to cull flowers from the big, greasy registers which lie on the marble counters."[1]

Add two years to Pardon's age, and James might have been describing Stephen Crane. James does not specify Pardon's motive in choosing a journalistic career at such a tender age; Stephen Crane was simply stepping into the family business. Stephen's older brother Townley ran a news bureau on the New Jersey shore, supplying the *New-York Tribune* and other newspapers with news from the popular summer resorts. Stephen began working for his brother's news bureau when he was sixteen, copying hotel registers in order to report on arriving guests.[2] This is not to say that Crane began life as a hack reporter, indifferent to poetry and fiction; his early literary ambitions were equal to those of Howells and James. However, almost everything Crane published for the first five years of his career appeared in newspapers, as did much of what he wrote afterward. When he completed a novel about a young Civil War soldier, he first took it not to a commercial publisher but to a newspaper syndicate, and *The Red Badge of Courage* made its initial appearance in newspaper pages. After the novel made him famous, he continued to write for newspapers.

Crane moved easily between journalism and fiction throughout his career. To take one representative twelve-month period, the year 1897, Crane began by publishing on January 7 a syndicated newspaper article about his experience in a shipwreck. Shortly afterward he wrote about the same episode for *Scribner's* magazine in a piece titled "The Open Boat." That spring he went to Greece, where he reported on the Greco-Turkish War for William Randolph Hearst's *New York Journal*, then moved to England, where he wrote a series of short works, including "The Blue Hotel" and "The Bride Comes to Yellow Sky."

Crane's activities during 1897 reveal a writer unconcerned, both professionally and artistically, with the distinctions between literature and journalism, artist and reporter, high culture and low that were so significant to Howells and James. At a time when most serious writers professed to be scandalized by Hearst's high-pitched newspaper sensationalism, Crane eagerly sought assignments as a celebrity reporter for the *Journal*. Crane gained experience in virtually every area of the late nineteenth-century literary and journalistic marketplace. He wrote for the genteel *Scribner's* magazine and the mass-circulation *New York Journal*. He published novels with the prestigious Appleton company and books of poetry with an obscure avant-garde Boston firm. Crane, who supported himself by his pen from the age of twenty, was willing to write for anyone who would pay him.

Operating indiscriminately within the literary marketplace, Crane produced work that defies attempts to categorize it as literature or journalism, high culture or low. To take only his 1897 output, close examination yields numerous questions: Is "The Open Boat" an article or a short story? Is the Greco-Turkish War work "A Fragment of Velestino" journalism or art? What is the relation of "The Blue Hotel" and "The Bride Comes to Yellow Sky" to Crane's 1895 newspaper reporting from the West?

Crane's career as journalist and novelist and the writing he produced do not seem to fit any of the paradigms established by critics who have explicated the links between journalism and literature in America. The journalist-authors discussed by Shelley Fisher Fishkin in *From Fact to Fiction: Journalism and Imaginative Writing in America* were all late bloomers who first produced mediocre poetry or fiction. Their great works—which, Fishkin argues, were shaped by their newspaper experience—came only after years of false starts. But Stephen Crane produced his best work at a startlingly early age. He was twenty when he wrote *Maggie*, twenty-two when he completed *The Red Badge of Courage*, and twenty-three when he published the poems collected in *The Black Riders*. Nor does Crane's career fit the pattern explicated by Larzer Ziff and Ellen Moers in their discussions of 1890s metropolitan journalism. As Ziff puts it, newspaper city rooms served as a school for would-be novelists at the turn of the century; Moers writes that modern realist fiction "burst from the seed of the newspaper sketch." Many critics have assumed that Crane's career fit the Ziff-Moers paradigm and have regarded his New York City sketches as "warm-ups for novels," in the words of Tom Wolfe. However, attention to chronology complicates any effort to treat Crane's journalism as preparation for literature; Crane wrote most of his New York sketches *after* he published his Bowery novel *Maggie*. As Christopher Benfey has recently pointed out, throughout his career Crane's journalistic experiences followed his imaginative projections. Crane first wrote about poverty and war in *Maggie* and *The Red Badge of Courage* and then did newspaper reporting in the slums and on the battlefield.[3]

The chapters that follow will consider the complex relation between Crane's journalism and fiction dealing with New York City, the American West, and the battlefield. This chapter treats Crane's work between 1890 and 1892, when he was eighteen to twenty years old. During those years newspapers published almost all of Crane's writing. His journalism falls into three categories: articles from the New Jersey shore; sketches dealing with the history and folklore of Sullivan County, New York; and a series of short stories set in Sullivan County that describe the camping adventures of four friends.

These early newspaper pieces seem distant from the concerns of Crane's best-known fiction. Crane's most famous novels and short stories are set in the slums, the battlefield, and the Wild West. In contrast, his early journalism treats middle-class resorts on the New Jersey shore and a rural county in downstate New York. However, these early newspaper articles are important in understanding Crane's work.

Most significantly, the articles reveal how the young Stephen Crane flourished within the fact-fiction discourse of 1890s journalism. Journalistic discourse at the turn of the century was different from the newspaper conventions that have dominated since the 1920s. Twentieth-century newspaper producers and readers, under the sway of the ideology of journalistic objectivity, have insisted on drawing sharp distinctions between journalistic fact and literary fiction. Newspaper reporters and readers of the

1890s were much less concerned with distinguishing among fact-based reporting, opinion, and literature. Readers of front-page reporting on politics expected nineteenth-century journalists to interpret events according to their paper's editorial philosophy. (The *New York Press*, where Crane published most of his New York City sketches, proclaimed beneath its masthead that it was "New York's Largest Republican Newspaper.") The inside pages and Sunday feature sections, where virtually all of Crane's journalism appeared, indiscriminately mixed national and metropolitan reporting, short fiction, and realistic sketches that gave little indication of their verifiability.

The fact-fiction discourse that dominated in 1890s newspapers proved fruitful terrain for the young Stephen Crane. His New Jersey shore reports not only give resort news but are suffused by Crane's distinctive ironic voice. His Sullivan County sketches blend fact and folklore in a subtly disorienting brew. Within the fact-fiction discourse of 1890s journalism Crane experimented with approaches and techniques that would influence all his work to come.

Stephen Crane began his career as a summer reporter for the New Jersey Coast News Bureau. Townley Crane's bureau was part of a vast system of newsgathering that provided northeastern newspapers with resort news. During the late nineteenth century news from Saratoga, Newport, the New Jersey shore, and other resorts for the middle and upper classes appeared regularly in major newspapers' Sunday editions from July through September. Resort news had two primary functions: to give the names of visitors and to promote the resort. Most articles consisted of little but lists of new arrivals and the hotels at which they were staying. An 1890 *New-York Tribune* article from the Crane news bureau, almost certainly written by Stephen Crane, concludes with fifty-two paragraphs listing fifty-two visitors at Avon-by-the-Sea, New Jersey; the young reporter's task was to comb hotel registers and come up with variations on his initial entry: "George H. Delamater, of Meadville, Penn., is registered at the Avon Inn." We can observe Crane, like a sportswriter reporting his fiftieth baseball game of the season, doggedly coming up with variations on a formula: "is a guest at "; "has signed his name on the books of"; " is spending his summer outing at"; "enjoys the gayety at."[4] One or two paragraphs boosting the resort generally preceded the lists of names. A typical article from the Crane news bureau—this one from Long Branch and almost certainly not by Stephen—begins, "The balance of the season promises to be unusually brilliant and lively. There is to be a grand flower and children's carnival next Tuesday and Wednesday that will surpass anything ever known in the history of 'the Summer Capital.'"[5] Although a modern reader is likely to be amused by the Victorian hyperbole of such passages, Townley Crane's bureau was actually rather restrained in its promotion of New Jersey resorts. An article from Saratoga, New York, printed in the *Tribune* a few weeks earlier begins, "More perfect weather than that of the present week never before smiled on this richly-endowed mineral water foothill section of the Adirondacks. The meteorological conditions have been simply superb, and were highly enjoyed by the thousands of visitors luxuriating at this cosmopolitan resort."[6]

Appearing on newspaper pages filled with dozens of examples of such unabashed boosterism, Stephen Crane's articles are distinctive for their irony. The earliest article that can reliably be identified as his, published in 1890 when Crane was eighteen, is a remarkably assured performance.[7] The article's dateline is Avon-by-the-Sea, a New Jersey coast resort famous for its adult school, the Seaside Assembly. After opening with a description of the assembly, the article mentions another summer gathering at Avon, the American Institute of Christian Philosophy. As the aggressively irreverent son of a minister, Crane never let pass an opportunity to satirize the clergy. He writes,

The learned members of the institute are already making their appearance with their baggage at the hotels and boarding houses. The guests claim that they can tell the members of the institute from afar by a certain wise, grave and reverend air that hangs over them from the top of their glossy silk hats to their equally glossy boots. A member gazes at the wild tossing of the waves with a calm air of understanding and philosophy that the poor youthful graduate from college, with only a silk sash and flannel suit to assert his knowledge with, can never hope to acquire. When he learns to row on the lake or river, to his philosophical mind he is only describing an arc from the rowlock as a centre, with a radius equal to the distance between the fulcrum or rowlock and the point of resistance, vulgarly known as the tip end of the oar. When he "catches a crab" and goes over backward, he gets up and, after rubbing the back of his head, he calmly returns anew to what he calls a demonstration of the principles of applied force. He watches the merry dancers at the hotel hops with an air that says: "Vanity, vanity, all is vanity." Yet he has no doubt in his own mind, from certain little geometric calculations of his own, that he could waltz in such a scientific manner, with such an application of the laws of motion, that the best dancers would, indeed, be surprised.

This passage by the teenaged Stephen Crane reveals many characteristics that would mark his subsequent New Jersey shore reporting. First, he converts qualities that the institute members and most other people would consider to be internal and essential—such as the members' wisdom and gravity—into superficial signifiers created by their clothes and behavior: the self-created "air" associated with glossy silk hats and boots. Crane also satirizes the members' moral censoriousness, as they spout Bible verses while watching a hotel dance. Finally, he delights in exposing the ministers' pretension. He contrasts their air of calm philosophy with the unruly power of nature in the "wild tossing of the waves." And he undercuts their certainty that rowing is merely an application of applied force by the description of a Christian philosopher fumbling his oars and falling over backward.

The irreverence that Crane displays in this piece would mark much of his New Jersey shore reporting. His home base of Asbury Park proved fertile ground for a satirist. Asbury Park, named for the first Methodist bishop in the United States, was a middle-class family resort under the firm control of James F. Bradley, a moralistic businessman who founded the town in 1870 and owned the boardwalk, the beach, and much of the real estate. To the south Asbury Park was bordered by Ocean Grove, a resort wholly owned by the Methodist Camp Meeting Association and established as a place where sea bathing and evangelism could be combined, or, as one of the founders put it, where Methodists could find both "rest and . . . salvation."[8] All vehicles were prohibited in Ocean Grove on Sunday, while tobacco and liquor were banned completely. Crane found much to satirize in these pious middle-class resorts, but it is important to note the limits of his irony. In the same article satirizing the Christian philosophers at Avon-by-the-Sea he also respectfully discusses the musicians and painters teaching at the Seaside Assembly. In all Crane's New Jersey coast reporting only two groups are invariably safe from his irony: artists—whether visual artists, musicians, or writers—and professional athletes. Whether reporting on the activities of "the well-known New-York tenor" Albert G. Thies, who "has a voice of great compass and sweetness," or of boxer James J. Corbett, possessor of a "gentlemanly bearing and quiet manners," Crane treats artists and athletes with respect.[9] The youthful Stephen Crane, scourge of the ministry and the middle class, was awed by artistic accomplishment and physical daring. Art and courage would remain obsessions in his writing for the rest of his career.

Crane's 1890 article on Avon-by-the-Sea can be confidently attributed to him by both style and content. Attribution of articles from the summer of 1891, when Crane was nineteen, is more difficult. The only article for which external evidence exists is a straightforward report of Hamlin Garland's Seaside Assembly lecture on William Dean Howells.[10] During the summer of 1891 Townley Crane's bureau supplied a number of articles to the *Tribune* that contain witty and mildly ironic descriptions; however, it seems unwise to attribute any glimmer of irony to Stephen.[11] It is just as likely that a sort of competition to produce witty phrases may have arisen among Stephen and the other writers at the news bureau as that Stephen alone is responsible for every attempt to enliven the generally dull summaries of resort news.

However, during the summer of 1892 the *Tribune* printed numerous articles that can be confidently identified as Stephen Crane's. These extravagantly and consistently ironic articles reveal that the twenty-year-old reporter had gained a mature stylistic confidence. Two years earlier Crane was still feeling his way as a writer. Just before publishing in the *Tribune* his witty send-up of the Christian philosophers at Avon-by-the-Sea, he had published in his school magazine an essay on writer-explorer Henry M. Stanley; the article is a standard hagiographic Victorian biography that concludes by extolling Stanley as "a great christian explorer."[12] In contrast, by 1892 Crane was working in a consistently ironic mode.

Crane's artistic transformation during the two-year period from 1890 to 1892 is remarkable but comprehensible. During this time Crane had attended and quickly dropped out of two colleges, turning his back on a standard career path and instead attempting to make his way as a writer. His mother had died soon after his twentieth birthday, an event that forced the beginning of independent adulthood. He had written a draft of a novel about a prostitute from the New York City slums, a daring work that would be published the next year as *Maggie: A Girl of the Streets (A Story of New York)*. And he had succeeded in publishing his Sullivan County tales and sketches in the *New-York Tribune*, the nation's most prestigious newspaper.

~~~~~

According to an intermittently reliable memoir by Willis Fletcher Johnson, an editor at the *Tribune*, Crane showed him the first of the Sullivan County sketches during the summer of 1891, when Crane was nineteen. The *Tribune* began publishing the tales and sketches in February 1892; fourteen pieces appeared over the next five months. All are set in the densely wooded hills of lower New York State's Sullivan County. Crane's older brother William owned a 3,500-acre tract in the county, adjacent to the 6,000-acre Hartwood hunting club, where Stephen spent considerable time hunting and camping during his youth.[13]

The Sullivan County pieces fall into two groups: nine are sketches about backwoods folklore; five are comic short stories about the camping mishaps of four friends. All appeared in the *Tribune*'s Sunday edition. Newspapers of the 1890s, particularly their Sunday editions, were capacious enough to welcome both folklore sketches and short stories; the papers contained a much greater variety of discursive forms than is seen in contemporary journalism. Typically, an 1890s Sunday edition of the *Tribune* contained twenty-four to twenty-eight pages divided into two or three sections. The first section was devoted to news reports, whereas the second and third sections were miscellanies with an indiscriminate mixture of literary and journalistic modes. Short stories, poems, serialized novels, and humorous anecdotes were scattered among historical essays, travel articles, book reviews, fashion notes, sports reports, resort news, and a variety of sketches.

The *Tribune* and other newspapers used few headlines or typographical markers that would flag a piece's generic status. Often the opening lines made a work's genre obvious. Crane cast all five of his Sullivan County short stories as frank fictions; one begins, "Four men once upon a time went into the wilderness."[14] However, his nine folklore sketches had a much more ambiguous status within the newspaper. Three sketches are historical works, describing encounters between the region's white settlers and its original inhabitants; the other six are hunting tales. Unlike the short stories, all the folklore sketches carried a dateline. The place is given as Hartwood, New York, or some other Sullivan County town; the date is generally a few days before publication. Although it is impossible to determine whether Crane or a *Tribune* editor inserted the datelines, they suggest that the sketches are "news"—timely reports of actual events. Yet the sketches' placement in the Sunday *Tribune*'s second or third section, which contained poetry and serialized novels along with news, qualifies readers' assumptions of the sketches' factuality.

The sketches' ambiguous status within the newspaper, as datelined articles appearing amid both news and fiction, nicely coincides with their ambiguity of content. The folklore tales, several of which describe fabulous hunting exploits, provided Crane with the opportunity to explore the truth status of narrative itself. The Sullivan County folklore sketches— whether their nominal subject is bears, panthers, or Native Americans—are fundamentally metafictions about storytelling. The fact-fiction discourse of the new journalism enabled Crane, whose mature work has been praised by postmodernist critics, to consider the nature of narrative truth from the beginning of his career.

The Sullivan County sketches dealing with Native Americans, set in the eighteenth century, are as much about the oral and literary traditions through which these stories were passed down as they are about the frequently violent relations between Native Americans and white settlers. The first of the Sullivan County sketches to be published in the *Tribune*, "The Last of the Mohicans," explicitly draws attention to the literary tradition through its frequent references to the James Fenimore Cooper novel of the same title. Crane contrasts Cooper's "noble savage" title character with the "demoralized, dilapidated," and alcoholic Native American whom Sullivan County storytellers claimed was actually the last of his tribe.[15] On the surface Crane's narrative seems to establish a simple contrast between truth and fiction, with the sordid Sullivan County reality set against Cooper's idealized portrait. Yet "The Last of the Mohicans" undermines this reading, for it opens not with a description of Cooper's character or the Sullivan County Indian but with a reflection on the veracity of Sullivan County's oral history. These traditional tales are often verified by "learned men," the narrator tells us, but he also describes how stories can become distorted as they pass from generation to generation: "Insignificant facts . . . have been known to become of positively appalling importance," the narrator explains, as stories are "told from mouth to mouth down the years." Crane's focus on the act of storytelling undercuts a simple fact-fiction distinction between the alcoholic Indian and Cooper's character; both, the tale reveals, are narrative creations.

Another of the Native American sketches, "Not Much of a Hero," focuses on the nature of narrative and upsets the dominant cultural discourse about Indian warfare. This brief biography of Tom Quick, a settler who gained fame as an Indian fighter, ends by considering the problem of determining who Quick was and what he represents. Was he, the narrator asks, an "Indian fighter" or "merely an Indian killer"?[16] "There are three views to be taken of 'Tom' Quick," the narrator says, and he goes on to consider the problems of determining the veracity of traditional tales and interpreting their meaning. His "views" of Quick include the possibility that the settler was an admirable character, "one of those sturdy and bronzed woodsmen who cleared the path of civilization"; an appraisal of him as "a monomaniac upon the subject of Indians"; and a condemnation of Quick as "purely and simply a murderer." The narrator refuses to choose among these three views, leaving us free to select the one we prefer. Our more likely response is a recognition of the uncertain veracity of any narrative—particularly the narratives about whites and Indians that were central to American culture in the early 1890s.

When Crane's story about Tom Quick appeared in the *Tribune* in 1892, the wars against the Plains Indians had only recently concluded; the battle of Wounded Knee, which marked the end of armed Indian resistance in the American West, took place less than two years earlier. Many historians regard Wounded Knee as the My Lai of the Plains wars; about two hundred Sioux, the majority of them women and children, were killed by U.S. troops in an orgy of violence.[17] Yet at the time newspapers, including the *Tribune*, reported Wounded Knee as a chapter in a larger narrative concerning manifest destiny and white superiority.[18] "Not Much of a Hero" is set in the eighteenth century, yet in its challenge to readers' certainty of how to read narratives about white and Indian warfare it responds powerfully to recent events.

Aside from his three sketches about Native Americans, all of Crane's other Sullivan County sketches are about hunting—more precisely, they are about hunting stories. Whereas William Faulkner would later use hunting stories in his 1942 novella *The Bear* as a way of uncovering mythic truths about humans and the natural world, Crane treats bear-hunting tales as fabrications that lead us to question the truth of any narrative. "The Way in Sullivan County" is representative of Crane's hunting sketches. "The way" in Sullivan County is hunting, we soon learn, but the way is also lying. Crane treats hunting and lying as inextricably bound activities. "One can buy sawlogs from a native and take his word that the bargain is square," the narrator tells us, "but ask the same man how many deer he has killed in his lifetime and he will stop working, take a seat on the snake-fence and paralyze the questioner with a figure that would look better than most of the totals to the subscription lists for monuments to national heroes."[19] Crane paints a comic picture of the "city man" who comes to Sullivan County, is astonished by the tales of hunting prowess that he hears, and then writes one of "those brief but lurid sketches which fascinate and charm the reading public." Crane's narrative then proceeds to offer a series of brief but lurid sketches of hunting exploits, such as an anecdote about a hunter who kills three bears all hiding behind a single log and another about hunters who kill a bear and a panther simultaneously. The difference between Crane's hunting sketches and those of the naive city man is that Crane frames his hunting stories within a larger metafictional narrative that draws our attention to the unreliability of any story.

In "Bear and Panther," another of the hunting sketches, Crane seems to be toying with the questions of verifiability raised by the sketch's journalistic context. "Bear and Panther" is an anecdote about hunters who witness a fight to the death between a bear and panther and then shoot the victor. Like the other hunting sketches, "Bear and Panther" begins with a dateline that seems to announce its status as news. Yet the dateline is followed by an opening that directly calls into question the narrative's veracity:

> Hartwood, N.Y., July 12.—Two or three men known individually as positively the oldest inhabitants of the county can tell stories of the time when the panthers used to haunt these woods and make desperate hunting. A story of a disturbance between a bear and a panther is their favorite, and as each oldest inhabitant insists upon telling it whenever a listener heaves in sight, it may be said to be well authenticated.[20]

This prefatory paragraph begins not with a story but with its tellers—men whom the narrator slyly brands as liars, because each claims positively to be the county's oldest inhabitant. By the second sentence the narrator has abandoned any claims for the story's truth. The tale's "authenticity" depends not on any verification—the anecdote that follows never identifies the hunters—but on its status as a frequently repeated narrative.

"Bear and Panther" deals with decades-old folklore. Yet Crane toys with issues of veracity even in recounting recent events. His long sketch

"Hunting Wild Hogs" describes people Crane knew first hand; one hunter he mentions is his brother William. However, the sketch gives much less attention to the well-known Sullivan County judge William Crane than to a local hunter, Lew Boyd, whom the narrator transforms into a legendary figure. The sketch's account of how Boyd tracked a boar for more than two hundred miles during a weeklong chase undermines its veracity by reminding us of the narrative's mythic qualities. Crane describes Boyd in the terms used for half-real, half-mythic American frontier heroes like Daniel Boone and Davy Crockett: "He is a six-foot-four-inch man, with broad shoulders, a good eye, and legs that have no superior for travel in a rough country."[21] Crane prefaces Boyd's exploit with reminders that hunting stories are narratives deliberately crafted to delight and frighten listeners. Before "Hunting Wild Hogs" ever mentions hogs, it talks about other hunters, their hunting stories, and the tellers' narrative skills. The sketch opens:

> If the well-worn and faded ghost of many an old scout or trapper of long ago could arise . . . , it could doubtless create a thrill by reciting tales of the panther's gleaming eyes and sharp claws. Mayhap, in a thousand varieties of chimney-corner, old, gnarled, and knotted forty-niners curdle the blood and raise the hair of their listeners with legends of the ferocious and haughty grizzly bear.

In the sketch's opening, panthers and grizzly bears are not so much game for hunters as they are subjects for storytellers. They function less as objects upon which the hunter can test his skill and courage than as literary constructs he can use to demonstrate his narrative technique. Sullivan County's wild hogs fill the same purpose. The sketch's narrator reminds readers, as he does in "The Way in Sullivan County," that wild game and lying are inextricably entwined. The narrator writes that after several wild hogs, imported from Europe, escaped from a fenced estate, "the great liar" appeared all over Sullivan County. "Children going to school were frightened home by wild hogs. Men coming home late at night saw wild hogs. It became a sort of fashion to see wild hogs and turn around and come back." The narrator concludes the story of Lew Boyd with a reminder that the most significant result of his exploit is not pork but prose: "The people of Sullivan County are wonderful yarn-spinners and they have some great additions to their list of tales. Doubtless for years to come those that know the story will tell to admiring listeners how 'Lew' Boyd chased the wounded wild hog for 200 miles."

The format and context of the publication of the Sullivan County sketches—as datelined articles in Sunday newspapers that mixed factual reports with fiction and anecdotes—may have stimulated Crane's experiments with the ways in which narratives lay claim to truth. He carried into his later work the metafictional concerns with the nature of narrative that mark the Sullivan County sketches. As Michael Fried and other critics have recently argued, much of Crane's work can be read as a reflection on the act of writing.[22] Although much of this recent criticism suggests that Crane was a postmodernist in Victorian clothing, it could be argued that Crane's awareness of the instability of narrative representation was a natural result of his practice of journalism and of his familiarity with the fact-fiction discourse of 1890s newspapers.

A few months after the *Tribune* published his first Sullivan County sketch in February 1892, Crane returned to Asbury Park for his seasonal job with the New Jersey Coast News Bureau. Perhaps buoyed by his success in publishing his Sullivan County sketches and short stories, Crane brought a distinctive ironic voice to numerous articles he wrote that summer. Crane seemed determined to escape his status as "Townley's kid brother," as the other shore reporters called him.[23] That summer he emerged as an artist determined to find material in the unpromising surroundings of middle-class New Jersey shore resorts.

Crane's first article of the 1892 season begins with an ironic assault on a favorite target, the Methodist ministers of Ocean Grove:

> The sombre-hued gentlemen who congregate at this place in summer are arriving in solemn procession, with black valises in their hands and rebukes to frivolity in their eyes. They greet each other with quiet enthusiasm and immediately set about holding meetings. The cool, shaded Auditorium will soon begin to palpitate with the efforts of famous preachers delivering doctrines to thousands of worshippers.[24]

As in his 1890 article on the Institute for Christian Philosophy, Crane mocks the ministers' moral censoriousness—their reflexive "rebukes to frivolity"—and in effect deconstructs their piety, portraying them as an assemblage of superficial signifiers, from their somber clothes to their black luggage. He turns even the experience of religious conversion—the raison d'être of the Ocean Grove assemblies—into a purely physical phenomenon through the comic image of a palpitating auditorium.

The following day's *Tribune* contained another Stephen Crane article. It begins,

> Pleasure seekers arrive by the avalanche. Hotel-proprietors are pelted with hailstorms of trunks and showers of valises. To protect themselves they do not put up umbrellas, nor even prices. They merely smile copiously. The lot of the baggageman, however, is not an easy one. He manipulates these various storms and directs them. He is beginning to swear with a greater enthusiasm. It will be a fine season.
>
> Asbury Park is rapidly acquiring a collection of machines. Of course there is a toboggan slide. Now, in process of construction, there is an arrangement called a "razzle-dazzle." Just what this will be is impossible to tell. It is, of course, a moral machine. Down by the lake an immense upright wheel has been erected. This will revolve, carrying little cars, to be filled evidently with desperate persons, around and around, up and down.[25]

Crane works in a sly dig at Asbury Park's propriety through his reference to the morality of the "razzle-dazzle." Yet what is notable about the article is the broad range of his ironic targets. Affluent hotel owners, working-class baggage porters, middle-class vacationers seeking thrills on a ride so novel that it had not yet received its name of "Ferris wheel"—all are subjected to the subtle deflation of Crane's finely tuned sarcasm.

During the summer of 1892 Crane let pass no opportunity to undercut pretension and reveal the humor lurking within the ordinary people and everyday events of New Jersey shore towns. However, the two articles quoted earlier, which were routine dispatches from the New Jersey Coast News Bureau, necessarily included large quantities of information resistant to ironic treatment; the articles report on the formation of an association of pastors' wives, additions to the Asbury Park Athletic Association grounds, and the arrival of dozens of summer visitors. However, later in the summer Crane had the opportunity to produce feature articles free of routine news. During the course of the season he wrote three long articles that are entirely ironic in tone, pieces in which Crane takes the stance of an anthropologist reporting on the Victorian middle class. In these three fea-

tures Crane reports on everyday life in a New Jersey shore resort in copi-
ous detail, with the distant, amused tone of a late Victorian adventurer
describing the habits of an African or Pacific island tribe.

"On the Board Walk," published in the August 14 *Tribune*, is a lengthy
discussion of Asbury Park, "the world of the middle classes." After describing the resort's milelong boardwalk and the enormous crowds that parade
there each summer evening, Crane sets out to analyze the various types to
be found in Asbury Park:

> The average summer guest here is a rather portly man, with a good
> watch-chain and a business suit of clothes, a wife and about three chil-
> dren. He stands in his two shoes with American self-reliance and, playing
> casually with his watch-chain, looks at the world with a clear eye. . . . All
> day he lies in the sand or sits on a bench, reading papers and smoking cig-
> ars, while his blessed babies are dabbling around throwing sand down his
> back and emptying their little pails of sea-water in his boots. In the
> evening he puts on his best and takes his wife and the "girls" down to the
> boardwalk. He enjoys himself in a very mild way and dribbles out a lot of
> money under the impression that he is proceeding cheaply.[26]

Like the Methodist ministers of Ocean Grove, the Asbury Park vacationer
is reduced to an assemblage of attributes: watch chain, clothes, wife, and
children. Crane satirizes the vacationer's delusions about his financial acumen yet treats the man's family life with the same indulgent affection that
the middle-class father extends to his children.

That mixture of satire and affection characterizes the entire article.
Crane moves from the portly family man to a description of the gentle
romances of "the long-famous 'summer girl'" and her "golden youth,"
then to a lengthy discussion of James A. Bradley, the millionaire founder
of Asbury Park. The eccentric and moralistic Bradley was one of Crane's
favorite targets. In "On the Board Walk" he describes at length Bradley's
boardwalk collection of curiosities—including an antique fire engine and a
marble bathtub—and offers a high-spirited textual analysis of the numerous signs that Bradley posted on the boardwalk, Victorian axioms such as
"Modesty of apparel is as becoming to a lady in a bathing suit as to a lady
dressed in silks and satins." Crane's witty explication of this "beautiful
expression of sentiment" concludes with the declaration that "'Founder'
Bradley . . . is not merely a man. He is an artist."

In a feature headlined "Joys of Seaside Life," Crane turns his attention from Asbury Park's middle-class vacationers to the itinerant entrepreneurs or "fakirs," as Crane calls them, who made a living entertaining or selling goods to the seaside guests. Crane treats the fakirs, most of whom were immigrants or African Americans, with the same combination of amusement and affection that he extends to his middle-class peers. The article ends with a hilarious description of a dancer that shows just how funny Crane, not usually thought of as a comic writer, could be. "The most terrific of all the fakirs, the most stupendous of all the exhibitions," he writes, "is that of the Greek dancer, or whatever it is." He continues:

> Two Italians, armed with a violin and a harp, recently descended upon the town. With them came a terrible creature, in an impossible apparel, and with a tambourine. He, or she, wore a dress which would take a geometrical phenomenon to describe. . . . When he, or she, with his, or her, retinue of Italians, emerged upon the first hotel veranda, there was a panic. Brave men shrunk. Then, he, or she, opened his, or her, mouth, and began to sing in a hard, high, brazen voice, songs in an unknown tongue. Then, he, or she, danced, with ballet airs and graces. The scowl of the assassin sat side by side with the simper and smirk of the country maiden who is not well-balanced mentally. The fantastic legs slid over the floor to the music of the violin and harp. And, finally, he, or she, passed the tambourine about among the crowd, with a villainously-lovable smile upon his, or her, features. Since then, he, or she, has become a well-known figure on the streets. People are beginning to get used to it, and he, or she, is not mobbed, as one might expect him, or her, to be.[27]

Crane's hyperbolic descriptions of the dancer, combined with the running joke about the entertainer's uncertain gender, result in a comic tour de force that demonstrates how, if he had chosen to follow a different path, Crane might have become a newspaper humorist on the order of his contemporaries George Ade or Finley Peter Dunne.[28]

Crane's final New Jersey shore article, published on September 11, 1892, is a feature devoted entirely to the "seaside hotel hop," which he calls "an institution peculiar unto itself."[29] In this piece Crane again takes the position of ironic anthropologist detailing middle-class customs. He characterizes the hotel hop as an event with "usually from 200 to 600 people looking on, and occasionally as many as six couples on the floor." He describes the types who frequent the hops, including the "summer girl," dancing-school children, and the hotel proprietor, who occasionally looks in, "rubbing his hands and beaming on the scene with an air that says, 'Enjoy yourselves, my people, these riotous festivities are given away with every package of twenty meal tickets.'"

Throughout his New Jersey shore articles we can see Crane satirically analyzing his class experience, exposing the foibles of Methodist ministers, summer girls, golden youths, and the family man on vacation. Crane saw clearly the pretensions and absurdities of his middle-class peers; he was just as ironic about other social classes. Crane was an equal opportunity satirist, poking fun at everyone from millionaire James Bradley to immigrant peddlers and entertainers. The *Tribune*'s editors seemed willing to enliven the columns of generally dull resort news with the young journalist's irony, and the newspaper's largely middle-class readers evidently did not object to his caustic depictions of their habits. However, late in the summer of 1892 Crane wrote an article—no more ironic than any of his usual contributions—that raised a furor and altered the direction of the young journalist's career.

Stephen Crane's most notorious New Jersey shore article, published on August 21, 1892, covers a parade of the Junior Order of United American Mechanics, a working-class nativist organization. The occasion called for nothing more than a brief notice of this self-proclaimed patriotic organization. The *Philadelphia Press* covered the event in a flattering article that begins, "The Junior American Mechanics of New Jersey owned the town today. The young patriots and their friends came down by the thousands, and celebrated 'American Day' in a very enthusiastic way."[30] Stephen Crane saw the event as a perfect opportunity for satire. His Asbury Park dispatch begins with three paragraphs on the parade:

> The parade of the Junior Order of United American Mechanics here on Wednesday afternoon was a deeply impressive one to some persons. There were hundreds of the members of the order, and they wound through the streets to the music of enough brass bands to make furious discords. It probably was the most awkward, ungainly, uncut and uncarved procession that ever raised clouds of dust on sun-beaten streets. Nevertheless, the spectacle of an Asbury Park crowd confronting such an aggregation was an interesting sight to a few people.

Asbury Park creates nothing. It does not make; it merely amuses. There is a factory where nightshirts are manufactured, but it is some miles from town. This is a resort of wealth and leisure, of women and considerable wine. The throng along the line of march was composed of summer gowns, lace parasols, tennis trousers, straw hats and indifferent smiles. The procession was composed of men, bronzed, slope-shouldered, uncouth and begrimed with dust. Their clothes fitted them illy, for the most part, and they had no ideas of marching. They merely plodded along, not seeming quite to understand, stolid, unconcerned and, in a certain sense, dignified—a pace and a bearing emblematic of their lives. They smiled occasionally and from time to time greeted friends in the crowd on the sidewalk. Such an assemblage of the spraddle-legged men of the middle class, whose hands were bent and shoulders stooped from delving and constructing, had never appeared to an Asbury Park summer crowd, and the latter was vaguely amused.

The bona fide Asbury Parker is a man to whom a dollar, when held close to his eye, often shuts out any impression he may have had that other people possess rights. He is apt to consider that men and women, especially city men and women, were created to be mulcted by him. Hence the tan-colored, sun-beaten honesty in the faces of the members of the Junior Order of United American Mechanics is expected to have a very staggering effect upon them. The visitors were men who possessed principles.[31]

Crane's last sentence reveals that the principal targets of his ironic assault are Asbury Park's summer visitors and permanent residents. The former are reduced by Crane's familiar metonymic technique to empty display forms for fine clothes, with empty smiles upon their faces. The latter are morally blinded by greed. In comparison, the marchers come off rather well. Yet Crane does not romanticize the working-class marchers. The references to their discordant music and slovenly marching undercut his praise of their dignity and honesty. As in *Maggie*, the novel he was working on during the summer of 1892, Crane sprays everyone with his irony, both the respectable and disreputable classes.

Crane's treatment of the three distinct social groups at the parade was unflattering to each, but only the marchers complained of their treatment by the ironic young journalist. Three days after Crane's article appeared, the *Tribune* published a letter from a member of the Mechanics that began, "Sir: I, as a member of the Junior Order of American Mechanics, take the liberty of writing to The Tribune in the name of all who belong to this patriotic American organization, in answer to the uncalled-for and un-American criticism published in The Tribune." In a demonstration of the dignity that Crane discerned in the marchers' gait, the writer continued, "We are not a labor organization, nor are we a military company, drilled to parade in public and be applauded for our fine appearance and precision; but we were appreciated for our Americanism and we were applauded for it." The *Tribune*'s editors responded with a fulsome apology: "We regret deeply that a bit of random correspondence, passed inadvertently by the copy editor, should have put into our columns sentiments both foreign and repugnant to The Tribune."[32] The apology continues for another few lines; the editorial staff was clearly aghast. The *Tribune*'s publisher, Whitelaw Reid, was at that moment campaigning as Benjamin Harrison's running mate in the 1892 presidential elections in a close race with the Democratic ticket of Grover Cleveland and Adlai Stevenson; the *Tribune* was obviously terrified of offending voters.

Controversy over Crane's column was not limited to the columns of the *Tribune*. Both of Asbury Park's newspapers commented on the affair. One reprinted the offending article and indignantly demanded an apology and a retraction. The other took a more indulgent view of the affair: "It is said that the *Tribune*'s regular letter-writer, J. Townley Crane, was engaged on something else last week, and delegated the task of writing the usual Sunday gabble to another. This young man has a hankering for razzle dazzle style, and has a great future before him if, [un]like the good, he fails to die young."[33] A persistent controversy in Stephen Crane biography concerns whether the *Tribune* fired him as a result of the article. The editor responsible for New Jersey shore news insisted that Crane was not fired; several of Crane's friends, family members, and fellow journalists insisted that he was.[34] The evidence is inconclusive. Articles by Stephen Crane continued to appear in the *Tribune* for the next three weeks, although these articles—features rather than news reports—may have been written and submitted before the parade report appeared. What is unquestionable is that after the 1892 summer season ended, Crane did no more shore reporting and never again published in the *Tribune*.

Journalism of the 1890s enabled the teenaged Stephen Crane to experiment with narrative conventions, to explore his preoccupations with human character and the natural world, and to craft a distinctive ironic voice. At the same time, it allowed him to establish a professional career. Yet journalism also showed him the limits of the Victorian audience. Testing those limits, he found the *Tribune*, his principal outlet for publication, closed to him. When he moved to New York City in the fall of 1892, Crane would struggle to find new outlets in the literary marketplace. Over the next few years he became involved with private publication, the avant-garde press, commercial publishers, and a variety of other newspapers. Throughout the years between 1892 and 1896, when he completed and published *Maggie*, *The Red Badge of Courage*, and *The Black Riders*, Crane continued to write journalism.

CHAPTER 3

Reporting the City

NEW YORK JOURNALISM

The dual careers of reporter and novelist that Stephen Crane pursued after he moved to New York City in 1892 helped to shape a central myth of modern American literature: the role of the newspaper as training ground for novelists. According to the myth—not, I want to emphasize, a false tale but rather a narrative that both expresses and shapes cultural possibilities— ambitious young newspaper reporters on assignment in the city streets encountered a gritty and varied urban reality that could later serve as a source of literary material.

The myth developed with astonishing rapidity during the 1890s. At the beginning of the decade the role of the reporter-artist was still in its formative stage. In "The Literary Shop," an 1893 essay about the New York literary marketplace, editor and critic James L. Ford treated the reporter-artist as a not-yet-born phenomenon. "There are young men working in newspaper offices now who will one of these days draw true and vivid pictures of modern New York," Ford predicted.[1] A decade later editor George H. Lorimer said with the assurance of one looking back on a long-established trend, "The daily newspaper sustains the same relation to the young writer as the hospital to the medical student. It is the first great school of practical experience."[2]

What occurred during the 1890s to prompt the change from Ford's hopeful prediction to Lorimer's flat assertion that writers viewed newspapers as a tuition-free professional school? The answer lies partly in the greatly expanded employment opportunities for reporters that accompanied the rapid growth of metropolitan newspapers during the late nineteenth century. As newspaper circulation swelled during the era, so did the demand for reporters. However, 1890s newspapers did not simply hire more reporters; they began to hire a different kind of writer. Before 1890 the typical reporter was considered to be a cynical, lightly educated, hard-drinking male. During the 1890s the number of college graduates going into journalism increased dramatically, and many regarded city reporting as a stepping-stone to literature. Lincoln Steffens's *Autobiography* provides the best account of the change. As city editor of the *New York Commercial Advertiser* during the 1890s, Steffens refused to hire experienced journalists of the old school, preferring to recruit his reporters fresh from the Ivy League colleges. He looked, he wrote, for the college graduate who "openly or secretly, hoped to be a poet, a novelist, or an essayist." Steffens claimed he had no use for a reporter whose ambitions were limited to journalism. "My staff were writers," Steffens wrote in his *Autobiography*, "getting the news as material for poetry, plays, or fiction, and writing it as news for practice."[3] His staff included literary-minded Harvard graduates such as Hutchins Hapgood; Neith Boyce, one of the first female journalists; and Abraham Cahan, later to become famous as a novelist of New York's Jewish immigrants. Charles Dana, celebrated editor of the *New York Sun*, agreed with Steffens's description of the new breed of reporters. Reflecting on the changes he had seen during a long career in journalism, Dana said with an air of some surprise in an 1893 speech, "The number of intellectual young men who are looking at this new profession . . . is very great. I suppose that I receive myself every day . . . half a dozen letters from men, many of them college graduates, asking for employment."[4]

Steffens's and Dana's comments reveal the changes occurring in 1890s reporting and the construction of the myth of the reporter-artist. Stephen Crane's career was a major constituent of that myth. As H. L. Mencken said, the revelation that the wildly popular *Red Badge of Courage* had been written by a newspaper reporter "lifted newspaper reporting to the level of a romantic craft."[5]

The reviews of the second edition of Crane's novel *Maggie: A Girl of the Streets (A Story of New York)* reflect this romantic view of his newspaper experience. After completing the novel Crane was unable to find a publisher and issued the book himself in 1893; like most self-published works the novel went virtually unnoticed. However, when the success of *The Red*

Badge of Courage (1895) made Crane's name a valuable commodity, *Maggie* was reissued in a revised edition (1896), which was widely reviewed. By the time the revised *Maggie* appeared, Crane's career as a journalist-author was well known, and reviewers assumed that *Maggie*, set in the New York City slums, was based on Crane's experience as a New York reporter. Virtually every reviewer praised the novel's realism, and two reviewers described the book as photographic.[6] One writer claimed, "No newspaper man in New York, no one who is familiar with the life of the tenements, can deny the accuracy of the picture."[7] In their references to photography and newspaper reporters *Maggie*'s reviewers linked the worlds of journalism and fiction. Crane's novel, they implied, arose from his reportorial investigations of the slums; *Maggie* was the literary equivalent of a newspaper article or illustration.

Building on the perceptions of *Maggie*'s first readers, later critics assumed that a simple three-step process lay behind Crane's New York City writing: Crane observed New York's slums, wrote about what he saw in the newspaper, then used his newspaper sketches as raw material for his slum novels, *Maggie* and *George's Mother* (1896). As Tom Wolfe put it, Crane's Bowery sketches were "warm-ups for novels."[8] However, the relation between Crane's New York City journalism and fiction is not so simple as has been assumed. Both biographical investigation and literary analysis complicate any attempt to construct a genealogy for *Maggie* that moves from observation to journalism to fiction.

Although doubt has been cast on claims by Crane's fraternity brothers at Syracuse University that he wrote *Maggie* as a nineteen-year-old freshman in the spring of 1891, it seems certain that Crane completed a draft of the novel before he moved to New York City in the fall of 1892.[9] When Crane started *Maggie*, his knowledge of New York's mean streets was based on his teenaged excursions into the city from relatives' homes in New Jersey. All of Crane's New York City newspaper sketches followed his drafting of the novel, confounding any attempt to regard the journalism as a warm-up for *Maggie*.

Frank Norris, who was working as a journalist in San Francisco when *Maggie* appeared, was the first writer to call into question the notion that *Maggie* records Crane's observations in the slums of New York. Norris wrote perceptively in his review of the novel that Crane was drawing on a long tradition of slum literature: "Most of his characters are old acquaintances in the world of fiction. . . . In ordinary hands the tale of 'Maggie' would be 'twice told.'"[10] Subsequent scholars have identified the novel's debt not only to the world of fiction but also to the mass of nonfiction writing on the evils of slum life produced by reformers and clergy.[11] Crane's deeply religious family would have been familiar with the works of crusading Christian reformers like Charles Loring Brace and the Reverend Thomas DeWitt Talmage, both of whom wrote copiously about the problems of lower New York during the 1870s and 1880s, when Crane was growing up. In the early 1890s secular reformers such as Benjamin O. Flower and writers for his magazine, the *Arena*—where Crane later published—frequently railed against the slums.

Its plot and characters inherited from dozens of stories and sermons, *Maggie* can scarcely be identified as journalistic—or even, despite the many readers who have pinned the label on it, as realistic. Crane contributed to the confusion about his novel when he inscribed in several copies of the first edition, "[*Maggie*] tries to show that environment is a tremendous thing in the world and frequently shapes lives regardless."[12] The inscription implies that *Maggie* is a naturalistic text, a rigorous investigation into the effects of the New York City slums on their inhabitants. However, as D. H. Lawrence reminded students of American literature, one must trust the tale, not the teller.[13] Crane's title character seems virtually unaffected by her environment. She is, in the text's melodramatic phrase, a flower who "blossomed in a mud puddle," an icon of purity placed, improbably, in a monstrous family with a mother and father who regularly attack each other in alcoholic rages, smashing enough furniture over the course of the novel to fill a warehouse.[14] Crane's story of a poor and innocent virgin seduced and then driven into a life of prostitution fits snugly into the conventions of Victorian melodrama.

Maggie owes nothing directly to Crane's New York City newspaper sketches, which he wrote after drafting the novel. However, this is not to say that Crane's first novel has nothing in common with his journalism. *Maggie* reflects the same thematic and stylistic preoccupations evident in Crane's early newspaper writing about Sullivan County and the New Jersey shore. The early journalism and *Maggie* show three major continuities. First, *Maggie*, like the shore reports, is notable for its lack of overt moralistic commentary. Just as Crane's *New-York Tribune* articles avoid the tongue clucking about overly daring bathing suits or backroom gambling that was common in resort news, *Maggie* lacks the condemnations of drink, violence, and sexual misconduct that were standard in slum literature. Next, *Maggie* is remarkable for its irony; as Thomas Beer remarked, it is the first entirely ironic novel written by an American.[15] Maggie's drunken mother, who envisions herself as an excellent parent and a pious Christian; her truck-driving brother, who "menaced mankind" from street corners (20); her lover, an arrogant dandy—all are treated with the sharp-eyed irony that Crane used to describe middle-class vacationers at the New Jersey shore. Finally, the prose of *Maggie*, like that of Crane's early journalism, is strikingly fresh and original. A number of elements contribute to the distinctiveness of Crane's style in these early works. His writing abounds in startling figures of speech that evoke sharp images in readers' minds and, at the same time, move beyond the referents and draw attention to themselves as linguistic constructions. For example, in both Crane's journalism and in *Maggie* buildings become disconcertingly animate: a *Tribune* article describes a "palpitat[ing]" auditorium and tents that "rear their white heads under the trees,"[16] whereas a description of a slum in *Maggie* tells how "from a careening building, a dozen gruesome doorways gave up loads of babies to the street and the gutter" (11). Such deliberately disorienting descriptions follow one another in quick succession in Crane's work, joined by syntactically jerky sentences that are in turn assembled into short disconnected paragraphs. This abrupt style was a journalistic convention of the era. Shore reports got their unity from their setting rather than from a sustained narrative, and New Jersey Coast News Bureau reports commonly contained a half-dozen unconnected news items. However, the disconnected style that was conventional in a newspaper context appears radically new in *Maggie*.

Maggie is indeed related to Crane's early journalism, but the relation is more complex than early reviewers suggested. The myth of the reporter-artist implies a simple progression from observation to journalism to fiction. In addition, the myth places fiction at the top of an immutable literary hierarchy, with journalism below, serving as a stepping-stone to higher things. Critics of Stephen Crane's journalism have reinforced this hierarchical view. One of the first critics to examine Crane's newspaper journalism wrote of the inevitable conflict between "reportage and serious fiction" and concluded that the principal benefit of Crane's newspaper experience was to strengthen and sharpen his talent for "more serious creative work."[17] A more recent critic wrote approvingly of Crane's effort "to seek out the higher truths of fiction, beyond the bare facts of journalism."[18]

The notion that journalism traffics in bare facts lies behind Walter

Benjamin's elegant dismissal of journalism in his 1936 essay "The Storyteller." Characterizing journalism as information, Benjamin contrasts it
with storytelling and the novel and concludes that it threatens both forms.
"Every morning brings us the news of the globe," Benjamin writes, "and
yet we are poor in noteworthy stories."[19] Benjamin compares the journalist, who deals with verifiable information, with the storyteller, who offers
wisdom. Storytellers, Benjamin notes, fall into two types, whom he dubs
the peasant and the seafarer. The peasant, rooted in a single location, tells
stories whose roots are in local tradition; the seafarer brings tales from distant lands. Both kinds of storytellers offer tales that possess an authority
derived not from their verifiability but from their inherent narrative satis-
factions.

Recent theorists of narrative have disputed Benjamin's sharp distinction
between story and information. Benjamin used as his example of information a comment from the founding editor of the French newspaper *Le
Figaro*, who spoke of the importance to his readers of "an attic fire in the
Latin Quarter" (88). Theorists have pointed out that an article on a local
fire may be important to readers not because, as Benjamin assumed, it provides information that enables them to get "a handle [on] what is nearest"
(89) but precisely because the reporter shapes his report of the event according to timeless storytelling formulas. Michael Schudson has demonstrated
that Northrop Frye's scheme of literary classification in *The Anatomy of
Criticism* can be applied as easily to the newspaper's front page as to the
plays of Shakespeare. To take the story of the attic fire as an example, a
reporter may cast the event as a tragedy, in which lives or property are lost.
Alternatively, another observer of the same event might shape his report as
a comedy that emphasizes the joyous tears of the survivors who embrace one
another outside the burning building. A reporter focusing on the rescues
performed by a fire fighter might move into the realm of romance in depicting larger-than-life heroism, whereas an account that emphasized bureau-
cratic bungling in the municipality's response to the event and its aftermath
would construct an ironic narrative that could be seen as a satire. The point
is that even front-page news articles inevitably use storytelling conventions
as surely as do the folk tales of peasants and seafarers.[20]

Using Benjamin's terms, we can describe Crane's New York City journalism as the work of a seafarer-storyteller. Benjamin wrote that the seafarer conveyed tales over great distances, telling his hearers about lands
they would never visit. Crane's New York articles were, for the most part,

read by inhabitants of that city. Yet in writing about the New York City slums for a largely middle-class readership, Crane was in effect bringing intelligence from a distant land. By the 1890s, with a population of more than 1.5 million, New York City had become divided into "villages" based on income and ethnicity. Although these villages may have been geographically contiguous, the socioeconomic distances between them were enormous. Crane's New York City sketches bridge distances that are geographically insignificant but socially and cognitively vast.

The scarce documentation of Crane's life before *The Red Badge of Courage* made him famous has long frustrated biographers, and our scanty knowledge of his early newspaper work is equally frustrating for anyone interested in the development of his art. We know that Crane wrote for the *New York Herald*, the *Newark Daily Advertiser* and, most likely, other newspapers between 1891 and 1893, but it is extremely difficult to identify with any certainty what pieces might be Crane's among thousands of unsigned newspaper articles. Melvin Schoberlin, who wrote an unfinished biography of Crane in the 1940s, pored over all the newspapers for which Crane might have written and identified several articles as Crane's on the basis of subject matter and style. However, all his identifications are highly conjectural.[21] In the absence of other evidence it seems best to read the articles that Schoberlin singles out in the *Herald* and the *Daily Advertiser* as examples of newspapers' interest in documenting lower-class urban life. In New York City newspapers of the early 1890s one can find a wealth of articles that show how Crane worked within a tradition of news and feature writing about the city's vast immigrant population.

In an article about Crane's "lost" newspaper writings, based on Schoberlin's identifications, Thomas A. Gullason sensibly treats most of the identifications as conjectural. However, he regards one New York City feature as "unmistakably by Crane."[22] If Schoberlin and Gullason are correct, this article, published in the *Herald* in July 1891, when Crane was nineteen, would be his earliest New York City sketch. Gullason reprints the *Herald* article in full, thus performing a valuable service in making the piece more widely available. However, it is not certain that the article is by Crane. Titled "Where 'De Gang' Hears the Band Play," the article describes a band concert at Tompkins Square on the Lower East Side of Manhattan. As is typical of many 1890s newspaper sketches, the piece blends observation of the Tompkins Square scene with obviously created characters, whom we first meet in their tenement house apartment. The sketch focuses on two characters, a brother and sister whom it dubs "Mag" and "Jimmy." The closeness of these names to those of the brother and sister in Crane's *Maggie* makes Gullason certain that the piece is by Crane; however, it seems just as likely that Crane chose the names of his novel's characters for their typicality. Although the *Herald* sketch, like much of Crane's work, includes carefully rendered vernacular dialogue, it also includes a pompous narrative voice unlike that found in Crane's other sketches. "Where 'De Gang' Hears the Band Play" seems best viewed not as an addition to the Crane canon but as part of the fact-fiction discourse in which Crane and other 1890s newspaper writers were immersed.

The same page of the Sunday *Herald* on which "De Gang" appears contains a second sketch about working-class recreation, "Typical Scenes in a Summer Garden"; the garden is actually a working-class beer garden and dance hall. Both "De Gang" and "Summer Garden" are mildly condescending portraits of the poor at play, excursions into territory presumably unfamiliar to the *Herald*'s middle-class readership. In both sketches a resolutely middle-class narrator serves as guide, interpreting lower-class experience for his readers. The author of "Summer Garden" makes his presence felt throughout the piece and even explicitly portrays himself as tour guide. "Step inside this shrub-decked doorway with me," he writes near the sketch's opening, "divesting yourself in advance of social prejudice and oversqueamishness in the matter of dress and conventional politeness, and see how some of our fellow beings enjoy the pleasures that a slender purse can afford."[23] The author of "De Gang" is not so explicit a presence in his sketch; fascinated with immigrant dialect and vernacular speech, he devotes much of the article to quoting those present at the Tompkins Square concert. Still, the sketch's narrative voice provides a middle-class perspective that mediates the street scene and interprets its significance, as is evident in the opening paragraph of "De Gang": "Hard featured is the 'tough youth.' Hard mannered is the tough girl. She abounds on the east side. Down around Tompkins square she and her striped jersey are particularly prevalent. There are *musicales* in Tompkins square these hot summer nights—band concerts they are called—and great is the rejoicing thereabouts each season at the advent of the band."[24] The elaborate diction of phrases such as "great is the rejoicing thereabouts . . . at the advent of the band" calls attention to the presence of the narrator—a well-educated middle-class writer who inhabits a world distinct from, and superior to, the Bowery milieu of Mag, Jimmy, and the other working-class characters in the sketch. In contrast, the narrator of "The Broken-Down Van," the earliest New York City sketch that we can be certain is Crane's, rigorously avoids interpreting the street scene he presents to readers.

"The Broken-Down Van," published in the Sunday *New-York Tribune* on July 10, 1892, describes what ensues when a horse-drawn furniture van loses a wheel on a crowded rush-hour street in a poor downtown neighborhood. The sketch begins, "The gas lamps had just been lit and the two great red furniture vans with impossible landscapes on their sides rolled and plunged slowly along the street."[25] Proper nouns are entirely absent from this lead, and the sketch never reveals the exact location and date of the events it describes or the participants' names. In its lack of specifics the sketch fits squarely into the conventions of 1890s feature articles. The *Tribune* printed the piece under the heading "Travels in New-York," its title for an irregular Sunday series of features about the city. With its details of the van drivers' efforts to replace the wheel, hampered by the traffic surging past them and the unsolicited advice of passers-by, Crane's piece resembles numerous other humorous newspaper sketches. What distinguishes "The Broken-Down Van" is the way in which it pushes at the bounds of its conventional comic format by subtly introducing the vice, crime, and sexual and economic exploitation that exist in lower Manhattan, all presented without authorial commentary.

"The Broken-Down Van" opens by describing the flow of traffic through city streets. Its first paragraph mentions not only the two furniture vans but two modes of late nineteenth-century mass transportation: the streetcar and the elevated railway. These forms of rapid—at least for the era—transit had a profound effect on the way passengers perceived the city, for they made it possible for middle-class workers to travel between home and workplace while minimizing their encounter with the areas through which they passed. By the 1890s New York City's distinct districts separated their inhabitants not only by geography but by income, race, and ethnicity. Increasingly, New Yorkers in different parts of the city were strangers to one another, and new forms of urban transportation abetted that estrangement.

"The Broken-Down Van" puts a brake on movement through the city. When the van breaks down, the streetcars behind it are forced to a halt. The passengers—and Crane's readers—come to an abrupt stop in the middle of one of New York's poorest neighborhoods. Taking advantage of this static observation point, the sketch offers details of urban life that someone passing through could easily overlook. The moment when the van loses its wheel illustrates the sketch's narrative strategy:

> Just then the left-hand forward wheel on the rear van fell off and the axle went down. The van gave a mighty lurch and then swayed and rolled and rocked and stopped; the red driver applied his brake with a jerk and his horses turned out to keep from being crushed between car and van; the other drivers applied their brakes with a jerk and their horses turned out: the two cliff-dwelling men on the shelf half-way up the front of the stranded van began to shout loudly to their brother cliff-dwellers on the forward van; a girl, six years old, with a pail of beer crossed under the red car horse's neck; a boy, eight years old, mounted the red car with the sporting extras of the evening papers; a girl, ten years old, went in front of the van horses with two pails of beer; an unclassified boy poked his finger in the black grease in the hub of the right-hand hind van wheel and began to print his name on the red landscape on the van's side; a boy with a little head and big ears examined the white rings on the martingales of the van leaders with a view of stealing them in the confusion; a sixteen-year-old girl without any hat and with a roll of half-finished vests under her arms crossed the front platform of the green car. As she stepped up on to the sidewalk a barber from a ten-cent shop said "Ah! there!" and she answered "smarty!" with withering scorn and went down a side street.

Chronologically, this passage covers only a few minutes; grammatically, most of it is one long sentence. Yet the excerpt reveals an astonishing variety of New York street life, a world of child labor, petty crime, and vice that was normally overlooked by middle-class New Yorkers.

The normally hidden lower-class world revealed by the passage includes a swarm of unsupervised children in various activities. Two boys engage in petty crimes of vandalism and theft, while two girls carry pails of beer. Other children are already at work: a boy sells newspapers; a teenaged girl, dressed immodestly by the era's standards (she wears no hat), carries clothing from her sweatshop job and adeptly brushes off sexual advances from strangers. Remarkably, the narrator avoids comment on any of these activities, all of which violate the era's ideals of childhood. The passage displays a rigorous moral neutrality reinforced by a neutrality of grammar and syntax. The long central sentence is constructed of parallel independent clauses, interchangeable in their structure. The children working, carrying beer, or committing petty crimes receive the same textual emphasis as drivers applying their brakes or shouting to one another.

The dispassionate observation of the passage continues throughout "The Broken-Down Van," which alternates between the drivers' comic efforts to repair the van and the street life swirling about them. Children hawk newspapers and carry beer; a drunk sings; pawnbrokers look out of their shops; the 10-cent barber keeps trying to pick up women. One woman the barber approaches has a black eye; in this case too the narrator refuses comment and speculation, leaving readers to draw their own conclusions.

"The Broken-Down Van" is filled with the physical details of poverty, vice, and exploitation. That subject matter was common in 1890s newspapers. Not so common is the complete absence in the sketch of any moralistic commentary. Most newspaper sketches of the era dealing with lower New York and its poor inhabitants fall into two categories, both marked by frequent moralizing. One category consists of monitory articles that warn readers of the dangers to be encountered in the city. The *New York Press*, where Crane published the majority of his city sketches, made something of a specialty of the monitory genre, with an article in practically every Sunday issue detailing the deceptions and crimes practiced on unsuspecting members of the middle class. For example, "Sharks That Search New York for Prey" is the headline on an article about confidence men, who have not, according to the author, "conscience, honor, or scruples."[26] This article was followed a week later by a classic in the genre of deceptive appearances. "Verily, this is a queer town and a crooked one," the article begins. Its lengthy headline reads in part, "Good Samaritans Are Often Duped / It Is Even Dangerous to Do Good in This Big and Crooked Town / Don't Be Too Kind Hearted / You Are Likely to Be Assaulted, Robbed, Swindled and Locked Up if You're Accommodating."[27] Such articles reinforced the mystery and otherness of the New York poor, treating them as menacing figures best regarded from a considerable distance.[28]

Other features fall into the category of the sentimental crusade to aid the poor. Although he did not initiate the genre, Jacob Riis gave crusades a boost with the publication of his 1890 book *How the Other Half Lives*, based on articles that he wrote as a police reporter for the *Tribune, New*

York Sun, and Associated Press. All the major New York City newspapers featured crusades for worthy causes, ranging from shelters for homeless women to Coney Island excursions for slum children to a Free Bread Fund for the unemployed.[29] In many cases such crusading articles unquestionably aided the immigrant poor of lower New York. The sentimental crusade genre could improve material conditions, but it did nothing to lessen the cognitive distance between classes. The genre depicted the poor as victims in need of middle-class philanthropy. In Jacob Riis's phrase the poor were "the other half." In the writing of Riis and his peers among New York City journalists the poor remained unchangeably "other."

In place of the moralistic and sentimental perspectives common in 1890s journalism "The Broken-Down Van" offers a morally neutral visual perspective in which crime and vice are as much a part of city life as traffic jams. Working within the traditional form of the comic sketch, Crane upsets audience expectations and offers to the middle- and upper-class readers of the eminently respectable *Tribune* a new way of perceiving city life.

"The Broken-Down Van" has a typical local color subject, but the narrator is a dispassionate observer who withholds judgment on the scene. Crane's "Heard on the Street Election Night," published in the *New York Press* after an 1894 New York City election, is a formally innovative piece that dispenses with a narrator altogether. Reflecting Crane's interest in vernacular speech, "Heard on the Street" consists solely of disconnected fragments of overheard conversation. The sketch's headline reveals that it contains "Passing Remarks Gathered in Front of 'The Press' Stereopticon," a projector that flashed election results on a wall.[30] The sketch dispenses with any setting of the scene, physical description of the speakers, or other narrative connection.

Crane did not repeat the experiment of relying solely on dialogue. However, all his early New York City sketches can be seen as narrative experiments in point of view. For example, "Coney Island's Failing Days" is narrated largely from the point of view of a character whom Crane invented and dubbed "the stranger." In his lengthy monologue the self-described "philosopher" ruminates upon the "great mournfulness that settles upon a summer resort" at the end of the season, as he strolls around Coney Island on an autumn Sunday.[31] The stranger is well traveled and world weary—an attractive pose for a twenty-two-year-old writer who had never journeyed more than fifty miles from his birthplace of Newark, New Jersey.

Crane used the stranger as a character in two other sketches published, like "Coney Island," in the *New York Press* during the fall of 1894. These two "stranger" sketches, along with other sketches published at the same time, are notable for their vision of urban life as warfare. Crane had recently completed the manuscript of *The Red Badge of Courage*, and his sketches depict various New York City settings as if they were Civil War battlefields. "In a Park Row Restaurant" makes the comparison explicit. It begins, "'Whenever I come into a place of this sort, I am reminded of the battle of Gettysburg,' remarked the stranger." In the comic sketch that follows, both the stranger and the unnamed first-person narrator compare the noon rush hour at a downtown restaurant to warfare, and the stranger claims that the excitement is akin to the adventures he experienced as a sheriff in the Wild West. The narrator describes entering customers as "invad[ers]," speaks of "volley[s]" of viands served "with such speed and violence that it often resembled a personal assault," and reports that the sounds from the kitchen resemble "the cries . . . of a regiment under attack."[32]

The loquacious stranger is virtually silent in "When Every One Is Panic Stricken," a sketch about a tenement fire. The sketch achieved a certain notoriety when it received its first modern reprinting in a collection edited by R. W. Stallman and E. R. Hagemann, who labeled it a hoax. "This . . . fire never occurred," Stallman and Hagemann wrote in an editorial note, and they claimed Crane had duped the *Press*'s editor.[33] Stallman and Hagemann are correct that the sketch does not describe an actual fire, but there is no evidence that it was intended as a hoax or that the *Press*'s editor was unaware of the sketch's true nature. The sketch appeared in one of the Sunday *Press*'s supplementary sections, which contained a miscellaneous assortment of news, fiction, and feature articles. One subheadline reads, "A Realistic Pen Picture of a Fire in a Tenement"—a signal that the *Press* offered the article as an artistic representation of a typical urban event rather than as a factual report. The evidence suggests that Crane, his editor, and his readers understood the article to be part of the fact-fiction discourse of 1890s journalism.

Like Crane's other Sunday newspaper urban sketches, "When Every One Is Panic Stricken" never names the location or any participants in the event it treats. Crane's interest is not in timely news but in the timeless battle against nature, as exemplified in a tenement fire. "The Open Boat" (1897) is generally regarded as Crane's most significant treatment of the power of nature, but the theme is present in his Sullivan County sketches and New Jersey shore journalism, and it is at the center of "When Every One Is Panic Stricken." Crane uses an extravagance of metaphors that turn the fire into a satanic, bellicose monster. The sketch emphasizes the fragility of the urban environment in the face of natural forces. Crane describes the crowd as "fascinated by this exhibition of the strength of nature, their master after all, that ate them and their devices at will whenever it chose to fling down their little restrictions."[34] The language suggests that the city, the locus of civilization, is only a temporary stay against nature's power. The sketch is filled with similar passages that turn the fire into a synecdoche of natural power; nature becomes a slave in revolt against human attempts to subdue it.

If Crane is fascinated by the bellicose aspects of fire, he is equally interested in its aesthetic dimensions. Nowhere is Crane's fascination with color more evident than in this sketch. The sketch begins with a view down a dark side street toward the illuminated avenue, where "the tiny black figures" of pedestrians passing across the intersection "made an ornamental border on this fabric of yellow light." Suddenly, a police officer runs toward a fire alarm box at the corner, where a lamp sheds "a flicker of carmine tints upon the pavement." Once the narrator sees the fire, he describes the flames as "a deep and terrible hue of red, the color of satanic wrath, the color of murder." The narrator and the stranger function as appreciative aesthetes throughout the sketch: "Ah, look at 'em! Look at 'em! Ain't that great?" the stranger says as the fire fighters arrive on the scene, sounding like a spectator at a well-staged melodrama.

The sketch is so concerned with the aesthetic and bellicose aspects of the fire that it sacrifices what we think of as standard journalistic concerns: human-interest stories, information about material conditions, even narrative coherence. The sketch ends with the narrator and the stranger walking away from the still-burning fire, looking over their shoulders to admire "the red glimmer from the fire shin[ing] on the dark surging crowd over which towered at times the helmets of police." The sketch provides no information on the human and economic costs of the fire. We never learn whether anyone was killed or injured. We hear nothing about those left homeless. We do not find out whether the fire was contained or spread to other buildings. We learn nothing about the value of what was destroyed. Most surprising, early in the sketch Crane tells of a policeman plunging into the burning building to rescue a baby, but we never find out if he is successful. Taking advantage of the freedom offered by the Sunday news-paper's fact-fiction discourse, Crane writes a sketch that abandons con-ventional journalistic and narrative concerns and focuses instead on his aes-thetic preoccupations and his thematic interest in the human struggle against nature.

"When Every One Is Panic Stricken" also devotes considerable atten-tion to the behavior of the crowd that gathers to watch the fire, struggling against the line of police to get a better view. The crowd's heartless behav-ior in the face of tragedy is the primary theme in another New York City sketch from the same period, "When Man Falls a Crowd Gathers." The sketch describes an Italian laborer who has a stroke and falls unconscious to the sidewalk, causing a crowd to gather around him. In describing this scene Crane was using a familiar urban trope: a surging crowd pressing around a fallen person. Except for the gender of the fallen person, an 1881 drawing from the cover of *Frank Leslie's Illustrated Newspaper* could serve as illustration for Crane's sketch, right down to the burly policeman hold-ing back the crowd. What is distinctive in Crane's treatment of this event is his vision of urban life as warfare. "There were men who nearly created a battle in the madness of their desire to see the thing," he writes, and he says that the lone policeman who arrives on the scene "charged the crowd as if he were a squadron of Irish lancers."[35] Like his other New York sketches, "When Man Falls" offers no proper names that would allow one to verify that the event actually took place, and an indignant reader wrote to the *New York Press* to complain that the sketch was not realistic; New Yorkers, the writer insisted, were quick to offer help to those in distress.[36] However, in his sketches Crane was at least as concerned with aesthetic and thematic issues as he was with realistic portrayal.

Crane's depiction of common urban events as warfare, evident both in *Maggie* and in his newspaper sketches, was not unique during the 1890s. A long-standing American tradition associated urban life with violence—a tradition that gained strength during the labor strikes of the 1870s, inten-sified after the Chicago Haymarket bombing in 1886, and reached its peak during the economic depression of the 1890s, when U.S. Attorney General Richard Olney warned, in a phrase that was to be often repeated, that the nation was at "the ragged edge of anarchy."[37] Many of Crane's contemporaries echoed Olney's prophecy of incipient urban violence. The best known of the doomsayers was the Reverend Josiah Strong, whose chapter on city life in his best-selling jeremiad *Our Country* (1886) is an

FIGURE 3.1 "A Fair Pedestrian Overcome by the Heat" from *Frank Leslie's Illustrated Newspaper*, August 27, 1881.

apocalyptic warning of future violence. Jacob Riis titled one of the chapters in *How the Other Half Lives* (1890) "The Man with the Knife"; the chapter turns a slum dweller who goes berserk on Fifth Avenue into an image of the potential for violent revolt among the urban poor. Readers of the era were well prepared for Crane's grim portrayals of brutal slum dwellers and heartless crowds.

Yet if Crane's emphasis on the violence inherent in New York's tenement districts was a familiar theme, his treatment of the poor is still distinct from that of other urban writers. I have already discussed how Crane's journalism differs from the two most common categories of newspaper feature articles about New York's poor: monitory articles warning of urban dangers and sentimental crusades to aid the poor. His writing also differs from the major ideological and literary approach to the poor in the late nineteenth century: Christian moralism. Christian moralism can be defined as the belief that poverty resulted from the moral failings of individuals, predominantly intemperance and idleness. Joined to this belief in the individual origins of poverty was the conviction—central to the ideology of Protestant evangelicals, marginal among more secularized writers— that the embrace of Protestant doctrine formed the basis for moral regeneration.[38] Christian moralism saturates writing about the poor during the 1890s, including newspaper journalism. Crane's 1894 articles on the New York poor appeared in the Sunday *New York Press* alongside feature articles such as one headlined "Poverty's Sunny Side / How to be Happy Though Poor Shown by Famous People / Adversity Is a Good Thing if You've Nerve to Fight It." The first two of the famous people to be featured in this article were the prominent New York City clergymen Chauncey M. DePew and T. DeWitt Talmage. The former observed, "If [a person in adversity] preserves his cheerfulness, doesn't drink, doesn't become a tramp, doesn't 'drop out,' but does the best he can to find a place that will hold him and support him, he will get there." The latter concluded his observations, "It is to throw us back upon an all comforting God that we have this ministry of tears."[39]

DePew and Talmage exemplify their era's dual emphases on individual effort and religious redemption. The Christian moralism that they advocated formed the basis for virtually all writing about the poor in the Gilded Age. All nineteenth-century urban reformers shared a belief in the need for moral regeneration; however, they offered differing proposals for reform. Stephen Crane came to maturity at a time when a bewildering variety of cures for the disease of urban poverty were being prescribed. The would-be physicians included Charles Loring Brace, who advocated removing poor children from the slums and sending them to live with western farm families where, he assumed, the pervasive atmosphere of agrarian self-reliance would turn them into model citizens; Jane Addams, who worked to regenerate the slums through her work at Hull-House; Jacob Riis, who pushed for improved housing conditions; and Christian socialist Benjamin O. Flower, who promoted a variety of reform measures in the pages of his journal, the *Arena*.

Stephen Crane reported in the *New-York Tribune* on an 1892 lecture by Jacob Riis, and Crane published sketches and short stories about the New York poor in Flower's *Arena*. These actions show his sympathy with reform efforts of his era; however, his journalism is remarkably free of theories about the origins of poverty or proposals for reform. It is impossible to draw from Crane's work any coherent political agenda. Although Crane is clearly interested in improving social conditions, his work gives no sign of how reform might be accomplished. Rather, Crane is concerned with angles, not arguments, to borrow Christopher Benfey's phrase.[40] He is interested in *perspectives* on the poor, and his journalism about the New York slums can be seen as a collection of experiments in point of view.

"The Men in the Storm," a sketch published in the *Arena*, is as much about points of view as it is about the homeless men who are Crane's subject.[41] Set in the midst of a blizzard, the sketch begins by deconstructing the narrative convention of the middle-class narrator. After briefly describing the blizzard in its first paragraph, the sketch continues, "All the clatter of the street was softened by the masses [of snow] that lay upon the cobbles until, even to one who looked from a window, it became important music."[42] What follows details the observations of this "one" safely ensconced behind a window. The observer draws "recollections of rural experiences" from the sight of men shoveling snowdrifts. He finds the lighted shop windows "infinitely cheerful." And he discerns "an absolute expression of hot dinners in the pace of the people" hurrying toward home (662). The sketch emphasizes the solid assumptions of this middle-class observer, a person with sufficient means to be familiar with rural scenes, with the pleasures of shopping in cheerfully lighted stores, with hot dinners and a comfortable home. The text comments, "As to the suggestion of hot dinners, he was in firm lines of thought, for it was upon every hurrying face. It is a matter of tradition; it is from the tales of childhood" (663). The sketch underlines the observer's conviction of the universality of his experience and beliefs. Yet it also subtly suggests that his beliefs are based on a childish naïveté. The narrative sets up this middle-class onlooker, the better to undercut him in the next paragraph, which reads in full: "However, in a certain part of a dark West-side street, there was a collection of men to whom these things were as if they were not. In this street was located a charitable house where for five cents the homeless of the city could get a bed at night and, in the morning, coffee and bread" (663). From this point on "The Men in the Storm" abandons the complacent middle-class observer and thrusts readers into the midst of the homeless men in the street waiting for the charity to open, into a world where the benign assumptions of the comfortable observer are not simply wrong but irrelevant—"as if they were not."

In writing about a group of homeless men waiting at twilight for the

doors of a charity to open Crane took on a familiar subject. Numerous
reporters observed breadlines at about the same time as Crane, including
Jacob Riis, who published an article on police lodging houses in the *New
York World* in 1893. Like Crane's feature, Riis's article is set in a winter
storm, and its opening may have served as a model for "The Men in the
Storm." Riis's article begins, "Strung along the iron railing in front of the
Mulberry street police station stood on one of the recent stormy evenings
a line of ragged, shivering men and women. It had been there, at first a little knot at the locked area door, since before the twilight set in, and now
it was fast deepening into the darkness of night."[43] Despite the similarity
of their openings, Riis's sketch soon moves in a quite different direction
from Crane's. In his third paragraph Riis introduces two young men,
"decently dressed mechanics" out of a job, who are contrasted with the
"hardened old tramps" who make up most of the men in line. The first half
of Riis's lengthy article takes the perspective of the two mechanics, showing their disgust at conditions in the police station lodgings for the homeless. The last half is a bogus interview with Riis himself—the *World* printed
the sketch unsigned—in which he offers solutions to the bad conditions in
the police lodgings and to the "tramp nuisance" that, he says, underlies the
whole problem.

By adopting the point of view of the mechanics and then including his
lengthy self-interview, Riis provides readers with a firm, resolutely middle-
class perspective on the homeless men and women seeking shelter. In contrast, Crane's sketch abandons any stable narrative point of view, deliberately unsettling readers as it moves from one perspective to another. The
sketch opens with the point of view of the "one" who watches from a window, then abandons this observer, and thrusts readers into the midst of the
crowd of men. The anonymous third-person narrator is seemingly located
somewhere in the crowd, yet he does not long maintain a single perspective. He speculates about how the crowd might appear from directly
above, briefly takes the perspective of a merchant staring down at the men
from the window of a dry goods shop across the street, and then shifts back
into the crowd of men as they taunt this well-dressed observer.

"The Men in the Storm" rejects both a stable narrative position and any
solution to the problem of the homeless men. The sketch's silence on
larger issues of homelessness, poverty, and unemployment is remarkable,
considering both the context of 1890s journalism and the venue in which
the sketch appeared. "The Men in the Storm" was published in the

October 1894 issue of the *Arena*. Like other articles in the progressive monthly, "The Men in the Storm" is a work of social protest, for it implicitly challenges an economic system that divides Americans into comfortable observers and the impoverished homeless. Yet the sketch stands out from most articles that Flower, a Christian socialist, published in his journal. Just as "The Broken-Down Van" rejects the prevailing middle-class moralism of the staid, solidly Republican *Tribune*, "The Men in the Storm" rejects the *Arena*'s moralistic condemnations of social injustice. Crane's sketch is more subtly—and more fundamentally—radical, for it questions concepts of free will and human identity shared by the producers and readers of both the *Tribune* and the *Arena*.

"The Men in the Storm" locates its subjects not only within the mean streets of 1894 New York City but within a timeless, unlocalized landscape that is depicted as a battleground between a powerful and pitiless nature and weak, insignificant humankind. Like the characters in Crane's well-known short story "The Blue Hotel," set in a howling Nebraska blizzard, the men in the New York storm are battered by natural forces that seem to determine their behavior. Every action they take in the sketch is controlled by the desire to protect themselves from the cold of the storm and to find food and shelter. Frequently, the language of the text reduces them to animals engaged in a Darwinian struggle. Crane appropriates the language of nineteenth-century biological determinism in his comment, "With the pitiless whirl of snow upon them, the battle for shelter was going to the strong" (666).

Yet Crane does not allow this determinist perspective to stand as single stable explanation; it is only a temporary point of view. The storm that beats upon them may determine the men's behavior, but their identity depends upon the fluid language and shifting narrative perspective of Crane's text. The men's very humanity is provisional in the narrator's hands. Viewed from above, they are nothing but "a heap of snow-covered merchandise" (664). From ground level the narrative transforms them through metaphor and simile. The sketch is dense with figures of speech that either fracture the men into outerwear or body parts—they are in close succession "a heap of old clothes" and a "collection of heads"—or that suppress their humanity: they are a "mass," "wave," "stream," "sheep," "grass," "ogres," and "fiends." Through its shifting, dehumanizing descriptions of its subjects "The Men in the Storm" calls into question the identity of not only these homeless tramps but also the well-dressed merchant, the "one" who observes, and Crane's readers. In its challenges to a society that identifies people on the basis of social and economic class, "The Men in the Storm" fits in squarely with the *Arena*'s reformist perspective. Yet Crane's sketch outflanks the magazine's usual reform articles, calling into question not only class hierarchy but stable human identity.

Crane confronts the questions of free will and identity raised by "The Men in the Storm" even more directly in his paired sketches "An Experiment in Misery" and "An Experiment in Luxury," published on successive Sundays in the *New York Press* in April 1894. The experiment, a common newspaper device during the 1890s, was the report of a journalist who participated in some uncommon experience in order to write about it. Joseph Pulitzer's *World*, New York City's largest newspaper in 1894, included at least one experiment in virtually every Sunday newspaper during the months before Crane published his two experiments. Most often, the *World*'s experiments entertained readers with a report of some exotic, dangerous, or glamorous occupation, such as when *World* reporters worked briefly as a lion tamer, fire fighter, and extra in a popular melodrama.[44] However, the earliest journalistic experiments were exercises in muckraking, aimed at reforming social ills. Elizabeth Cochrane, who became one of the *World*'s most popular reporters under her pen name Nellie Bly, helped to make the experiment a widely practiced form after 1887, when the *World* hired her to feign insanity, get herself committed to New York's public "lunatic asylum," and write about her experience. Her series of articles, later published as *Ten Days in a Madhouse* (1887), was highly popular and resulted in a grand jury investigation into the asylum's management.[45]

Many critics of Crane's "Experiment in Misery," his best-known newspaper sketch, assume that Crane's approach to reporting on the homeless—disguising himself as a homeless man—was a journalistic novelty. However, Nellie Bly and dozens of other reporters had paved the way. What may be the first nineteenth-century journalistic experiment took an approach almost identical to Crane's. In 1866 British journalist James Greenwood donned shabby clothes to gain entrance to one of London's municipally sponsored shelters for homeless men and published the result of his experiment in the *Pall Mall Gazette* as "A Night in a Workhouse."[46] In the United States Josiah Flynt began publishing his articles about his travels as a tramp in 1891; they were collected as *Tramping with Tramps* (1893). While Flynt was tramping, Princeton graduate Walter A. Wyckoff set off from a friend's Long Island estate, working his way west across the country as a manual laborer and regularly publishing magazine articles on his experiences, which were gathered in the two volumes *The Workers: An Experiment in Reality* (1897–98). In the months just before Crane's "Experiment in Misery" appeared in the *New York Press*, the same newspaper published two sketches by reporters who donned old clothes and pretended to be homeless people.[47] By the time Crane's sketch appeared, it had become so common for middle-class writers to conduct experiments in poverty that a cartoonist parodied the trend in a drawing published in the *New York World* on the same day that Crane's sketch was published in the *Press*. Titled "The Demon Realism," the cartoon shows two men digging a ditch. One has the simian features that illustrators of the era often used to depict working-class Irish characters; the other is a tall, skinny "dude." Printed below the drawing is their dialogue:

LABORER: Yez don't look like a mon as has done much av this kind av wur-rk.

PAPERWATE: No; I am an author of realistic fiction, and I have to accumulate experiences of various kinds.

LABORER: (*rather hazy*) Begob! So that's what brought yez to it? It must be as bad as dhrink![48]

Presumably, what enabled Crane to publish his contribution to this well-worn genre was his idea of pairing his "Experiment in Misery" with a companion "Experiment in Luxury"; the two sketches were published on successive Sundays in the *New York Press*. Whereas Crane dressed as a homeless person and slept in a Bowery flophouse for his first experiment, for the second he donned a dinner jacket and reported on his meal at the home of a Fifth Avenue millionaire, the father of a college friend. Crane's paired experiments are unique, although the juxtaposition of poverty and wealth was a common trope in the era.[49] His paired sketches treat a familiar theme, yet they are free of the moralizing, sentimentality, and proposals for reform that were common to other discussions of the contrast between misery and luxury. Instead, Crane uses a conventional newspaper form to conduct experiments in perception and identity. Crane's journalistic experiments play on the scientific connotations of the word and show how the successive catalysts of poverty and wealth transform the consciousness of the experimenting reporter.

Laborer—Yes don't look like a mon as has done much av this kind av wur-rk.
Paperwate—No; I am an author of realistic fiction, and I have to accumulate experiences of various kinds.
Laborer (rather hasy)—Begob! So that's what brought yes to it? It must be as bad as dhrink!

FIGURE 3.2 "The Demon Realism" from the *New York World*, April 22, 1894.

"An Experiment in Misery" appeared in the *New York Press* on April 22, 1894. Although the *Press* had printed other experiments in which the reporter impersonated a poor person, the timing of "An Experiment in Misery" ensured that readers would see it as a politically charged document; it appeared at the height of a national hysteria caused by the march on Washington of Coxey's Army. The widespread unemployment following the 1893 financial panic had galvanized Jacob Coxey, an Ohio businessman with an interest in economic reform, into action. He organized a group of unemployed men—largely wanderers who at the time were dubbed tramps—to march from Ohio to Washington, D.C., where Coxey intended to present to Congress his scheme for eliminating unemployment through public works projects. Coxey's Army, as it came to be known, left Massillon, Ohio, on March 25, 1894. By April 22, when Crane's sketch appeared, the army was less than one hundred miles from Washington, provoking widespread disdain and panic among the middle and upper classes. Throughout the spring of 1894 denunciations of Coxey and his followers filled newspapers—including the *New York Press*.[50] The hysterical edge to much of the press coverage can be attributed less to Coxey's rather modest demands than to the wave of violent strikes and anarchist agitation that characterized the 1880s and 1890s and to the rising crescendo of public nervousness about what was known as the "Tramp Menace."

The American tramp was largely a creation of the 1870s, when an economic depression and the rapid expansion of the nation's railway system combined to create a large class of unemployed men who relied on the trains for a nomadic way of life. Within a few years the tramp rivaled the Indian as a sort of national bogeyman, a locus for the strains and fears generated by the expanding, unstable, and unjust economic system of the United States. By 1877 the dean of Yale Law School was fulminating, "As we utter the word *Tramp*, there arises straightaway before us the spectacle of a lazy, incorrigible, cowardly, utterly depraved savage."[51] Jacob Riis, who had gone on the road after he immigrated to the United States in 1870, was one of the most strident critics of the tramp, peppering his newspaper articles and books with denunciations.[52]

The combination of two decades of warnings against the Tramp Menace, an immediate crisis of massive unemployment, and the approach of Coxey's Army to the nation's capital meant that Stephen Crane's experiment among New York City's homeless appeared at a moment when fears had reached a fever pitch. Remarkably, for Crane these fears were as if they were not. Crane wrenches the tramp out of the immediate context of economics, politics, and journalistic hysteria. Never acknowledging the "tramp problem," "An Experiment in Misery" instead focuses on problems of perception and understanding. Crane writes as if the common concerns of Riis and other writers—the tramp as threat to morality, property, and social order—did not exist. Instead, he is concerned with the middle-class person's lack of knowledge of the tramp's inner life.

Although most journalistic experiments were written as first-person reports, Crane uses third person and, avoiding proper names, casts himself as "the youth." The technique allows Crane to present this thinly disguised version of himself as a character akin to the protagonist of the novel that he had just completed in the spring of 1894. Like Henry Fleming in *The Red Badge of Courage*, who is most often called "the youth," the young man in "An Experiment in Misery" begins as a naïf but is educated by his searing experiences.

"Misery" opens with the youth's reflections as he and a friend observe a tramp. "I wonder how he feels," the youth says to his friend. "I suppose he is homeless, friendless, and has, at the most, only a few cents in his pocket. And if this is so, I wonder how he feels."[53] Crane's opening emphasizes through repetition its epistemological concerns: "I wonder how he feels." His friend replies that his question can be answered not by theory but only by empirical test. "You can tell nothing of it unless you are in that condition yourself," the friend advises. "It is idle to speculate about it from this distance." Their distance from the tramp is twofold: both spatial and cognitive. Crane's experiment in misery is an attempt to bridge both distances.

The sketch almost immediately confronts the youth's epistemological queries; he tells his friend that he intends to dress in "rags and tatters" in order to "discover [the tramp's] point of view." He borrows an outfit from an artist friend and late on a rainy night begins "a weary trudge toward the downtown places, where beds can be hired for coppers." The sketch continues, "By the time he had reached City Hall Park he was so completely plastered with yells of 'bum' and 'hobo,' and with various unholy epithets that small boys had applied to him at intervals that he was in a state of profound dejection, and looked searchingly for an outcast of high degree that the two might share miseries." Already, at the commencement of his experiment, the young man has abandoned his confident, reflective stance and is profoundly dejected. Oppressed by the middle-class disdain expressed in the boys' taunts, he seeks an alliance with a member of the other half; the experimental transformation of his consciousness has begun.

As the sketch continues, the young man loses all will, turning from a middle-class experimenter who deliberately embarks upon a project into a plastic creature controlled by his environment. When he spots a saloon that advertises "Free hot soup tonight," he is "caught by the delectable sign" and "allowed himself to be swallowed" by the saloon's swinging doors. The verbs emphasize the young man's passivity and the corresponding power of his surroundings.

When he leaves the saloon, the youth meets a drunken tramp whom the narrator dubs "the assassin." Serving as a sort of derelict Virgil to the youth's Dante, the assassin leads the young man to a seven-cent lodging house where they spend the night. Crane's description of the youth's sleepless night is an artistic tour-de-force, a barrage of violent metaphors that, taken together, reflect the young man's disoriented mental state. Crane uses deliberately startling similes—the odors in the room assail the young man "like malignant diseases with wings"; the sleeping men heave and snore "with tremendous effort, like stabbed fish"—that disconcert the reader, leaving us as vulnerable and open to change as the young man.

As Benedict Giamo points out, the youth's sleepless night serves as an initiation ceremony, signaling his change from one identity to another.[54] When he leaves the tramp lodging house in the morning, the youth "experienced no sudden relief from unholy atmospheres. He had forgotten all about them, and had been breathing naturally and with no sensation of discomfort or distress." The youth's acceptance of the lodging house stench signals a change in physical perception; by the end of the sketch all his perceptions are similarly changed.

The sketch concludes as the youth and the assassin walk to City Hall Park, where they sit down "in the little circle of benches sanctified by traditions of their class." With the plural possessive pronoun the narrator subtly places the experimenter in the same socioeconomic class as the professional tramp. The passage that follows reveals how an experiment that initially involved a change only of clothing and sleeping place has become a transformation of consciousness:

> The people of the street hurrying hither and thither made a blend of black figures, changing, yet frieze-like. They walked in their good clothes as upon important missions, giving no gaze to the two wanderers seated upon the benches. They expressed to the young man his infinite distance from all that he valued. Social position, comfort, the pleasures of living, were unconquerable kingdoms. He felt a sudden awe. . . .
>
> He confessed himself an outcast, and his eyes from under the lowered rim of his hat began to glance guiltily, wearing the criminal expression that comes with certain convictions.

The young man has become so distanced from the middle-class people with whom he formerly identified that he can no longer see them as individuals; they have become a "blend of black figures." And just as the affluent customarily stare past the homeless, not really seeing them or recognizing their common humanity, the young man no longer recognizes the middle-class passers-by as three-dimensional people; they are transformed into a flat frieze, a metaphor that suggests something foreign, exotic, and archaic. The young man has completely assumed the perceptions of the outcast tramp. The passage reveals that he has also assumed the tramp's convictions, ideas about social inequality that the larger society would consider criminal.

Like "The Men in the Storm," "An Experiment in Misery" never directly addresses the issues that were central to other discussions of poverty and unemployment in the 1890s: the Tramp Menace, politics, economics, morality, public safety, property rights, charity, reform, and revolution. It would not have been possible to advocate radical political and economic change in the pages of the *New York Press*; the newspaper proclaimed in its masthead its allegiance to the Republican Party. Yet, like "The Men in the Storm," "Misery" is a fundamentally radical work that challenges belief in a stable identity. It portrays the young man as a creature of his environment who assumes a completely new consciousness as his circumstances change. The sketch obliterates distinctions between social classes, showing how easily a member of the "respectable" classes can be transformed into a tramp.

The companion sketch, "An Experiment in Luxury," also reveals human identity as provisional and fluid. In this sketch the young man of "Misery" dines at the Fifth Avenue home of a college friend, son of a millionaire. Together, these two sketches form Crane's purest work of literary naturalism. Critics have long argued about the extent to which Crane can be classified as a naturalist, a debate that has centered on the question of whether *Maggie* actually demonstrates the environmental determinism that Crane implied in his inscription: "[*Maggie*] tries to show that environment is a tremendous thing in the world and frequently shapes lives regardless." Whatever one's conclusions about *Maggie*, "An Experiment in Misery" and "An Experiment in Luxury" vividly demonstrate the power of environment to shape lives. The young man of these paired sketches is a completely plastic creature whose surroundings determine his consciousness. At the conclusion of "Misery" he shares the tramp's criminal convictions; in "Luxury" he adopts plutocratic views. On successive Sundays the young man rockets among the middle, lower, and upper classes, assuming a new identity and consciousness as easily as he dons a tattered overcoat or a dinner jacket. Crane uses the conventional form of the journalistic experiment for radical ends, upsetting his audience's beliefs in class divisions as natural and inevitable.

Although "An Experiment in Misery" had been preceded by dozens of similar journalistic experiments, "Luxury" uses a novel strategy in extending to the wealthy the same experimental treatment that reporters normally used for workers, tramps, and other marginalized or exotic social groups. Newspapers of the 1890s generally treated the wealthy in respectful, frequently adulatory pieces describing their homes, social events, and recreations. The *New York Herald*, a newspaper for which Crane wrote for a time, carried in every Sunday edition during 1894 a huge half-page illustration of some society event, the participants depicted in the flattering style of Charles Dana Gibson. In contrast, Crane's sketch is cheerfully irreverent. It includes a cheeky, unflattering portrait of the millionaire's wife, describing her as "a grim old fighter . . . a type of Zulu chieftainess who scuffled and scrambled for place before the white altars of social excellence."[55]

Like "Misery," "Luxury" begins by focusing on the changes that this experiment induces in the youth's consciousness. But whereas "Misery" records the young man's steady change from a middle-class perspective to the assumption of an outcast's perceptions and convictions, in "Luxury" the youth's perceptions swing back and forth. The youth enters the millionaire's Fifth Avenue mansion "with an easy feeling of independence," but he is quickly awed by the supercilious servant who opens the door. Once in his friend's room he assumes the self-satisfaction of the wealthy, a complacency undercut by the narrator's irony:

> Presently he began to feel that he was a better man than many—entitled to a great pride. He stretched his legs like a man in a garden, and he thought that he belonged to the garden. . . .
> In this way and with this suddenness he arrived at a stage. He was become a philosopher, a type of the wise man who can eat but three meals a day, conduct a large business and understand the purposes of infinite power. He felt valuable. He was sage and important.

In his friend's comfortable room the youth takes on the perspective of the wealthy and powerful, but as soon as they descend to the family's drawing room, he loses his "delightful mood" and mentally bows down before the splendor embodied in the mansion's lavish decor.

In his quick changes of consciousness the youth reveals his similarity to Henry Fleming of *The Red Badge of Courage*. The youth's swings between pride and envious humility are as quick and unpredictable as Henry's flickering alternations between bravado and cowardice in the period before his first battle. Henry's uncertainty comes from his attempts to answer the question of whether he will run in battle. The young man in "Luxury" is attempting to divine what the narrator calls the "eternal mystery of social condition." The phrase occurs as the youth and his college friend talk before dinner, and the narrator describes the youth's state of mind: "He was beginning to see a vast wonder in it that they two lay sleepily chatting with no more apparent responsibility than rabbits, when certainly there were men, equally fine perhaps, who were being blackened and mashed in the churning life of the lower places. . . . The eternal mystery of social condition exasperated him at this time." The passive verbs of the youth's reflection—"were being blackened and mashed"—abet the mystery of poverty; it is not clear if the poor are maimed by an outside force or simply by the "churning life" of their environment. However, a later passage near the end of the sketch uses active verbs that shed light on the mystery. "Theologians had for a long time told the poor man that riches did not bring happiness," the youth reflects. "And when a wail of despair or rage had come from the night of the slums they had stuffed this epigram down the throat of he who cried out and told him that he was a lucky fellow." The active agents in this passage are not the wealthy but the purveyors of ideology. Visiting his rich friend, the youth can find no direct evidence of violence in this comfortable mansion; however, he comes to see the common wisdom of the dominant ideology—exemplified in the maxim that riches do not bring happiness—as a violent response to a violent threat. "Theologians," the transmitters of moral maxims, brutally stuff self-serving ideological defenses down the throats of slum dwellers whose rage threatens the status quo. The youth's reflection reveals that the mystery of social condition is created by ideology, which cloaks social processes in moralistic maxims.

The theme of class struggle that is latent in "Misery" and explicit in "Luxury" underlies another sketch published a few months later. Its theme links it to the two "Experiments," although its subject involved an excursion outside New York City. S. S. McClure, owner of a newspaper syndicate and publisher of the magazine that bore his name, commissioned Crane and an artist friend to visit a coal mine near Scranton, Pennsylvania; the resulting sketch was published in *McClure's* magazine and in several newspapers. In part, "In the Depths of a Coal Mine" is a particularly powerful working out of a central Crane theme, which he states with unusual explicitness. "The meaning of it all," he says of the mine, is "the endless battle between man and nature"—a battle that receives its best-known description in Crane's short story "The Open Boat."[56] In "Coal Mine" Crane illustrates his theme through an extended metaphor of the mine as a monster that devours men. His sketch opens with a metaphoric description of the huge coal-sorting sheds called "breakers": "The 'breakers' squatted upon the hillsides and in the valley like enormous preying monsters, eating of the sunshine, the grass, the green leaves" (195). This metaphoric treatment of the mines continues throughout the sketch, and the narrator's descent into a mine becomes a journey into the belly of a beast.

The elevator ride that the narrator and his artist companion take into the mine is a disorienting plunge into blackness: "The will fought a great battle to comprehend something during this fall, but one might as well have been tumbling among the stars" (200). This free fall serves as transition to a strange world of fantastically heightened perceptions. If the mine is a monster, the miners are fearsome, blackened creatures described as "spectres," "ghouls," and "wolves." The earth that surrounds them fairly pulses with malevolence. With "the strength of a million giants" it has "the little men at its mercy." Usually resting in massive calm, it sometimes becomes "exasperated" and snuffs out the men's lives, crushing them "like a bug." The narrator's tour through the mine is a Stygian journey into a hellish region where "little men" are at the mercy of omnipotent nature.

Yet if Crane casts the miners as warriors in a timeless battle of nature, he also locates them firmly in a contemporary struggle between labor and capital. With an attention to economic detail unusual in his work he gives the workers' exact wages: a miner gets $3 a day; his assistant gets $1.25; the boys who pick slate from the coal earn 55 cents a day. Juxtaposed to Crane's fantastically heightened descriptions of the men's brutal, dangerous work, these earnings—paltry even by 1894 standards—seem grimly ludicrous.

Crane's sympathy for the miners and disdain for their employers is subtly but unmistakably evident in the published version of "In the Depths of a Coal Mine." The first draft, preserved in manuscript, is explicit about his class allegiance. "When I had studied mines and the miner's life," he writes in the first draft, "I wondered at many things but I could not induce myself to wonder why the miners strike and otherwise object to their lot."[57] He continues, "One cannot go down in the mines often before he finds himself wondering why it is that coal-barons get so much and these miners . . . get proportionately so little" (606). In a powerful passage later in the manuscript he writes:

> If all men who stand uselessly and for their own extraordinary profit between the miner and the consumer were annually doomed to a certain period of danger and darkness in the mines, they might at last comprehend the misery and bitterness of men who toil for existence at these hopelessly grim tasks. They would begin to understand then the value of the miner, perhaps. Then maybe they would allow him a wage according to his part. (607)

All these passages are missing from the published version. According to Corwin Linson, the illustrator who accompanied Crane to the coal mine, the writer was angered when he saw his article in print. "The birds didn't want the truth after all," Linson quotes Crane as saying. "Why the hell did they send me up there then? Do they want the public to think the coal mines gilded ballrooms with the miners eating ice-cream in boiled shirtfronts?"[58] According to Edwin Cady, Linson is not an entirely reliable source, and it is not clear if the political outbursts in the manuscript draft were cut by *McClure's* editors or by Crane himself.[59] However, even in its published version, "In the Depths of a Coal Mine" remains a powerful work, revealing how Crane was able to use the journalistic discourse of his era for both artistic and political ends.

Not only the discourse of the era's newspapers but also the social role of the reporter enabled Crane to write so memorably about exploited workers and the urban poor. The work of Crane's literary mentor William Dean Howells stands in illuminating contrast. During the 1890s Howells occasionally wrote nonfiction pieces on the same subjects of unemployment and poverty in lower New York City that absorbed his young friend. Although his subject matter is similar to Crane's—a midnight breadline, Lower East Side tenements, street beggars—Howells's use of the belles lettres essay resulted in radically different work.[60] In his essay about a winter's night breadline, for example, Howells observes the men from the vantage point of a comfortable carriage, from which he never alights. Howells remains in the role of the genteel literary observer. The real subject of his New York essays is not the poor so much as it is the unbridgeable gulf between the essayist and those he sees. In contrast, the routines of newspaper work discouraged a distant observer's stance. Crane was following the lead of dozens of other reporters when he plunged into the midst of a crowd of homeless men waiting to enter a shelter or donned shabby clothes to seek out a Bowery lodging house.

～

Crane took a hiatus from New York journalism in January 1895, when he left the city for a five-month tour through Mexico and the American West, sponsored by the Bacheller newspaper syndicate. He did not return to urban journalism until the summer of 1896, when he wrote a dozen articles over the course of several months. By mid-1896 Crane's life had changed radically. With the publication of *The Red Badge of Courage* in 1895 he went from being a struggling freelance journalist and unsuccessful novelist to being one of the most highly acclaimed writers in England and the United States. Much of his early journalism had been published anonymously; now Crane's name was featured prominently in the headlines. And instead of publishing his work in an obscure magazine like the *Arena* or a second-tier newspaper like the *Press*, Crane worked as a celebrity author for the nation's two largest newspapers, Joseph Pulitzer's *New York World* and William Randolph Hearst's *New York Journal*, while also syndicating his articles nationwide.

A number of the 1896 New York articles reveal Crane's concern with the poor and marginalized—he visited a police court, an opium den, and Sing Sing prison—but a few are purely comic sketches about well-known aspects of New York City life. The funniest of these, "In the Broadway Cars," purports to describe a typical day's occurrences aboard the cable cars running along the city's main thoroughfare. The sketch begins quietly, describing the janitors and porters who board the cars to go to their jobs in the predawn gray of the morning. As the sun rises, so does the sketch's comic temperature. Crane begins a barrage of hyperbole that continues throughout the sketch. Writing about the abandoned speed at which the cars supposedly travel, Crane says, "It is a great ride, full of exciting action. Those inexperienced persons who have been merely chased by Indians know little of the dramatic quality which life may hold for them."[61] Picking up a theme from his 1894 New York City sketches, Crane goes on to depict a cable car ride as a violent encounter akin to warfare, but he does so with playful comic exuberance:

Suppose you are in a cable car, clutching for life and family a creaking strap from overhead. At your shoulder is a little dude in a very wide-brimmed straw hat with a red band. If you were in your senses you would recognize this flaming band as an omen of blood. But you are not in your senses; you are in a Broadway cable car. You are not supposed to have any senses. From the forward end you hear the gripman uttering shrill whoops and running over citizens. Suddenly the car comes to a curve. Making a swift running start, it turns three hand-springs, throws a cart wheel for luck, bounds into the air, hurls six passengers over the nearest building, and comes down a-straddle of the track. That is the way in which we turn curves in New York.

Meanwhile, during the car's gamboling, the corrugated rim of the dude's hat has swept naturally across your neck, and it has left nothing for your head to do but to quit your shoulders. As the car roars your head falls into the waiting arms of the proper authorities. The dude is dead; everything is dead. The interior of the car resembles the scene of the battle of Wounded Knee, but this gives you small satisfaction.

In his best-known works Crane brings a quiet wit into his descriptions of people in violent, threatening situations: the slums, a battlefield, an open boat. In "In the Broadway Cars" he brings allusions to violence into a description of everyday occurrences, displaying a comic exuberance that recalls Mark Twain. Two other sketches written at the same time, "New York's Bicycle Speedway" and "The Roof Gardens and Gardeners of New York" are similar to "In the Broadway Cars"—playfully humorous sketches about common New York City scenes.

"Stephen Crane in Minetta Lane," another of the 1896 sketches, is in the same comic genre; however, the sketch is likely to be much less appealing to a modern reader. "Minetta Lane" recounts the history of a Greenwich Village street that served as a gathering place for criminals during the post–Civil War decades when the district was largely inhabited by African Americans. The area had a reputation for violence, and Crane uses comic hyperbole to convey Minetta Lane's fearsome reputation: "The razor habit clung to [the inhabitants] with the tenacity of an epidemic, and every night the uneven cobbles felt blood. . . . A man in a boiler iron suit would walk down to City Hall and look at the clock before he would ask the time of day. . . . They killed a sailor man every day and the pedestrians went about the streets wearing stoves for fear of the handy knives."[62]

Although the humor in this passage is not racially based, much of the sketch relies on racial stereotypes for its comedy. Describing a "large . . . and very hideous . . . negro named Bloodthirsty," wanted by the police for murder, Crane writes, "Bloodthirsty was particularly eloquent when drunk, and in the wildness of a spree he would rave so graphically about gore that even the habituated wool of old timers would stand straight." The dehumanizing reference to old timers' wool standing on end picks up stereotypes from nineteenth-century blackface minstrel shows. In much of the sketch Crane's habitual interest in vernacular speech strays into minstrel show parody. Quoting an elderly resident on the changes in Minetta Lane, he writes, "Why, disher' Lane ain't nohow like what it useter be— no indeed, it ain't. No, sir! 'Deed it ain't! Why, I kin remember dey des was a-cuttin' an' a'slashin' 'long yere all night. 'Deed dey was! My—my, dem times was diff'ent!"

Lewis Erenberg has noted that two stereotypes of African Americans were common in nineteenth-century minstrel shows.[63] One was "Jim Dandy," an urban black who habitually drank and fought. The Jim Dandy figure permeates the depiction of blacks in "Minetta Lane," which is filled with descriptions of hard-drinking, impulsively violent men like Bloodthirsty. Yet, like the minstrel shows, "Minetta Lane" contains a competing racial stereotype, that of the "happy darky." The sketch, which focuses on the threat of ghetto violence, contains that threat through its humor and its insistence that despite their potential for violence, African Americans are fundamentally harmless. The last paragraph begins, "But they are happy in this condition, are these people. The most extraordinary quality of the negro is his enormous capacity for happiness under most adverse circumstances. Minetta Lane is a place of poverty and sin, but these influences cannot destroy the broad smile of the negro, a vain and simple child but happy."

Readers familiar with Crane's complex and sympathetic portrayal of Henry Johnson, the principal African American character in his short story "The Monster," may be surprised by the blatant Jim Dandy and "happy darky" stereotypes of "Minetta Lane." However, given the pervasiveness of minstrel show stereotypes among white Americans in the post-Reconstruction era, it is more surprising that so few racial and ethnic stereotypes are to be found in Crane's New York City journalism. His contemporary Jacob Riis stands in illuminating contrast. *How the Other Half Lives*, Riis's most widely circulated work, uses racial or ethnic stereotypes on virtually every page. Race serves as Riis's fundamental analytic tool in discussing the New York poor. *How the Other Half Lives* is divided into chapters based on race and ethnicity. In Riis's account supposedly innate characteristics—German industriousness, Jewish greediness, Chinese barbarism—are more powerful determinants than economics or environment. Like other political progressives of his era, Riis took Anglo-Saxon superiority as a given, and he assumed that racial and ethnic differences largely accounted for the poverty of African Americans and immigrants.[64]

In contrast, racial and ethnic considerations are virtually absent from Crane's New York City writing. The ethnicity of the characters in his two Bowery novels, *Maggie* and *George's Mother*, is never specified. Among his newspaper sketches, aside from "Minetta Lane," only "When Man Falls a Crowd Gathers" mentions its characters' ethnicity, and there the two central characters' Italian speech is used to emphasize the threatening nature of the crowd, which speaks in a language that the fallen man's companion imperfectly understands. During a period when virtually all white Americans shared racist assumptions, and when many intellectuals and writers used racial and ethnic differences as a means of explaining economic and social inequality, Crane's general indifference to race is remarkable.

In the fall of 1896, when he reported on Minetta Lane, Crane also wrote a number of sketches about the Tenderloin district, New York City's Gilded Age center of entertainment and vice. The district was known for its gaudy dance halls, gambling, prostitution, and police corruption; it supposedly received its name from a police captain who said with relish on his transfer into the district, "I've had nothing but chuck steak for a long time, and now I'm going to get a little of the Tenderloin."[65]

Crane knew the Tenderloin intimately—he had lived in various locations within the district—and the *New York Journal*, which had recently come under the ownership of the exuberant William Randolph Hearst, arranged with the newly famous young novelist to write a series of Tenderloin sketches. The *Journal* published Crane's first Tenderloin sketch with great fanfare in its Sunday edition, giving the brief piece a full-page spread that was filled out with three large illustrations. Despite the *Journal*'s enthusiasm—the headline reads in part, "The First of a Series of Striking Sketches of New York Life by the Famous Novelist"—Crane completed only three Tenderloin pieces for the *Journal*, and they are among the weakest of his New York City writings.[66] The form of the sketch allowed journalists great flexibility, and for the *Journal* Crane used the form as a visual artist uses a sketchbook: a place for rough fragments.

Crane's first two sketches for the *Journal* were miscellaneous collections of brief pieces: reflections on the Tenderloin's reputation, scenes of drunks in cafes, a short story about a working-class couple in a dance hall. Crane's final Tenderloin piece for the *Journal* was a longer short story, a senti-mental tale about an ailing opium addict and his selflessly devoted sweet-heart. During his New York years it seems that Crane sold his weakest fic-tion to newspapers; all his stories of higher quality appeared in magazines. Crane's newspaper fiction is consistently disappointing; however, his reporting, enlivened by the creative tension inherent within the fact-fiction discourse, is generally intriguing.

A Tenderloin piece written for the McClure newspaper syndicate in May 1896, "Opium's Varied Dreams," illustrates Crane's newspaper reporting at its best. Opium was legal in much of the United States until the twentieth century and was widely used in patent medicines, but the custom of smoking the drug, introduced into the United States by Chinese immigrants, generated a widespread anti-opium hysteria. By the 1890s the drug was associated with a myth that held that any non-Chinese person who tried the drug faced degrading addiction and almost certain death.[67] In its obligatory section on the mysteries of Chinatown a popular book on New York City held that "indulgence in opium destroys the Chinaman far less surely, quickly, and completely than the Caucasian. To Americans in particular it means swift and certain degradation."[68] Jacob Riis made the same point in *How the Other Half Lives*: "The Chinaman smokes opium as Caucasians smoke tobacco, and apparently with little worse effect upon himself. But woe unto the white victim upon which his pitiless drug gets its grip!" Riis continued, "From any other form of dissipation . . . there is recovery; for the victims of any other vice, hope. For these there is nothing but death—moral, mental, and physical death."[69]

In place of Riis's moral fulminations "Opium's Varied Dreams" uses the journalistic technique of the experiment to puncture the myths about opium. As was his habit, Crane does not use first person in the article, but the piece makes clear that the writer has visited opium dens and has tried the drug. Crane undercuts readers' fears about the drug by humorously recounting the distasteful sensations of a first-time smoker: "When a man arises from his first trial of the pipe, the nausea that clutches him is some-thing that can give cards and spades and big cassino [sic] to seasickness. If he had swallowed a live chimney sweep he could not feel more like dying."[70] Throughout the article Crane uses his experimental knowledge of the drug to debunk the myths about opium.

Crane's debunking begins with his opening sentence: "Opium smoking in this country is believed to be more particularly a pastime of the Chinese, but in truth the greater number of the smokers are white men and white women." In the rest of the article he explodes other myths about smokers, the opium pipe, the process of smoking, and effects of the drug. He quotes an opium smoker's defense of his habit without appending moralistic comment. And he offers a long section full of how-to instructions for smoking opium. Throughout this section he uses homely analogies that remove the exotic aura from opium and domesticate the drug. He writes that heated opium exactly resembles molasses, describes a tool used to prepare it for smoking as "a sort of sharpened darning needle," and compares smokers clustered around an opium den lamp to people gathered around a campfire.

Just as "An Experiment in Misery" used the form of the journalistic experiment to illuminate the lives of homeless men at a time of national hysteria about tramps, "Opium's Varied Dreams" offers experimental knowledge about the drug in place of conventional moralistic condemnations. The article boldly challenges Victorian conventions, and it must have taken a certain bravery—or foolhardiness—for Crane to offer the piece to the McClure syndicate under his signature. It is interesting to note that the syndicate distributed with the piece an illustration of two women smoking the pipe, which various newspapers captioned either "Victims of Despair," "Fair Victims of the Pipe," or "Foolish Victims of the Harmful Drug."[71] Nowhere does Crane discuss female opium smokers; the illustration and its caption serve to place Crane's article within a frame of sentimentalism and morality, as if to make up for the article's lack of those qualities. Even more interesting is that the *New York Sun*, alone among the seven newspapers nationwide that printed the article, removed Crane's byline. There is no evidence as to why the *Sun* printed the article anonymously—the other newspapers included Crane's name in the headline—but we can speculate that one of Crane's many acquaintances on the *Sun* staff may have removed the byline in order to protect the young writer's reputation in his home city of New York. If so, the effort proved futile. Before the year came to an end, newspapers in New York and across the country printed accusations that Stephen Crane was an opium addict.

The accusations stemmed from Crane's work as a reporter. In search of material for his *New York Journal* Tenderloin sketches, in the early morning hours of September 16, 1896, Crane sat with two young female actors—"chorus girls"—in a popular Tenderloin cafe. While they chatted, a young woman who called herself Dora Clark joined them, and around two in the morning the four of them left the cafe together. Within minutes, while Crane was helping one of the women onto a streetcar, a plainclothes policeman arrested Dora Clark for soliciting as a prostitute.

As Crane stood dumbfounded and the remaining chorus girl screamed in hysterics, the policeman hauled Clark to the local station. The policeman, Charles Becker, was later to become famous as one of the most corrupt officers on a notoriously corrupt police force. Eventually executed for his part in the murder of a gambler, in 1896 Becker was engaged in a campaign to harass Clark because of an insult she had given to a fellow officer. As Crane was soon to find out, Dora Clark was indeed a prostitute; however, he knew that she had done nothing to warrant her arrest on the morning of September 16.[72]

Later that day Crane appeared in court to testify to Dora Clark's innocence. The anguish that the appearance caused him is revealed in an extraordinary article about the affair that he wrote for the *Journal*, "Adventures of a Novelist."[73] Throughout the article Crane refers to himself in third person as "the reluctant witness," and he recounts his internal debate as he tried to decide whether to risk his reputation by testifying on behalf of a prostitute. Fortunately, Crane's reporter colleagues rallied to his defense, and newspaper stories about his court appearance were uniformly favorable. Three newspapers referred to Crane's personal "red badge of courage" in their headlines about the episode, and the phrase cropped up in the text of other articles.[74] Unfortunately, this was not to be the end of the affair.

Dora Clark—young, quick-tempered, and impulsive—decided to press charges against Becker in a police commission court and asked Crane to testify again. The reluctant witness agreed. This time Becker, his lawyer, and the New York City police force knew of Crane's intended testimony well in advance, and they set to work gathering information to discredit Clark's witness. Clark's suit was tried on October 16, 1896; Crane underwent a brutal cross-examination by Officer Becker's lawyer. The newspapers could do little to contain the damage. The headline in the *New York World* is representative:

CRANE HAD A GAY NIGHT
RACY STORY BROUGHT OUT IN THE TRIAL OF BECKER . . .

DORA CLARK'S CHAMPION
A JANITOR TESTIFIED THAT THE NOVELIST LIVED WITH A
TENDERLOIN GIRL
AN OPIUM SMOKING EPISODE[75]

Becker's lawyer questioned Crane extensively about his sexual history and his use of opium; Crane repeatedly refused to answer on the grounds that "it would tend to degrade me."[76]

Crane never wrote about his reactions to his ordeal on the stand. Given the anguish he displayed about his brief unchallenged testimony in the first trial, the experience of the second trial may have been too overwhelming to describe. Understandably, the experience made him eager to leave New York, and within a few weeks of the second trial Crane departed the city on assignment for the Bacheller newspaper syndicate. For the rest of his life he made only brief visits to New York. From this point on virtually all of Stephen Crane's journalism was journalism of travel and war.

CHAPTER 4

The Shape of a Cloak
and a Point of View

TRAVEL JOURNALISM

Early in his career Stephen Crane was determined to write travel journalism. In August 1892, barely out of his teens and still working for his brother Townley's New Jersey Coast News Bureau in Asbury Park, Crane wrote to the American Press Association, trying to arrange a journalistic excursion to the South and West. Although the young journalist threw considerable bravado into his letter—"I have written special articles for some years for the Tribune and other papers"—his gambit was unsuccessful.[1] However, Crane did not abandon his quest to write travel journalism. In 1895 the Bacheller newspaper syndicate agreed to fund the trip that Crane had conceived of earlier, with an excursion to Mexico thrown in.

The syndicate's willingness to bankroll the young writer came from the success of his first piece for Bacheller: an abridged version of *The Red Badge of Courage*. The newspaper's importance in the late nineteenth-century literary marketplace—and in Stephen Crane's career—is revealed in the fact that the first place Crane thought of for publication of his Civil War novel was the newspaper. Crane originally took the manuscript of *Red Badge* to the S. S. McClure newspaper syndicate in the spring of 1894. When McClure kept the manuscript for six months without giving him a decision, Crane retrieved his novel and submitted it to Irving Bacheller, who arranged for its publication in the *New York Press* and several other newspapers in December 1894.[2]

Crane departed on his journalistic excursion in January 1895. He was away from New York for almost four months, stopping in Nebraska, Arkansas, New Orleans, Texas, and Mexico City. It is questionable whether the Bacheller firm earned back the money it advanced, because it syndicated only a dozen articles and sketches. However, the trip proved to be a gold mine for Crane, who wrote at least five other articles that remained in manuscript. In addition, he later used his western and Mexican experiences for fiction, producing eight short stories about the region, including two of his greatest, "The Blue Hotel" (1898) and "The Bride Comes to Yellow Sky" (1898).

Crane returned to travel journalism after he settled in England in the summer of 1897, writing a series of letters from London. That fall he also capitalized on an Irish vacation with another series of sketches. Altogether, Crane wrote about two dozen travel pieces from the West, Mexico, England, and Ireland. Much of this travel writing is not at the level of his New York City journalism. The routines of metropolitan reporting—in particular, the popular form of the "experiment"—stimulated some of Crane's best writing. Dressing as a tramp, descending into a coal mine, smoking opium in the Tenderloin, Crane immersed himself in others' lives through his newspaper work. Crane's fascination with the lives of those on the margins of society and his interest in issues of identity and perception fueled the resulting sketches. His best New York journalism combines a social reformer's outrage at poverty and oppression, a scientific naturalist's fascination with the effect of environment on character, a philosopher's interest in epistemology, and an artist's concern with the complexities of rendering points of view through the medium of language.

In contrast, nineteenth-century travel journalism promoted superficiality. The typical travel "letter" in 1890s newspapers was little different from the Parisian letters that Henry James had attempted unsuccessfully in the 1870s: a random collection of a traveler's observations, united only by the writer's sensibility and location. Crane's letters from Mexico City, Arkansas, Texas, and London are akin to James's from Paris: fragmented miscellanies. James at least had the advantage of familiarity with French language and culture. Crane was innocent of any knowledge of the Spanish language or Mexican history; on his western trip he was hampered by the fact that he could spend only a few days in each location; in England he had to produce great quantities of prose at a fast clip in order to support the lavish lifestyle that he and his companion, Cora Howorth Stewart, had adopted. In the first of his Irish sketches Crane acknowledged the inherent superficiality of travel journalism: "The shape of a cloak is handier to the eye than is a point of view," he wrote.[3]

The wonder is that among much hurried, indifferent writing, Crane produced in the travel form some superior pieces that both portray the novel shape of a foreign cloak and capture differing points of view. His western and Mexican sketches offer a different perspective on these regions than do his short stories, and they illuminate the popular formulas on which Crane relied in his fiction. His reporting from both Mexico and Ireland rivals his New York City journalism in its sympathy for the oppressed. His "London Impressions" is a formally experimental tour-de-force. And his two accounts of his shipwreck off the coast of Florida demonstrate Crane's brilliant handling of his era's journalistic fact-fiction discourse.

Readers familiar with Crane's western short stories—"The Blue Hotel," "The Bride Comes to Yellow Sky," "Twelve O'Clock" (1899), and "Moonlight on the Snow" (1900)—are likely to be surprised by his reporting from Nebraska and Texas. The short stories are melodramatic and violent, the characters quick with knife and revolver. The journalism features not a single weapon, and the principal characters are farmers, bureaucrats, and businessmen.

Certainly, Crane's sole article from Nebraska, "Nebraska's Bitter Fight for Life," differs from his great short story set in that state, "The Blue Hotel." "The Blue Hotel," a complex work about West and East, violence and moral responsibility, takes place in a howling midwinter blizzard. In contrast, the newspaper article concerns a summer drought. Although "Nebraska's Bitter Fight for Life" ignores the human violence that preoccupied Crane in his fiction, it treats other concerns central to his writing and can stand among his greatest short works. Crane's travels in Nebraska gave him the opportunity to join national myth—what Henry Nash Smith calls the "myth of the garden" of the American West—with his personal vision of a powerful, seemingly malevolent nature.[4]

Traveling west of Pennsylvania for the first time in his life, Stephen Crane arrived in Lincoln, Nebraska, on February 1, 1895. He stayed in the state two weeks, gathering information on the drought of the previous summer that had led to a near famine in the state's central counties. His account of the drought, "Nebraska's Bitter Fight for Life," was widely syndicated on February 24. The piece contains a quantity of pure reporting that is unique in Crane's work. Crane's New York City feature articles are almost devoid of proper names. In contrast, for "Nebraska" Crane interviewed and quoted at length Governor Silas A. Holcomb and relief commission head L. P. Ludden, and he included a wealth of statistics on rainfall and weather. However, the interviews and statistics are contained within a romance narrative that features heroic farmers struggling against both the grand cruelties of an omnipotent nature and the petty chicanery of unscrupulous profiteers.

Crane establishes his romance in the opening sentence of his article. Datelined "Eddyville, Dawson Co., Nebraska," the article begins, "The vast prairies in this section of Nebraska contain a people who are engaged in a bitter and deadly fight for existence."[5] He goes on to paint an idyllic picture of Nebraska agriculture before the 1894 drought and a stirring portrait of the farmers' heroism. The article's third paragraph contains both themes:

> In June, 1894, the bounteous prolific prairies of this portion of Nebraska were a-shine with the young and tender green of growing corn. Round and fat cattle filled the barnyards of the farmers. The trees that were congregated about the little homesteads were of the vivid and brave hue of healthy and vigorous vegetation. The towns were alive with the commerce of an industrious and hopeful community. These mighty brown fields stretching for miles under the imperial blue sky of Nebraska had made a promise to the farmer. It was to compensate him for his great labor, his patience, his sacrifices. Under the cool, blue dome the winds gently rustled the arrays of waist-high stalks. (409)

This description could have been lifted from one of the many 1880s publications intended to promote settlement in the Great Plains. Speculators' optimism and heavier-than-usual rainfall in the 1880s helped to shape expectations that the northern Great Plains could be transformed into a fertile garden. One Nebraska booster and amateur scientist even concocted a theory that cultivation of the land would promote rainfall, condensing his notion into a potent slogan: "Rain follows the plough."[6] The drought of 1890 upset that theory and led to a Populist revolt, a midwestern political earthquake. The 1894 drought was even worse: the lowest recorded rainfall of the nineteenth century, combined with a blast-furnace heat wave in July that withered virtually every scrap of vegetation in the central counties. The financial panic of 1893 and the ensuing national depression had left banks too shaky to lend money to the distressed farmers. The 1890 farm crisis had led to a Populist political uprising in Nebraska, but the severity of the 1894–95 crisis created only suffering and despair.[7]

In his article Crane ignores the bad weather and political upheaval of 1890 in order to paint his portrait of an undisturbed agrarian utopia in June 1894. The effect is to make the ensuing drought and heat wave seem unexpected, capricious, and cruel. He closes his narrative of the drought with a melodramatic image of farmers versus nature: "The farmers helpless, with no weapon against this terrible and inscrutable wrath of nature, were spectators at the strangling of their hopes, their ambitions, all that they could look to from their labor. It was as if upon the massive altar of the earth, their homes and their families were being offered in sacrifice to the wrath of some blind and pitiless deity" (410).

The quotation's second sentence reads like a prose adaptation of a poem in *The Black Riders* (1895), the book Crane had just completed and sent to his publisher. Many poems in *The Black Riders* depict a war between an audacious humankind and a vengeful Old Testament God. The opening lines of three poems give a powerful sense of the book's angry theology:

Blustering god,
Stamping across the sky
With loud swagger,
I fear you not.

A god in wrath
Was beating a man;
He cuffed him loudly
With thunderous blows
That rang and rolled over the earth.

*"And the sins of the fathers shall be visited upon the heads of the children,
even unto the third and fourth generation of them that hate me."*
Well, then, I hate Thee, unrighteous picture;
Wicked image, I hate Thee;
So, strike with Thy vengeance
The heads of those little men

Who come blindly.
It will be a brave thing.[8]

"Nebraska's Bitter Fight for Life" may have little in common with Crane's "The Blue Hotel," but it shares his poetry's vision of humanity beset by a bullying deity. The difference between article and poems is that *The Black Riders* offers no clear resolution to its mordant dramas, whereas Crane's religious despair in "Nebraska" is tempered by his embrace of the myth of the western garden. He refuses to leave his narrative of the 1894–95 crisis with the farmers in defeat. For all the irony regarding physical courage contained in *The Red Badge of Courage*, throughout his life Crane was unironically admiring in the presence of men of action, as in his Asbury Park paean to boxer Jim Corbett. In the peroration of "Nebraska" Crane writes,

> The final quality of these farmers who have remained in this portion of the State is their faith in the ultimate victory of the land and their industry. They have a determination to wait until nature, with her mystic processes, restores to them the prosperity and bounty of former years. . . . In the meantime, they depend upon their endurance, their capacity to help each other, and their steadfast and unyielding courage. (419–20)

His closing sentences offer an image of human triumph and leave intact the myth of the western garden.

After departing Nebraska in February 1895, Crane traveled to Hot Springs and New Orleans, then stayed briefly in Galveston and San Antonio. His articles about the two Texas cities record his surprise at their modernity; San Antonio "presents a totally modern aspect to the astonished visitor," he writes. Both articles use the trolley as an emblem of modernity. He calls the trolley "terrible and almighty" and writes that both Texas and Nebraska have "come to an almost universal condition of yellow trolly-cars with clanging gongs and whirring wheels, and conductors who don't give a curse for the public."[9] Except for the Alamo, Crane can find no trace of Texas's distinctively western roots.

Crane's journalism and fiction record two different visions of the West, two differing interpretations of its significance. His article on Nebraska portrays only two groups: the farmers of the central counties, whom he depicts as heroes engaged in a struggle with nature, and the people of

Lincoln, the state capital, who are involved in government and business. His Texas articles feature derby-hatted citizens riding on trolleys. That is, in "Nebraska" the winning of the West is an ongoing narrative about farming families supporting themselves in a difficult environment. In Crane's Texas articles the winning of the West is a purely historical narrative; its only contemporary trace is San Antonio's Alamo. In contrast, Crane's western short stories depict the winning of the West as a contemporary struggle between forces of modernity and violent white males.

"The Bride Comes to Yellow Sky," one of Crane's best-known stories, illustrates most clearly the clash between modernization and archaic male violence. The story's protagonist is Jack Potter, a Texas sheriff returning to Yellow Sky in a Pullman railway car with his eastern bride. His antagonist is Scratchy Wilson, a gunslinger on a tear who wants to fight Potter. But when Wilson sees the sheriff unarmed, in his good clothes, with his bride by his side, the gunfighter dejectedly lowers his pistol and shuffles off. All Crane's other short stories about the American West similarly pit emblems of modernity against embodiments of western violence.

Crane's observations of the West, as recorded in his journalism, are of a world of late Victorian farmers and businessmen. His fiction takes place not in this observed world but in what Richard Slotkin has called the "mythic space" of the West, a space defined not by geography or history but by the literary formulas of the dime novel and commercial popular culture.[10] Crane alters the hackneyed gunfighter formulas of popular fiction by locating his conflict not among western characters—heroic gunfighters versus evil gunslingers or marauding Indians—but between representatives of the mythic West and emblems of the modern East. However, this revised version of the western is not unique to Crane. As John Cawelti points out, Crane was working within a "new western" tradition established by Mark Twain and Bret Harte, which features a cultural dialectic between West and East.[11] Crane's western short stories, particularly "The Blue Hotel" and "The Bride Comes to Yellow Sky," are superb. But they are not, as many critics have suggested, dependent upon Crane's experience in the West; his journalism depicts that experience. Rather, the western stories rely on formulaic literary depictions of situations that by 1895 were not to be found by a touring journalist.

Crane's Mexican short stories are even more rigidly formulaic, sharing a common plot. In each a white American male is the innocent target of unprovoked Mexican threats. The Mexicans are blustering, sneaky, and aggressive, but they are also cowardly, afraid of even the implication of Anglo violence. In two stories ("One Dash—Horses" [1896] and "Five White Mice" [1897]) the Mexicans withdraw in the face of Anglo courage. In "A Man and Some Others" (1897) they are defeated in a gunfight with two Anglos, despite a four-to-one advantage.

The white Americans' status as innocent victims of Mexican aggression makes Crane's Mexican short stories part of what Richard White has termed the "American iconography of the frontier," a mythic narrative that transforms white conquerors into victims of the people they conquered.[12] Popular representations of the West such as Buffalo Bill's Wild West presented their white characters as victims of Indians, a narrative strategy that turned the conquest and appropriation of Indian lands into a defensive action on the part of whites. Similarly, Crane's stories of Anglo-Mexican conflict serve to mask white territorial aggression. At the same time, they shore up white masculinity, threatened by the forces of modernity, through their demonstrations of the warrior virtues of Anglo-Saxon males.[13]

One of the few extended analyses of Crane's Mexican fiction is by Raymund Paredes, who surveys every reference to Mexicans in Crane's fiction and concludes, "There are few characterizations of the Mexican in serious American literature less flattering than Crane's. His Mexicans perpetuate a traditional Yankee stereotype; they are wicked, drunken and cowardly. Their only function in Crane's stories is to provide an odious comparison—to glorify the powerful Anglo by serving as grotesque foils for his tedious exhibitions of courage and ingenuity."[14] One critic has attempted to argue that Paredes misses the stories' irony and that they are actually an attack on Anglo racism, but the irony is not apparent to this reader.[15] Paredes' assessment seems fundamentally correct. Where it falls short is in Paredes' privileging of the fiction and failure to consider Crane's Mexican journalism. The journalism complicates our view of Crane's attitude toward Mexicans and calls into question Paredes' implication of unrelieved racism in Crane's Mexican writing.

Crane completed eight newspaper articles during his two months in Mexico. If his Mexican fiction can be seen as simple and racist, his Mexican journalism is more complex in its attitude toward Mexicans and in its thematic concerns. The attitude toward Mexicans displayed in Crane's journalism is most often jocular and condescending. The Mexicans of the travel journalism are not the violent figures of the short stories, but they are quaint, amusing figures eager to fleece visiting Americans when opportunity arises. Yet Crane's gentle gibes at the Mexicans encountered on tourist rounds alternate with a sympathetic perspective that is remarkable in work by a nineteenth-century North American. Crane frequently shows a remarkable sensitivity to the plight of Mexico's impoverished Indian majority. For example, a tourist-oriented article about the dollar-to-peso exchange rate and consumer-goods prices ends with a stark and moving paragraph that shows compassion for the Mexican working class and over-turns stereotypes of the lazy Mexican: "The Mexican laborer earns from 1 real (6 ¼ cents United States) to 4 reals (25 cents United States) per day. He lives mostly on tortillas, which are beans. His clothing consists of a cot-ton shirt, cotton trousers, leather sandals, and a straw hat. For his wages he has to work like a horse."[16]

In a similar fashion Crane's other Mexican journalism combines jocular condescension with efforts to comprehend the Mexicans' point of view. Those efforts culminate in "The Mexican Lower Classes," an extraordi-nary work that Crane never sent to the Bacheller syndicate; it remained in manuscript until 1967, when R. W. Stallman found it among Crane's papers and published it. "The Mexican Lower Classes" is unique among Crane's travel journalism—less a record of observations than an inquiry into observation, less travel writing than a meditation on travel writing. The piece begins with a reflection on the difficulties of understanding a foreign point of view: "Above all things, the stranger finds the occupations of foreign peoples to be trivial and inconsequent. The average mind utterly fails to comprehend the new point of view."[17] Crane goes on to detail the seeming futility of the lives of Mexico's impoverished Indians and an American's shock at seeing "a brown woman in one garment crouched list-lessly in the door of a low adobe hut while a naked brown baby sprawls on his stomach in the dust of the roadway" (435–36).

Crane's encounter with extreme poverty was akin to that of thousands of other Americans, before and since, who have traveled in underdevel-oped nations. That encounter frequently produces judgment, disdain, condescension, and pity—all of which Crane manages to avoid. Instead, he writes about the temptation to judge and the difficulties of understanding. "The most worthless literature of the world," he writes near the article's opening, "has been that which has been written by the men of one nation concerning the men of another" (436). Crane resists the arrogance of facile judgments and superficial understanding, and he lays out a strict pro-gram for the travel writer: "It seems that a man must not devote himself for a time to attempts at psychological perception. He can be sure of two things, form and color. Let him then see all he can but let him not sit in literary judgment on this or that manner of the people" (436).

In the rest of his article Crane does not restrict himself to form and color. But he does withhold judgment, and he prefaces every generalization with a qualifier: "I cannot perceive any evidence"; "As far as I can perceive" (437). "The Mexican Lower Classes" uses more first person than almost anything else Stephen Crane ever wrote. It is easy to see why Crane, who habitually wrote about himself in the third person in his journalism, decided not to publish the piece. Crane's perceptions, his temptations to judgment, and his efforts to restrain his conclusions are the real subject of this piece. The article gives a direct avowal of Crane's thinking that distinguishes it from anything he published in his lifetime.

"The Mexican Lower Classes" is extraordinary in political as well as artistic terms. Contrasting the seemingly stoic attitude of Mexico's poor with the "savage and scornful" mien of American slum dwellers, Crane offers a vision of impending class warfare that is franker than anything in his New York City journalism:

> The people of the slums of our own cities fill a man with awe. That vast army with its countless faces immovably cynical, that vast army that silently confronts eternal defeat, it makes one afraid. One listens for the first thunder of the rebellion, the moment when this silence shall be broken by a roar of war. Meanwhile one fears this class, their numbers, their wickedness, their might—even their laughter. (436)

Such statements show Crane's sensitivity to social injustice, whether in the New York slums, the Pennsylvania coal fields, or the Mexican countryside.

Crane's compassion for the Indians suffuses "The Mexican Lower Classes," yet he rigorously refuses glib generalizations about their condition. In his concluding paragraph he writes, "I refuse to commit judgment upon these lower classes of Mexico. I even refuse to pity them" (438). Crane writes in an Irish travel sketch cited earlier that "the shape of a cloak is handier to the eye than is a point of view." In "The Mexican Lower Classes" he acknowledges that, given vast differences in language, culture, and material conditions, grasping a foreign people's point of view may be impossible. "Form and color" (or "the shape of a cloak"), self-examination, and an attention to the limitations of language may be the best and truest path for the writer encountering a culture radically different from his own.[18]

~~~

After he returned from Mexico in May 1895, it would be two years before Crane wrote any substantial amount of travel journalism. The opportunity came when he and his companion, Cora, decided to settle near London in June 1897. Crane soon produced a long article titled "London Impressions," which was published in three successive issues of the English *Saturday Review* and which Crane's agent offered, unsuccessfully, to the *New York Journal*.

"London Impressions" is an extraordinary work that, like "The Mexican Lower Classes," implicitly challenges conventional travel writing. As Richard Brodhead has pointed out, the elite U.S. magazines of the late nineteenth century had an enormous appetite for travel journalism, publishing one or more travel articles in every issue. The function of those articles, Brodhead suggests, was to enable the burgeoning American upper class to define itself; travel—particularly European travel—was a "class-signifying leisure habit" at a time when even white-collar workers received no paid vacation.[19] However, Crane's "London Impressions" was useless for such signifying practices, as confirmed by his inability to find a U.S. publisher for the piece. "London Impressions" rigorously avoids the picturesque, typical, and touristy. Instead, it is an exercise in perception, a linguistic equivalent of Claude Monet's series of Impressionist renderings of a single scene.

"London Impressions" is different from anything else Crane wrote. It seems to be a deliberate exercise, with Crane setting self-imposed limits within which he must work. Monet frequently set such limits for himself, making multiple paintings of the same location in different conditions of light, as in his series of paintings of Rouen Cathedral; Crane's limits in "London Impressions" are temporal. Most of this lengthy article describes the brief period between arriving in the London train station and reaching his hotel by cab. Crane divided the piece into eight sections, which were published in three installments. Four sections describe the cab ride; the narrator does not actually arrive at his hotel until the eighth installment. A conventional tactic would have been for Crane to describe the landmarks he observed from his cab's window; a writer could easily wring five hundred words out of passing Buckingham Palace, another five hundred link-ing a grubby side street to recollections of *Oliver Twist.* But Crane avoids this approach. For one thing, it is night, and a dense wet fog is over the city. Crane notes that in the darkness each person in the passing carriages "sat in his own little cylinder of vision," and he limits himself to what he can sight within his cylinder.[20] "London Impressions" is a record of perception. The first half of the title, "London," is ultimately much less significant than the second, "Impressions." The focus is on the perceiving consciousness. If that consciousness is sufficiently fine—as Stephen Crane's was—the description of a cab ride can easily take four thousand words.

Crane notes in the first section of "London Impressions" that it would be "more correct" for him, as a travel writer, to describe St. Paul's, the Thames embankment, and the houses of Parliament. Instead, he devotes the first section to a porter and a cabman. "I was born in London at a railroad station," he writes, "and my new vision encompassed a porter and a cabman" (682). The sentence emphasizes his perceptual concerns. Erasing any prior knowledge he may have of London's history or architecture— such as the houses of Parliament that constitute a more correct subject for travel writing—he represents himself as an infant limited to sensory impressions. The next four sections describe the cab ride in impressionistic prose. A street is "like a passage in a monstrous cave"; street lamps "resembled the little gleams at the caps of the miners" (682). He devotes most of one section to the sounds of London, the next to the cab horse's gait, one to an accident in which another cab horse falls to the pavement, and another to reflections occasioned by the sight of a young man in a top hat.

Crane's lengthy record of his perceptions occasioned some derision. An article in the *San Francisco Wave* that may well have been written by Frank Norris commented on "London Impressions": "Mr. Crane has started in with his descriptions at the railway depot. The best that I can wish for him is that he may live long enough to reach his hotel." The *Wave* writer compared Crane to a locust in a grain elevator attempting to empty the silo by carrying off one grain of corn at a time.[21] The *Wave* article's subtitle reads, "The American Novelist Investigating England with a Microscope." Crane's technique in "London Impressions" can fairly be said to be microscopic, a minutely detailed perceptual record. In its slow-paced detail and its focus on the perceiving consciousness, the piece resembles Henry James's late travel writing, such as *The American Scene* (1907). Crane's most famous subjects—war, shipwreck, the Wild West—make him seem to many readers a very different writer from James, but as artists they had in common an interest in the processes of perception and in the representation of the individual consciousness. "London Impressions" is Crane at his most Jamesian. It seems to prefigure the friendship that developed between Crane and James a few months later, as well as Crane's admiration for James's early exercise in the microscopic late style, *What Maisie Knew* (1897).[22]

Crane's only other travel journalism from England was a series of miscellaneous letters published without byline in the *New York Press* and titled "The European Letters" in *The Works of Stephen Crane*.[23] These letters were submitted to the *Press* under the name Imogene Carter, the pseudonym that Crane's companion, Cora, used for her journalism. In a letter to his American agent written in October 1897, Crane said, "You might go to Curtis Brown, Sunday Editor of the *Press* and say how-how from me. Then tell him this *in the strictest confidence*, that a lady named Imogene Carter whose work he has been using from time to time is also named Stephen Crane and that I did 'em in about twenty minutes on each Sunday, just dictating to a friend. Of course they are rotten bad."[24] Crane was not being overly modest. "The European Letters" are unrelievedly mediocre collections of disconnected paragraphs dealing largely with fashions, the English royal family, and the doings of European aristocracy. Lillian Gilkes, who examined the handwritten drafts of the "Letters," concluded that Crane was exaggerating his contribution to Cora's articles. His participation in the letters "was on the whole minimal."[25] Crane wrote two short items, dictated a few others in whole or part, and added material to some of Cora's paragraphs. To the extent that Crane participated in and gave his approval to the "Letters," they show his contradictions. On the one hand, Crane was sympathetic to slum dwellers, coal miners, and the Mexican lower classes; on the other, he helped to write articles that reveal an unabashed infatuation with European aristocrats.

As he and Cora were producing "The European Letters," with their chronicles of the rich and famous, Crane wrote a travel piece that celebrates the British working man. When he and Cora set out for an Irish holiday in August 1897 in company with the writer Harold Frederic and his companion, Kate Lyon, they took a boat from Glasgow, Scotland. For the train journey there Crane arranged to ride in the locomotive with the engineer and fireman and to write about the experience for *McClure's*. "The Scotch Express" is in part an inquiry into the nature of courage. As he had done in "Nebraska's Bitter Fight for Life," Crane turns a representative of the common man, in this case the locomotive engineer, into a heroic figure. "For the exercise of temperance, of courage, of honesty," Crane writes, the engineer "has no equal at the altitude of prime-ministers."[26] "The engine-driver is the finest type of man that is grown," he writes later in the article. "He is the pick of the earth" (746). "The Scotch Express" romanticizes the engineer in the same way that Crane's journalism always romanticizes athletes, soldiers, and other men of action. At the same time, it offers a lengthy, vivid, impressionistic account of the three-hundred-mile train ride. Crane writes at one point,

> This valkyric journey on the back of the vermilion engine with the shouting of the wind, the deep mighty panting of the steed, the grey blur at the track side, the flowing quicksilver ribbon of the other rails, the sudden clash as a switch intersects, all the din and fury of this ride was of a splendor that caused one to look abroad at the quiet green landscape and believe that it was of a phlegm quite beyond patience. It should have been dark, rain-shot and windy; thunder should have rolled across its sky. (745)

In its impressionistic attention to perception—as in "the grey blur at the track side"—the passage is typical of all Crane's journalism. It stands out only in its unabashed joyous exuberance; the narrator of the piece is clearly having the time of his life.

Crane's good mood evidently continued throughout his three-week vacation in Ireland. He wrote five articles about Ireland that were published in an English newspaper, the *Westminster Gazette*, and in part in the *New York Journal*. These pieces, which Crane referred to as the "Irish Notes," are uniformly affectionate portrayals of the Irish. Possessed of an instinctive sympathy for the oppressed, Crane depicts the Irish people's indomitable spirit in the face of British occupation.

Crane expresses his theme of Irish resistance to the British with great subtlety and art in his first "Irish Note," "Queenstown." Even the title of the piece can be read as an announcement of his theme, for the name "Queenstown" had been imposed by the British upon the Cove of Cork in 1849, within the memory of many of Crane's readers.[27] With British domination suggested by the title, the piece continues the theme in its opening paragraph:

One by one, passengers in heavy rain-coats came on deck and turned their eyes toward the dripping coast-line of Ireland. In the thick rain-mist to the west gaunt capes were sleepily lifting their heads from the sea, and on these headlands were sometimes little buildings, implacably severe and grim, which denoted that a government had built them. Afterward a red buoy that appeared to be swimming against the tide shone amid the dim streets of a terraced city on the hillside. The form of H.M.S. *Howe* was flat against some long sheds at the water's edge. The buoy which had challenged towers and steeples rapidly subsided to its usual meek size.[28]

The passage reveals Crane's interest in visual impressionism through his depiction of a buoy that from a distant perspective appears larger than the town's towers and steeples but shrinks to its proper proportion as the packet boat passengers draw near. Woven into this purely visual approach is a subtle political commentary. The narrator notes that the "severe and grim" buildings on the headlands must be government constructions; his observation of her majesty's ship *Howe* reminds the reader that it was the occupying British government that built them.

Crane continues his subtle depiction of the British occupation through-out the piece, weaving the theme into his figures of speech, as when he notes that the heavy rain "would have gone through any top-coat but a sentry-box"—a reminder of British military presence (484). And he delights in contrasting nimble Irish wit with English stolidity. Describing his cab driver Jerry, the narrator writes, "His agile mind is a real type of the country; it moves with the rapidity of light from the past to the future, here, there and everywhere. . . . It would attempt forty games of chess at one time and play them all passably well" (486). Following this description of the cab driver, Crane ends the piece with another reference to the British naval vessel: "The rain disclosed the bay at last, and from the hill one could look down upon the broad deck of the *Howe*. Against the slate-colored waters shone the white pennant of the English navy, emblem of the man who can play one game at a time" (486). Crane implicitly con-trasts the Englishman's single-mindedness with the Irish people's mental agility and concludes by quietly predicting that Irish wit will triumph over British military might, as represented by the *Howe*, in the chess game of Anglo-Irish politics.

Crane wrote his "Irish Notes" in 1897, during an era of relative politi-

cal calm in Ireland. The violent Land Wars of the 1880s between impoverished Catholic tenants and Protestant landlords were a decade in the
past. The political movement for Irish independence had fallen apart early
in the 1890s after its leader, Charles Stewart Parnell, was accused of conducting an adulterous affair and died soon after. British prime minister
William Gladstone's second Irish Home Rule Bill was defeated in 1893.
When Gladstone resigned the next year and Conservatives took over the
government, any hope of Irish self-governance in the near future was
ended.[29] However, if conflict between the Irish and their British masters
was not overt in the late 1890s, it nevertheless existed beneath the surface
calm; it was to explode into violence two decades later in the 1916 Easter
Rising. Crane's subtle evocation of Irish rebelliousness and British force in
"Queenstown" was appropriate to the era, and he continued the theme in
the second of the "Irish Notes," "Ballydehob."

On its surface "Ballydehob" is simply a celebration of a typical Irish village. "There is in Ballydehob," Crane writes near the sketch's opening,
"not one thing that is commonly pointed out to the stranger as a thing
worthy of a half-tone reproduction in a book. There is no cascade, no
peak, no lake"—the listing of the charms lacking in Ballydehob continues.
But the passage ends with a subtle reminder of the British occupation of
Ireland: "[Ballydehob] is simply an Irish village wherein live some three
hundred Irish and four constables."[30] The constables were members of the
Royal Irish Constabulary (RIC), a semimilitary force whose members were
housed in barracks throughout Ireland and whose primary responsibility
was the suppression of anti-British activities. Crane mentions the RIC officers at two other points in the brief sketch—he observes that their primary
occupation appears to be trout fishing—and he takes a direct jab at the
English in one passage that derides the "average English tradesman with
his back-breaking respect for this class, his reflex contempt for that class,
his reverence for the tin gods" (487). However, the political implications
of "Ballydehob" are not limited to its references to the RIC and English
tradesmen. The piece as a whole is based upon a contrast between freedom
and regimentation that evokes the tensions between the Irish and English.

Crane's primary theme in "Ballydehob" is that the village's lack of obvious, picturesque attractions means that tour groups ignore it, and therein
lies its charm. Only one willing to break away from the guided tours can
find Ballydehob; the sketch depicts the relationship between the tour agencies and the independent traveler as parallel to that between the British and

the Irish. The tour agencies, like the British occupying Ireland, are rigidly militaristic. The piece opens, "The illimitable inventive incapacity of the excursion companies has made many circular paths throughout Ireland, and on these well-pounded roads the guardians of the touring public may be seen drilling the little travellers in squads" (486). Later in the opening paragraph the narrator describes "the tourists chained in gangs." He depicts tour guides as drill sergeants and prison guards from whom the traveler who wishes to see Ballydehob must "escape," break "like a Texan steer out of the pens and corrals of the tourist agencies" (486, 487). The narrator, who manages to escape from the agencies and visit Ballydehob, is subtly linked with the independent Irish of the village, who could flay with "their fast sharp speaking" the stolid English tradesman (487). Readers of "Ballydehob," by their textual presence in the village, are similarly linked with the Irish against both tourist agencies and English overseers.

Yet for all Crane's identification with the Irish throughout the "Irish Notes," he was not unrelievedly hostile to the English and their representatives. His third article in the series, titled "The Royal Irish Constabulary," is a politically complex piece. As with "Queenstown," his title alone carries political meanings. In 1897 the name of the Royal Irish Constabulary was still inseparably linked with the Mitchelstown Massacre of ten years earlier, when a group of constables fired into a crowd gathered for a land reform rally, killing three people.[31] The piece opens with an anecdote that depicts the RIC as both repressive and inept. Acting on an informer's tip, the RIC surround and break into a house after dark, finding only a single shotgun; the newspapers herald the action as the seizure of a "Veritable Arsenal." Crane follows up the anecdote by noting, "One cannot look Ireland straight in the face without seeing a great many constables. The country is dotted with little garrisons. It must have been said a thousand times that there is an absolute military occupation. The fact is too plain."[32]

Immediately after this paragraph that depicts the constables as an occupying force, Crane writes, "The constable himself becomes a figure interesting in its isolation" (489). In the rest of the sketch Crane goes on to offer a sympathetic portrait of the constables. Garrisoned in their small barracks, shunned by the local populace that refuses to acknowledge their existence, the constables are like lighthouse keepers. Their life, he writes, "looks to be . . . infinitely lonely, ascetic, and barren" (490). In the "Irish Notes" as a whole Crane's allegiance is unquestionably with the Irish, and he skillfully brings the reader to his anti-British stance. Yet at the same time, his instinctive sympathy for the underdog enabled him to treat members of the Royal Irish Constabulary, a sometimes brutal but perpetually isolated military force, with a generous compassion.

~~~

The final two pieces of travel writing that I examine came about unexpectedly; Crane had intended to write war correspondence. In November 1896 Crane traveled to Jacksonville, Florida, on assignment for the Bacheller syndicate in an attempt to gain passage on a "filibuster"—a gun-running ship—to Cuba. The Cuban guerrillas, fighting Spanish troops in the island's long-running war for independence, depended on U.S. supporters for arms and munitions; however, the U.S. government, officially committed to a policy of neutrality, tried to apprehend the filibusters and the reporters who sometimes accompanied them. Crane's plan was to sail with a filibustering ship and report from Cuba on the guerrilla war, but he spent several weeks in Jacksonville futilely trying to find an expedition. Finally, on New Year's Eve 1896 he succeeded. Registered clandestinely as an able-bodied seaman, Crane set sail on the *Commodore*, a vessel with an already substantial filibustering reputation.

Twenty-four hours after its departure the *Commodore* was sinking. Most of the crew and passengers—expatriate Cubans returning to fight the Spanish—escaped aboard three lifeboats. Crane, the captain, and two crew members left last, in a ten-foot dinghy. The four men spent almost thirty hours in heavy seas before they came ashore near Daytona; one man died when the boat swamped near the beach.

The experience resulted in two works: "Stephen Crane's Own Story," published in the *New York Press* and other newspapers four days after his rescue, and "The Open Boat," written within the next few weeks and published in the June 1897 *Scribner's* magazine.[33] The latter has become one of Crane's best-known works. Frequently reprinted and exhaustively analyzed, "The Open Boat" is usually categorized as a short story; "Stephen Crane's Own Story" is studied as journalistic background. In their analyses of "The Open Boat" many of Crane's most perceptive critics have quickly dismissed "Stephen Crane's Own Story," treating it mainly as an instructive contrast with "The Open Boat." A typical comment reads, "The documentary article sticks to the facts that can be related without the distortion or heightening that marks the distinction between reportage and art."[34]

"The Open Boat" is unquestionably a more powerful piece of prose than "Stephen Crane's Own Story." But careful reading reveals that the differences between the two works have nothing to do with distinctions between reportage and art, or fact and fiction. Critics who dismiss "Stephen Crane's Own Story" as an inartistic assemblage of facts come to the article with a set of powerful assumptions: anything appearing in a newspaper must be simple, factual, objective—assumptions that, as I have argued throughout this book, do not apply to the fact-fiction discourse of 1890s newspaper journalism. "Stephen Crane's Own Story" is no less artful a narrative than "The Open Boat," and "The Open Boat" is as factual as "Stephen Crane's Own Story." "The Open Boat," categorized by twentieth-century critics as fiction and frequently analyzed from a formalist, ahistorical perspective, appeared in *Scribner's* with the subtitle "A tale intended to be after the fact. Being the experience of four men from the sunk steamer Commodore" (728). That is, the work immediately announces its nonfiction status and uses a name—the *Commodore*—that would have been familiar to readers from the extensive newspaper coverage of the ship's sinking six months earlier. In terms of their circumstances of production and their initial appearances in print "Stephen Crane's Own Story" and "The Open Boat" have the same textual status, and readers of the time would have approached both works with similar expectations. "Stephen Crane's Own Story" appeared on a newspaper's front page, but the author's name and the possessive pronoun in the headline alerted readers to the article's subjective nature—a subjectivity common in 1890s newspapers. Similarly, the subtitle of "The Open Boat," with its inclusion of a ship's name so recently in newspaper headlines, signaled to readers of *Scribner's* that they were encountering a journalistic work.

Dozens of formalist readings of "The Open Boat" have praised the artistry of its opening paragraph: "None of them knew the color of the sky. Their eyes glanced level, and were fastened upon the waves that swept toward them. These waves were of the hue of slate, save for the tops, which were of foaming white, and all of the men knew the colors of the sea. The horizon narrowed and widened, and dipped and rose, and at all times its edge was jagged with waves that seemed thrust up in points like rocks" (728). The paragraph's literary qualities are obvious: the impressionistic emphasis on perception, the deliberate repetition ("None of them knew," "all of the men knew"), the use of simile. But the opening of "Stephen Crane's Own Story," far from "stick[ing] to the facts that can be related without . . . distortion or heightening," is equally literary. It begins,

It was the afternoon of New Year's. The *Commodore* lay at her dock in Jacksonville and negro stevedores processioned steadily toward her with box after box of ammunition and bundle after bundle of rifles. Her hatch, like the mouth of a monster, engulfed them. It might have been the feeding time of some legendary creature of the sea. It was in broad daylight and the crowd of gleeful Cubans on the pier did not forbear to sing the strange patriotic ballads of their island. (85)

Crane's use of simile is even more extravagant in his newspaper article than in the later magazine piece. In addition, this newspaper passage relies on repetition ("box after box," "bundle after bundle"), neologism ("processioned"), and litotes ("did not forbear to sing").

Throughout his "Own Story" Crane uses literary devices that overturn modern readers' assumptions that a newspaper article must be simple and objective. Like "The Open Boat" and much of his other writing, "Crane's Own Story" frequently uses epithets rather than proper names; "the cook," for example, is known only by that epithet. The newspaper article, like the rest of Crane's work, is also concerned with the impressionistic rendering of perception, as in the passage, "The State of Florida is very large when you look at it from an airship, but it is as narrow as a sheet of paper when you look at it sideways. The coast was merely a faint streak" (87). This passage not only reveals Crane's characteristic emphasis on visual perception (the "faint streak" of coastline) but also shows his concern with a variety of perspectives, such as the overhead view from a yet-to-be-invented airship.

"Crane's Own Story" is equally literary in its narration. One critic has written that "Crane's Own Story" is "told in a flat, technically 'objective,' first-person narrator's voice," but again this seems a case in which a reader's perceptions have been skewed by assumptions about newspaper journalism.[35] "Crane's Own Story" is no more objective than his other journalism—or than "The Open Boat." Throughout the newspaper piece Crane enters into the minds of other crew members, treating them, and himself, with the same comic irony that he uses with the alternately blustering and cringing Henry Fleming. When, less than two miles out of port, the *Commodore* becomes stranded on a sandbar, Crane writes, "It was to all of us more than a physical calamity. We were now no longer filibusters. We were men on a ship stuck in the mud. A certain mental somersault was made once more necessary" (86).

Determining the "literariness" of "Stephen Crane's Own Story" is easy enough. One can just as easily demonstrate the "journalistic" qualities of "The Open Boat." Generations of high school and college English teachers have approached "The Open Boat" as an ahistorical, universal exploration of the natural world and human community. However, readers encountering the work in *Scribner's* would have been conscious of the work's fidelity to the facts of the *Commodore* disaster: a captain, cook, oiler, and correspondent adrift for thirty hours; the rescue of three of the men by a bystander; the death of the fourth, Billie the oiler. In its reference to the captain's memory "of a scene in the grays of dawn of seven turned faces" (728), "The Open Boat" explicitly calls on readers' extratextual knowledge of the *Commodore*'s sinking; the line is intelligible only to those familiar with the newspaper accounts of seven men who died after their lifeboat foundered alongside the sinking ship.[36]

The generic labels traditionally assigned to these two works—fiction and nonfiction, art and reportage—obscure more than they reveal. Labeling "Crane's Own Story" as newspaper reportage, critics have been unable to perceive the piece clearly, so certain have they been that newspaper prose must necessarily be "flat," "unadorned," and "objective." Generic distinctions between fiction and journalism have served to direct critics, anthologists, teachers, and students away from one work and toward the other. Such attention may not necessarily be misplaced; as I have said, "The Open Boat" is unquestionably the more powerful of the two pieces. But the magazine piece is no more literary and no less journalistic than the newspaper article. Both texts can be seen as examples of Stephen Crane's masterful handling of the fact-fiction discourse of the American 1890s.

Examining Crane's travel journalism sheds light on neglected writing and illuminates canonical works like "The Open Boat" and the western short stories. However, as with Crane's New York City writing the relation between his journalism and fiction is complex, far different from the simple progressive model established by some critics in which observation leads to journalism that leads to fiction. That model is even more blatantly unhelpful in studying Crane's war writing. When he began writing *The Red Badge of Courage* in 1893, Crane had come no closer to battle than parade-ground drills at a boys' military academy. His direct experience of war would come on assignment as a newspaper reporter.

⁓

CHAPTER 5

After The Red Badge

WAR JOURNALISM

The hardcover publication of *The Red Badge of Courage* in 1895 turned Stephen Crane into an anomaly: an internationally famous writer on war who had never witnessed combat. Journalism gave Crane the means to resolve that contradiction. Within a year after *Red Badge* appeared, he attempted to become a war correspondent, a role that would engage him for much of the short time remaining in his life.

Crane's first efforts to report on war, late in 1896, led to his thirty hours in an open boat, an experience that did not dampen his ardor for war correspondence. He tried for weeks after his shipwreck to find another boat to Cuba in order to report on the rebellion there. When that effort was unsuccessful, he signed on with William Randolph Hearst's *New York Journal* to cover the short-lived Greco-Turkish War of 1897. That war over, he waited only a few weeks before making attempts to serve as correspondent in another war—any war. In quick succession he made and discarded plans to cover conflicts in India, South Africa, and the Sudan.[1] When the U.S. battleship *Maine* sank in Havana harbor early the next year, drawing the United States into a war with Spain, Crane was gleeful. Joseph Conrad, Crane's closest friend in England, described how Crane, "white-faced" with excitement at the imminent declaration of war, careened around London one day that spring searching for money to pay his passage to the United States. He had "to find £60 that day . . . at once, that instant," Conrad wrote, "lest peace should be declared and the opportunity of seeing a war be missed."[2] Conrad eventually pledged his future work as security for a loan. In his memoir of the episode Conrad mused about his responsibility for sending Crane to a war that undoubtedly hastened the young writer's death. However, Conrad concluded that any aid he gave was insignificant in Crane's decision. "Nothing could have held him back," Conrad wrote. "He was ready to swim the ocean."[3] Once in Cuba, Crane zealously sought out combat. He spent weeks aboard a hired tugboat covering the naval campaign, was the only correspondent to witness every land battle in Cuba, and remained in the Caribbean for months after Spain surrendered, covering the peace negotiations. He wrote, all together, fifty Spanish-American War dispatches for Hearst's *New York Journal* and Pulitzer's *New York World*, in addition to completing *Wounds in the Rain* (1900), a book of short stories and sketches about the war.

Crane's war correspondence fills a volume of his collected works, but critics have virtually ignored it. H. G. Wells established the dominant view of the war reporting in an essay he wrote shortly after Crane's death. Wells constructed a mythic narrative of Crane's post–*Red Badge* career that still shapes Crane criticism. In the life of Crane according to Wells, a young novelist who writes a brilliant imaginative account of the Civil War is lured from fiction into journalism by newspaper publishers eager to capitalize on his reputation. However, he is a complete failure as a war correspondent. Moreover, while traveling in foreign climes he contracts tropical diseases that bring on his lamentably early death. In a heavily ironic passage of his essay Wells writes,

> Since Crane had demonstrated, beyond all cavil, that he could sit at home and, with nothing but his wonderful brain and his wonderful induction from recorded things, build up the truest and most convincing picture of war . . . , it was clearly the most reasonable thing in the world to propose, it was received with the applause of two hemispheres as a most right and proper thing, that he should go as a war correspondent, first to Greece and then to Cuba. Thereby, and for nothing but disappointment and bitterness, he utterly wrecked his health . . . ; and I read even in the most punctual of his obituary notices the admission of his journalistic failure.[4]

Wells thought Crane's journalism beneath notice; the few critics who have given any attention to his war correspondence generally examine it for clues to his fiction.[5]

It is possible to take a different approach to Crane's war journalism. Instead of viewing Crane's interest in war reporting purely as a response to commercial pressures, we can locate Crane within the cultural forces of the 1890s that promoted both masculine ideals of the strenuous life and the war against Spain. Rather than using the journalism to throw light on the fiction, we can examine it on its own terms. If we can free ourselves of preconceptions about journalism's lower status within a hierarchy of literary value, we can take a fresh look at a body of work that deserves more than its reputation as a footnote to *The Red Badge of Courage*.

Crane wrote almost all his war correspondence for Joseph Pulitzer's *World* or William Randolph Hearst's *Journal*. These ambitious publishers frequently reminded readers of their celebrated writer's Civil War novel in the headlines that they attached to his dispatches. A typical example, published in the *World* during the Spanish-American War, reads, "The Red Badge of Courage Was His Wig-Wag Flag. Sergeant of Marines Signalling the Dolphin the Central Figure in Stephen Crane's Story of the First Fight at Guantanamo Bay."[6] Crane's publishers primed readers to expect connections between the famous writer's best-selling novel and his war journalism, and the correspondences between *Red Badge* and the war dispatches are many: a focus on individual acts of heroism, an impressionistic detailing of the process of perception, and frequent use of irony. However, the differences between *Red Badge* and the war journalism are even more striking. The war correspondence frequently romanticizes war and fighting men in a way that the more consistently ironic *Red Badge* does not. During the Spanish-American War this romanticizing led Crane to join in the jingoistic trumpeting of U.S. superiority common in 1898. However, in his final piece of war journalism, written a year after the Spanish-American War's conclusion, Crane rejected jingoism and produced one of his greatest works, an extraordinary autobiographical essay marked by daring stylistic experiments and by an avant-garde attention to the limits of language.

⁓

H. G. Wells was convinced that Crane became a war correspondent only in response to newspaper publishers' entreaties. John Berryman, who correctly noted Crane's eagerness to witness combat, developed a complex, highly speculative Freudian interpretation that located Crane's fascination with war in his family's psychological dynamics and in a violent incident he may have witnessed as a child. More recently, Christopher Benfey has traced Crane's desire to go to war after completing *Red Badge* to a repeated pattern within the author's life in which he first wrote about an experience, then attempted to live it.[7]

Another way to think about Crane's drive to experience warfare is to turn from his personal life to larger forces within American culture. For example, although Philip Rahv never mentions Crane in his famous essay "The Cult of Experience in American Writing," it would be easy enough to insert Crane into Rahv's line of writers from Whitman to Hemingway who placed a premium on "bare experience" rather than on ideas or values.[8] Rahv's broad-brush analysis, however, is largely ahistorical. It is possible to analyze Stephen Crane's urge for experience, and particularly experience of war, specifically within the conditions of the late nineteenth century.

If we focus on the 1890s, we can substitute for the general term "the cult of experience" the more historically specific notion of the cult of "the strenuous life." Theodore Roosevelt did not make his famous speech of that title until 1899, but the concept of the strenuous life permeated the United States of the 1890s. Vast numbers of middle- and upper-class males felt uneasy in the increasingly urbanized, mechanized, rationalized post–Civil War culture. In a culture where "personal meaning had dissolved in comfort and complacency," in T. J. Jackson Lears's phrase, people sought intense and "authentic" experience.[9] Men reacted against a genteel Victorian culture that they saw as soft and flaccid by turning for recreation to athletics, the outdoors, and heroic fiction. Football, boxing, camping, hunting, and romantic action novels all experienced a tremendous surge of popularity in the 1890s.

The ultimate expression of the strenuous life and the highest test for the male's heroic capacities was war. A generation removed from the horrors of the Civil War, many American men viewed that conflict nostalgically, as a testing ground for manhood denied to the veterans' children and grandchildren. T. J. Jackson Lears writes of this period, "As the rationalization of culture increasingly . . . reduced more and more existence to banal routine, life at war . . . sometimes seemed to promise authentic experiences no longer available in everyday life: the opportunity for moral and physical testing, the sheer excitement of life amid danger and death."[10]

Stephen Crane serves as exemplar of the quest for meaning and for masculine identity through the strenuous life and through war. His career from adolescence on can be seen as a reaction against genteel Victorian propriety, as embodied by his highly religious parents. When he was sixteen, Crane convinced his mother to allow him to transfer from Pennington Seminary, a Methodist institution formerly directed by his father, to a military school—an early sign of his lifelong interest in war and the strenuous life. Despite his small size—full grown, he was under 5'8" and 125 pounds—Crane was an enthusiastic outdoorsman and athlete. He spent long periods camping and hunting and was a highly regarded baseball player.

His fascination with war rivaled his enthusiasm for baseball. Crane's entire generation was absorbed with the Civil War. Young men during the 1890s commonly measured themselves against the earlier generation of soldiers. Crane's contemporary Carl Sandburg wrote of the 1890s, "Over all of us . . . was the shadow of the Civil War and the men who fought it to the end."[11] *Battles and Leaders of the Civil War* (1888), which Crane used as background for *The Red Badge of Courage*, was a phenomenal bestseller, although it was surpassed by *The Personal Memoirs of U. S. Grant* (1885), which became one of the best-selling American books of the nineteenth century.[12]

Crane, who wrote a best-seller on the Civil War before he had any personal experience of combat, presumably felt a need to authenticate his novel. If so sensitive a person as Joseph Conrad asked Crane at their first meeting if it was true that the young novelist had never witnessed combat, the question must have been repeated by dozens of others whom Crane encountered. His response to Conrad shows a certain testiness: "No. But the 'Red Badge' is all right."[13] When Conrad asked his question in the fall of 1897, Crane was able to assert his war novel's fidelity to truth with some authority, because he had just returned from his first experience as a war correspondent in the Greco-Turkish War. On his way to the war, he had told a London reporter that "he was off to Crete because, having written so much about war, he thought it high time he should see a little fighting."[14] Note that Crane did not say it was high time to fight but rather to *see* some fighting. It was the relatively new role of war correspondent that enabled Crane to see whether *Red Badge* was all right.

Reports of war have always been a journalistic staple, but until the midnineteenth century newspapers obtained their accounts of battles from participants. The Civil War produced the first American war correspondents. The role quickly became institutionalized. By 1897, when Crane set off to cover the war in Greece, he was able to join an entire cadre of U.S. correspondents.[15]

The Greco-Turkish War of 1897 lasted only one month, but the newspapers had ample opportunity to assemble correspondents in Greece before the formal declaration of war in April. The previous year had seen a rebellion in Crete against Turkish rule. Although Greece had achieved independence from the Ottoman Empire seventy years earlier, Crete was still under Turkish control. Early in 1897 an ambitious Greek prime minister sent ships and troops to Crete; once the troops were mobilized, war between Greece and Turkey was inevitable.[16]

Crane read about the incipient war in Greece while he was in Jacksonville, Florida, trying to get passage to the guerrilla war in Cuba after his rescue from the open boat. In March 1897 he abandoned the attempt, writing to his brother, "I have been for over a month among the swamps further south wading miserably to and fro in an attempt to avoid our derned U.S. navy. And it cant be done. I am through trying. I have changed all my plans and am going to Crete."[17] In New York on his way to Europe he acknowledged to an acquaintance, "Greece means nothing to me, nor does Turkey."[18] The important thing to Crane was the opportunity to witness war, to test his imagination against actuality.

Crane published a dozen dispatches in Hearst's *New York Journal*, the British *Westminster Gazette*, and other newspapers during the Greco-Turkish War. He was in a corps of more than one hundred correspondents, four from the *Journal* alone. In addition to Crane, the *Journal* hired Crane's companion, Cora Howorth Stewart, who under the pen name Imogene Carter sent a handful of brief dispatches to the newspaper that trumpeted her intoxication with her role as the war's only woman correspondent but revealed little about the war. The other two *Journal* correspondents were John Bass and Julian Ralph, both celebrated reporters. With Bass and Ralph covering political and military developments Crane was free to write lengthy feature articles on whatever subjects attracted him. His Greek dispatches include a comic sketch on the idiosyncrasies of the other correspondents and a sentimental account of finding a puppy on the battlefield.

His dispatches dealing more directly with the war reveal the qualities that would distinguish his reporting from both Greece and Cuba: a boyish romanticizing of war and fighting men, combined with a wide-ranging irony and an impressionistic attention to the process of perception. Crane's

FIGURE 5.1 Stephen Crane in war correspondent's garb, Athens, Greece, 1897. Stephen Crane Collection, Syracuse University Library, Department of Special Collections.

first article from Greece, "An Impression of the 'Concert,'" includes all these traits. Crane's material for this dispatch was unpromising. On his way to Athens Crane took an unexpected trip to Crete when his passenger ship detoured to deliver mail to the European battleships that were cordoning off the island. Crane spun this slight episode into a lengthy article that reveals his infatuation with war. He describes the massive warships and their officers with respect and even awe. The ships are "great steel animals." A Turkish officer "was rather tall and well made and had the face of a man, a man who could think, a man who could fight. He was fit for problems and he was fit for war, this fellow."[19]

Yet even as Crane romanticizes warriors and their armaments, he delights in puncturing illusions. Repeatedly, he contrasts romantic expectations with banal realities. For example, as his passenger ship approaches Crete, Crane parodies the passengers' expectations. "Surely," he writes, "a little decent excitement could be expected. Surely a few men in white kilts could have turned out and chased a few men in red fez up and down the hillsides." Instead, the "great high sun-burned island was simply as thrilling as a bit of good pasturage for goats" (6). The article's ironic stance is abetted by Crane's technique of juxtaposing the momentous and the mundane. In a recurring motif he counterpoints the appearance of the massive battleships with the crying of a colicky baby. He writes about his first full view of the fleet: "It was the fleet of the Powers; the Concert—the Concert, mind you, this most terrible creature which the world has known, constructed out of the air and perhaps in a night. This fleet was the living arm and the mailed hand of the Concert. It was a limb of Europe displayed, actual, animate. The babe who disliked the motion of the steamer continued to cry in the cabin" (7).

"An Impression of the 'Concert'" also contrasts romantic clichés with an impressionistic attention to perception. Crane notes that in contrast to the pictures in illustrated newspapers, "which appear always to have been sketched from balloons," the fleet is unimpressive to an approaching observer. The ships first appear as "some faint etchings on the distances. They might have been like masts, but they were more like twigs." Later, they resolve themselves into "a sort of prickly hedge" (6, 7).

Modern readers are likely to be struck not only by the combination of romanticism and irony in this article and in Crane's later war dispatches but also by the lavish use of first person and the frankly partisan stance in favor of the Greeks. A dispatch headlined "Stephen Crane Says Greeks

Cannot Be Curbed" is typical; in it Crane editorializes about the indomitable fighting spirit of the Greek people. However, in these regards Crane's work is squarely in line with that of the other reporters. Nineteenth-century newspaper readers were accustomed to a personal approach in war correspondence, and they did not expect neutrality. The Anglo-American public shared a Byronic sympathy for the Greek cause, and most of the English-language reporting on the war displays a pro-Greek bias.

The first-person pronoun received particularly heavy use in Crane's first actual battle dispatch, headlined "Crane at Velestino" in the *New York Journal*. Velestino, on Greece's northern border, was the site of the war's single major battle; Crane witnessed the last half of the three-day conflict. A week after "Crane at Velestino" appeared in the *Journal* and eleven other newspapers that subscribed to the Hearst syndicate, the *New-York Tribune* featured a clever parody:

> I have seen a battle.
> I find it is very like what
> I wrote up before.
> I congratulate myself that
> I ever saw a battle.
> I am pleased with the sound of war.
> I think it is beautiful.
> I thought it would be.
> I am sure of my nose for battle.
> I did not see any war correspondents while
> I was watching the battle except
> I.[20]

The parody is not entirely undeserved, but the *Tribune* may have been as influenced by the treatment that editors gave Crane's dispatch as by what Crane actually wrote. All dozen newspapers that printed Crane's article featured his name prominently in the headline, playing up the author's celebrity. The *Kansas City Star*'s layout was typical. Its headline read, "Crane's Story of a Battle / The Author of 'The Red Badge of Courage' Sees War," and the front-page article was accompanied by Crane's portrait.[21] Writing the piece, Crane was aware that his readers were likely to be as interested in the correspondent as in the war he reported; the internationally famous young author of *The Red Badge of Courage* obliged with a personal emphasis. "I had seen skirmishes and small fights, but this was my first big battle," he writes. He continues, "The roll of musketry was tremendous. . . . It was a beautiful sound—beautiful as I had never dreamed. . . . It was the most beautiful sound of my experience." The passage represents Crane's romantic infatuation with war at its height. Yet even when caught up by the glamour of his first experience of warfare, Crane counters romanticism with a corrective irony. His paean to the beauty of rifle fire is immediately followed by an ironic disclaimer: "This is one point of view. Another might be taken from the men who died there."[22]

This juxtaposition of romantic and ironic views was to become a structural commonplace of Crane's war journalism. For example, a dispatch headlined "Stephen Crane Tells of War's Horrors" describes how crowds reading a newspaper extra about a Greek victory shouted "Hurrah, hurrah for war!" as a seemingly endless procession of wounded soldiers on stretchers filed from a troop ship.[23] Crane's dispatches are filled with similar ironic juxtapositions, creating a dialectic between tributes to heroism on the battlefield and compassionate detailings of the suffering endured by both soldiers and civilian refugees.

Crane's colleague John Bass observed him under fire at the battle of Velestino for a *Journal* article that was published under the headline, "How Novelist Crane Acts on the Battlefield." After establishing Crane's reckless disregard of danger—Bass said that he casually lighted a cigarette while sitting on an ammunition box as shells exploded around him—Bass quoted two of the novelist's observations. The first was that the "interesting thing" about war is "the mental attitude of the men." The second was that the opposing soldiers seemed unreal: "They are shadows on the plain—vague figures in black, indications of a mysterious force."[24] Coming from the author of *The Red Badge of Courage*, which focuses on the "mental attitude" of a single soldier as he faces a mysterious foe, the comments are unsurprising. The dual concerns of individual perception and the mystery of war are clearly paramount in Crane's second dispatch about the battle of Velestino, which was published after the war's conclusion. The editors of a collection of Crane's war dispatches call it "perhaps the finest sketch he ever wrote as a war correspondent"; certainly, this brilliant article deserves to be better known.[25]

Generally reprinted under its title in the *Westminster Gazette*, "A Fragment of Velestino," the dispatch received a lengthy headline in the *New York Journal* that played up its differences from Crane's Civil War novel: "That Was the Romance, 'The Red Badge of Courage'—A Story. This is the Reality, The Battle To-day in Greece—a Fact."[26] Despite the *Journal*'s contrast of "story" and "fact," the dispatch has many similarities to *Red Badge*. Like the novel, the dispatch begins by placing warfare within the setting of a serene and indifferent nature: "The sky was of a fair and quiet blue. In the radiantly bright atmosphere of the morning the distances among the hills were puzzling in the extreme. The Westerner could reflect that after all his eye was accustomed to using a tree as a standard of measure, but here there were no trees. The great bold hills were naked."[27]

More significantly, both *Red Badge* and "A Fragment of Velestino" wrench battle out of its larger political and military contexts. Critics have often remarked on *Red Badge*'s silence about the political issues of slavery and secession that underlay the Civil War and about such fundamental military issues as the name of the battle in which Henry is engaged.[28] "A Fragment of Velestino" is similarly indifferent to broad ideological and military concerns. The dispatch never mentions the causes of the war, and, as in *Red Badge*, we do not even learn which side won the battle. At one point Crane directly addresses the reader's desire to know the battle's result. "People would like to stand in front of the mercury of war and see it rise or fall," he writes. But this is "an absurd thing for a writer to do" (37). After all, Crane reminds the reader, the soldier in the field is severely limited in his knowledge, and even most officers are ignorant of the larger picture while the battle is still going on.

In place of conventional summaries of victory and defeat "A Fragment of Velestino" focuses on the individual: both the individual soldier and the narrator. The sketch's opening vignette combines both concerns. After describing the landscape around Velestino, the narrator shifts to a view of the road:

> On the lonely road from Velestino there appeared the figure of a man. He came slowly and with a certain patient steadiness. . . . The man had a staff in his hand, and he used it during his slow walk. He was in the uniform of the Greek infantry, and his clothes were very dusty—so dusty that the little regimental number on his shoulder could hardly be seen. Under other circumstances one could have sworn that the man had great smears of red paint on his face. It was blood. It had to be blood; but then it was weirdly not like blood. It was dry, but it had dried crimson and

brilliant. In fact, this hue upon his face was so unexpected in its luridness that one first had to gaze at this poor fellow in astonishment. (28–29)

The passage contains two dramas. The first is the story of the narrator's cognition, the process of perceiving a man with red paint on his face and then realizing that the soldier has been shot in the head and is covered with his own blood. The second is, simply, a war story—that is, a story that confronts squarely war's central purpose, the injuring of bodies.

The obvious but often-overlooked point that war is about injured bodies has been brilliantly illuminated by Elaine Scarry in *The Body in Pain*. Stephen Crane makes the same point in "A Fragment of Velestino." Scarry notes that most writers on war try to repress the centrality of injuring. "But if injury is designated 'the by-product,' what is the product?" she asks.[29] Crane anticipates Scarry's language in his story of the injured Greek soldier. He writes:

> Behind him was the noise of the battle, the roar and rumble of an enormous factory. This was the product. This was the product, not so well finished as some, but sufficient to express the plan of the machine. This wounded soldier explained the distant roar. He defined it. This—this and worse—was what was going on. This explained the meaning of all that racket. Gazing at this soldier with his awful face, one felt a new respect for the din. (29)

The repetitious language of the passage mimics the machinelike aspects of war, an automated process for producing . . . what? The passage, a complete paragraph, will answer only, "This." The pronoun's antecedent is largely absent from the paragraph. Readers must supply the missing antecedent, not just linguistically but imaginatively, conjuring up in our minds the horrifying image of the bloody man.

In the same way that Crane wants readers to share in his process of perception, as he sees a man with red paint on his face and then interprets it as blood, he also wants readers to share his broader confusion about the battle he witnesses. Parodying conventional descriptions of battle, he writes of an infantry charge, "The Turks did not come like a flood, nor did the Greeks stand like adamant." Instead, he continues, "It was simply a shifting, changing, bitter, furious struggle, where one could not place odds nor know when to run" (42).

The structure of the piece as a whole conveys the same sense of confusion and disorientation. In his comments to John Bass, Crane mentioned the unreality and mystery of the Turkish forces, a theme emphasized in "A Fragment of Velestino." At a distance the Turks are simply "a dark line." As they approach the Greek forces, they remain inscrutable: "These little black things streaming from here and there on the plain, what were they? What moved them to this? The power and majesty of this approach was all in its mystery, its inexplicable mystery. What was this thing? And why was it? Of course Turks, Turks, Turks; but then that is a mere name" (40). In this passage the narrator recognizes and acknowledges his inability to explain the war. In place of conventional summary or analysis he offers readers a series of disconnected, fragmented vignettes. The structure and content of "A Fragment of Velestino" imply that war is without a single stable meaning; its reality is best conveyed not by abstract analysis but by the random recollections of one individual.

The vignettes of which "A Fragment of Velestino" is composed are deliberately minor events that combine the horrific and the absurd. Describing the bloody-faced soldier, the narrator notes that a comrade has bound his wound with a bandage that looks exactly like something a New England grandmother might use to remedy her boy's toothache. When a soldier in the trenches is shot in the face, the narrator describes how a dazed comrade pulls out of his pocket a hunk of bread and a handkerchief to press against the wound, then, looking about him helplessly, holds the bread in one hand, not wanting to lay it down in the dirt. Another anecdote recounts how an officer, irate when a befuddled soldier brings him a bottle of wine instead of the field glasses he asked for, absentmindedly keeps the bottle in his hand as he gestures orders to fire. Resisting any simple interpretation, these anecdotes convey the contradictions and complexity of war.

For the most part, "A Fragment of Velestino" and Crane's other dispatches confirm his remark to Joseph Conrad: the Greco-Turkish War showed him that *Red Badge* was "all right." However, Crane's first article about the battle of Velestino contains one significant contradiction of the novel. In *Red Badge* Henry Fleming swings wildly between extremes of fear and bravery. The book's narrative consists largely of Henry's interior debates about courage and cowardice, and his actions are equally erratic. He flees from his first battle, but in a subsequent fight, possessed by a demonic fury, he keeps firing and swearing frantically even after the enemy has disappeared. However, in Greece Crane observed that the private soldiers were stolid men who "fought with the steadiness of salaried bookkeepers."[30] Crane elaborated this observation in his sole short story about the Greco-Turkish War, "Death and the Child" (1898), which contrasts a hot-blooded civilian who volunteers to go into the trenches with the impassive regular soldiers who surround him. The businesslike attitude of the regular soldier would strike Crane even more strongly during the Spanish-American War and become a central theme of his writing about that conflict.

~~~

Crane reported on the Spanish-American War for Joseph Pulitzer's *New York World* and William Randolph Hearst's *New York Journal*, the two representatives of the "yellow press" that many believe to be responsible for the Spanish-American War. According to popular history, a circulation war between Pulitzer, who had made the *World* the largest-circulation newspaper in the United States, and Hearst, who bought the *Journal* in 1895 to challenge Pulitzer's dominance, led the two publishers to provoke public hysteria in favor of a war certain to lead to even higher circulations. Certainly, Hearst did everything he could to further the impression that he was responsible for the war, swashbuckling around the Caribbean in his yacht and actually capturing a boatload of Spanish sailors, meanwhile running in his newspaper a front-page slogan that asked, "How Do You Like the Journal's War?"

Recent historians of the Spanish-American War have revised the popular view that the yellow journals were responsible for the war, devoting attention instead to political and economic causes. One recent massive history of the war devotes exactly one sentence to yellow journalism's contribution to war fever: "'Yellow journals' only rode the wave of feeling; they did not create it."[31] However, if the newspapers did not create the war, their coverage once the fighting broke out was remarkable. More than two hundred reporters, photographers, and artists covered the war in Cuba, including the era's most famous journalists.[32] Stephen Crane won praise as the best of them all. The intensely competitive Richard Harding Davis, who frequently denigrated Crane in private letters, acknowledged in print that Crane "distinctly won the first place among correspondents" of the war as the person who saw "more of the war, both afloat and ashore, than . . . his rivals, and who [was] able to make the public see what he saw."[33]

If Crane was the best of the Spanish-American War correspondents, in his background he was completely typical of them. An extraordinary number of the men who covered the war were, like Crane, ministers' sons; every correspondent aboard the newspaper dispatch boat on which Crane spent several weeks during the war had a minister father. A recent study of Spanish-American war correspondents offers a composite biography that fits Crane perfectly: the typical reporter was "the agnostic son of a Protestant minister, a drop-out from the genteel tradition who put his faith in science, social progress, and the superiority of American know-how."[34] As this description suggests, correspondents were, for the most part, earnest reformers who saw the war as a progressive crusade. In the months leading up to the Spanish-American War the press portrayed Cubans as innocent victims of Spanish cruelty. U.S. aid to the outnumbered Cuban insurgents was consistently presented not as an imperialist venture but as a humanitarian mission. If to Stephen Crane the war was in part a continuation of his adventurous travels in the American West, it was also an extension of his journalistic experiments in the New York City slums, an opportunity for social reform.

The Spanish-American War correspondents also regarded themselves as soldiers. Virtually all correspondents, including Crane, carried a sidearm, and they considered themselves full military participants. During the battle at Cuzco, for example, Crane served as an aide to the commanding officer and was cited in the official report.[35] His action was not at all unusual. Examples abound of correspondents who functioned as aides and engaged in combat. Richard Harding Davis assisted Theodore Roosevelt during the Rough Riders' first battle; one of Hearst's reporters led a charge on a Spanish blockhouse and captured its flag; and a *World* colleague of Crane's regularly acted as a translator for the military and led reconnaissance missions.[36]

Given their intense identification with the U.S. military, it is not surprising that correspondents shared the jingoistic perspective common among Americans in 1898. Stephen Crane was no exception. His first Spanish-American War dispatch, "The Terrible Captain of the Captured Panama," filed from Key West just two days after war was declared, is a boasting and bellicose attack on the cowardly captain of a captured Spanish ship. The dispatch makes unpleasant reading. Crane turns the captain of the Spanish passenger ship, who had boasted about his disdain for the U.S. Navy before leaving New York, into a symbol of old, decadent, cowardly Spain. "His face was yellow and lined like an ape's," Crane writes. The point of the article is that the captain stumbles when he is led ashore, his weak knees betraying his fear; thus, the article concludes, New York is "avenged."[37] None of Crane's subsequent dispatches contains such an ugly personalized attack on the Spanish; however, virtually all have some degree of patriotic trumpeting of the U.S. cause. Although Crane had said before going to the Greco-Turkish War that he cared nothing for either Greece or Turkey, the partisan conventions of nineteenth-century war correspondence led him to champion the Greek cause. In a war against an enemy of the United States the partisanship turned to strident jingoism.

The naval campaign that marked the early stages of the Spanish-American War from April to June 1898, before U.S. troops landed in Cuba, offered reporters relatively few opportunities to demonize the Spanish, because the enemy remained largely invisible; the only naval engagements during the war's opening weeks were minor. Starting within a few days of the war's declaration, Crane spent six weeks aboard various small boats chartered by the *World* and wrote ten dispatches during this period. Most convey the boredom experienced by both sailors and reporters as they waited for the Spanish fleet to make a move. "Inaction Deteriorates the Key West Fleet" is the headline of a typical Crane dispatch from this period of the war.[38]

The first U.S. Army regiments did not land in Cuba until the end of June. However, on June 10, 650 marines established a camp at Guantánamo Bay. Stephen Crane was with them, and he spent a horrific night with the marines when they came under heavy attack. His article about the episode is headlined "In the First Land Fight Four of Our Men Are Killed." This brief dispatch praises the unflinching behavior of the marines, acknowledges the courage of the Spaniards, and contains one sensational charge: that the bodies of two of the dead marines "were stripped of shoes, hats, and cartridges and horribly mutilated."[39] Two days later, on June 15, the *World* ran a front-page follow-up story about the charge. The four-column headline reads, "Mutilation of Our Marines Too Horrible for Description; Universal Sentiments of Horror Expressed at the Dastardly Work of the Spanish Butchers at Guantanamo."[40] Crane had nothing to do with the follow-up story. The day before it appeared he had cabled, too late to make the *World*'s June 15 edition, a retraction of his original article. It begins, "The story of the mutilation of the bodies of the two young privates of Captain Spicer's company of marines, which was sent in on Saturday last, is now found to be entirely untrue. The officers and men of the party which recovered the bodies were misled by the frightful tearing effect of the Mauser bullets when deflected by anything like brushwood, or from close range."[41]

With this, his second article from the Cuban land campaign, Crane began his career as a journalistic counterpuncher. As the Cuban campaign continued, Crane increasingly shaped his dispatches in opposition to the work of other correspondents. Most strikingly, while virtually every other journalist in Cuba celebrated the exploits of Teddy Roosevelt's Rough Riders and other volunteer regiments, Crane refused to join in the collectively constructed romance of the dashing American volunteer.

In the popular historical imagination the Spanish-American War was won by volunteers like Theodore Roosevelt and his Rough Riders, an elite volunteer cavalry regiment composed of western cowboys and eastern bluebloods. In fact, volunteers comprised only a fraction—about 15 percent—of the troops that fought in the crucial Santiago campaign. The remainder were regular army soldiers.[42] In 1898 the U.S. Army consisted of only 28,000 men. After war was declared against Spain in April 1898, President William McKinley called for 125,000 additional troops, to be composed of national guard regiments and volunteers. Roosevelt's Rough Riders, the most famous of the volunteer regiments, was one of the few to see active duty in Cuba; most volunteers got no closer to Cuba than Florida, where they remained snarled in logistical difficulties. The Spanish-American War was, for the most part, both fought and won by the navy, the marines, and the regular army. Yet contemporary newspapers focused overwhelmingly on the volunteers. Most newspapers concentrated on the hometown national guard regiment. Even small newspapers strained resources to send a reporter to the war, his task limited to reporting on the activities of the local volunteers.[43]

The major New York City newspapers also championed the volunteers, although they slighted the city's national guardsmen in favor of the handful of upper-class easterners serving under colonels Leonard Wood and Theodore Roosevelt in the Rough Riders. While the troops were still in the United States waiting transport to Cuba, the New York newspapers featured frequent and lavish spreads on the Rough Riders. When Stephen Crane was under fire at Guantánamo, one of only two reporters with the marines there, his newspaper, the *World*, featured lengthy articles with headlines like "Rough Riders Will Play Polo in Cuba"—although in fact the Rough Riders' horses were left behind in Florida for lack of room in the transports.

The same issue of the *World* carried an illustrated article on "How the Rough Rider Looks in His Uniform."[44] A few days later the *World* carried a full-page feature on a prominent New York City volunteer; the headline read, "John Jacob Astor, Richest Soldier in the U.S. Army. One day's work he performs. The discomforts. The experiences in camp life."[45]

The New York newspapers' infatuation with the Rough Riders' aristocratic volunteers continued once the troops reached Cuba. Two days after the disembarkment near Santiago the Rough Riders and two regular army regiments engaged Spanish troops in a skirmish at Las Guásimas. The New York papers went into paroxysms over one of the sixty-eight U.S. casualties in that fight: the death of Hamilton Fish Jr., a recent Columbia University graduate, son of a prominent New York City family, and grandson of President Grant's secretary of state. The *World* and other New York City newspapers featured Fish's name in headlines about the battle, and for days afterward they printed lengthy illustrated features on the young volunteer soldier. A *World* headline from June 26, two days after Fish's death, is typical: "Young 'Ham' Fish Died like a Hero. Had Found a Soldier's Career Best Suited to His Adventurous Spirit. His Courage Never Doubted. Only Twenty-Five, He Had Shown His Grit When He Was a College Oarsman."[46]

Stephen Crane, by nature an ironist and parodist, worked against the grain of this romance with the high-born volunteer. By the time the Rough Riders disembarked in Cuba, Crane had already accompanied the marines in two battles. Accustomed to the ways of these professional soldiers, Crane was appalled by what he perceived as the amateurism of the Rough Riders. His brief cabled dispatch on the skirmish at Las Guásimas differs dramatically from other newspaper accounts of the battle. Ignoring the death of Hamilton Fish, the leadership of Theodore Roosevelt, and the laudatory themes common to other accounts of the battle, Crane portrays the Rough Riders as brave but incompetent. His dispatch opens by implicitly attacking Roosevelt's leadership: "Lieutenant-Colonel Roosevelt's Rough Riders, who were ambushed yesterday, advanced at daylight without any particular plan of action as to how to strike the enemy." The article ends with the statement, "It was simply a gallant blunder," a remark that deftly combines both praise and criticism.[47] Crane was even blunter in a long follow-up article about Las Guásimas sent by mail and published ten days later. There he calls the Rough Riders "this silly brave force."[48]

Roosevelt and other observers challenged Crane's assertion that the Rough Riders had unknowingly walked into an ambush.[49] But Crane never changed his view. Instead, in a third article about Las Guásimas he engaged in a fit of self-flagellation for giving any attention at all to the volunteers. He explained that all five correspondents present at the battle had been with the Rough Riders, although a regular army regiment had also been involved and had suffered heavy casualties. But "when it comes down to action," he wrote in a spirit of self-chastisement, "no one out of five correspondents thought it important to be with the First Regular Cavalry." He continues:

> And their performance was grand! Oh, but never mind—it was only the regulars. They fought gallantly of course. Why not? Have they ever been known to fail? That is the point. They have never been known to fail. Our confidence in them has come to be a habit. But, good heavens! it must be about time to change all that and heed them somewhat. Even if we have to make some of the volunteers wait a little.[50]

This passage is the first announcement of what was to become a major theme of Crane's Spanish-American War writing: the nobility of the regular soldier.

Crane engaged the issue of volunteers and regulars most directly in an editorial he wrote for the *World* titled "Regulars Get No Glory." The article combines a paean to the regular soldier with a bitter attack on journalists' and the public's infatuation with upper-class volunteers. "The main fact that has developed in this Santiago campaign," Crane writes, "is that the soldier of the regular army is the best man standing on two feet on God's green earth." But the public, Crane charges, is indifferent to the regular soldier and instead "wants to learn of the gallantry of Reginald Marmaduke Maurice Montmorenci Sturtevant, and for goodness sake how the poor old chappy endures that dreadful hard-tack and bacon. Whereas, the name of the regular soldier is probably Michael Nolan and his life-sized portrait was not in the papers in celebration of his enlistment."[51]

After the war Crane's tribute to "Michael Nolan" in his *World* editorial developed into a full-blown romance of the regular soldier. Crane extended his Greco-Turkish War observation that the soldiers fought with the steadiness of bookkeepers, developing a portrait of the regular army soldier as a stolid workman, unfailingly brave under fire. "Marines Signaling Under Fire at Guantanamo," an article written shortly after the war's conclusion and published in *McClure's* magazine, is devoted to celebrating the courage of enlisted marines. Crane described several marines who had to stand isolated on a ridge, completely exposed to heavy enemy fire, in order to send semaphore signals to a navy ship anchored offshore. In an extremely dangerous situation the marines acted merely like men "intent upon . . . business," according to Crane. The article ends with a lengthy description of Sergeant John H. Quick, who served as a signalman during the battle at Cuzco. Crane describes Quick as he stood signaling while Spanish troops aimed their fire at him: "I watched his face, and it was as grave and serene as that of a man writing in his own library. He was the very embodiment of tranquillity in occupation. He stood there amid the animal-like babble of the Cubans, the crack of rifles, and the whistling snarl of the bullets, and wig-wagged whatever he had to wig-wag without heeding anything but his business. There was not a single trace of nervousness or haste."[52] Sergeant Quick was later awarded the Congressional Medal of Honor for his actions at Cuzco. According to Quick's commanding officer, Crane's article influenced the decision to give him the decoration.[53] The writer who had ironically bestowed on Henry Fleming an undeserved red badge of courage—a wound incurred by a knock on the head from another soldier—in this case unironically celebrated a soldier's courage, helping him to win the nation's highest award for military heroism.

When he wrote "Marines Signaling Under Fire," Crane was composing the short stories about the Spanish-American War collected in *Wounds in the Rain*. "The Price of the Harness," the lead story in the collection, has as its central character a regular army soldier named Nolan—the same name as the representative soldier in Crane's newspaper article "Regulars Get No Glory." "The Price of the Harness" extends the tributes to courage in "Marines Signaling Under Fire" into full-blown romanticizing of the regulars. The story begins as Nolan and the other men in his squad are clearing a road through the Cuban bush. At the end of the day they head for camp: "They swung up the hill in an unformed formation, being always like soldiers, and unable even to carry a spade save like United States regular soldiers. As they passed through some fields, the bland white light of the end of the day feebly touched each hard bronze profile."[54] The passage's final metaphor both describes the men's sunburned faces and converts them into heroic two-dimensional icons stamped onto a coin or medal. When, on the next morning, the soldiers trade their shovels for rifles, the tributes to their heroism become more intensely extravagant:

> There was something distinctive in the way they carried their rifles. There was the grace of an old hunter somewhere in it, the grace of a man whose rifle has become absolutely a part of himself. Furthermore, almost every blue shirt sleeve was rolled to the elbow, disclosing fore-arms of almost incredible brawn. The rifles seemed light, almost fragile, in the hands that were at the end of these arms, never fat but always with rolling muscles and veins that seemed on the point of bursting. And another thing was the silence and the marvelous impassivity of the faces as the column made its slow way toward where the whole forest splut-tered and fluttered with battle. (7–8)

The admiration for the regulars in this passage slides into homoerotic infatuation. As Susan Jeffords observes of Vietnam literature, the erotic attraction of the masculine body is so threatening to the male heterosexual writer that he displaces it by portraying the body in scenes of violence—think of the bare torso of Sylvester Stallone's Rambo character, criss-crossed with bandoliers.[55] In Crane's passage the erotic quality of the soldiers' arms, with their tumescent muscles and veins, is safely framed by the references to rifles and to battle; the body fluid about to "splutter" is blood.

The infatuation with soldiers displayed in "The Price of the Harness" and some of Crane's other Spanish-American War fiction and journalism seems a long way from *The Red Badge of Courage*. The narrator of *Red Badge*, despite his access to Henry Fleming's thoughts, remains at an ironic distance from his character. At the novel's end Henry may conclude that he is a now a man, but it is not apparent that the narrator agrees with him. In contrast, the narrator of "The Price of the Harness" is uncritically admiring of his characters' bodies and equally infatuated with their thoughts. In this passage, which comes as Nolan begins the charge up San Juan Hill that will prove fatal to him, the narrator enters Nolan's consciousness:

> He heard a shout. "Come on, boys! We can't be last! We're going up! We're going up." He sprang to his feet and, stooping, ran with the oth-

ers. Something fine, soft, gentle, touched his heart as he ran. He had loved the regiment, the army, because the regiment, the army, was his life—he had no other outlook; and now these men, his comrades, were performing his dream-scenes for him; they were doing as he had ordained in his visions. (26–27)

The passage is representative of the narrative attitude in "The Price of the Harness." Crane is frequently ironic in his Spanish-American War writing, but the irony is always directed against civilians or volunteers, never against the regular soldiers.

If Crane's attitude toward soldiers in his Spanish-American War writing seems quite different from his treatment of Henry Fleming in *The Red Badge of Courage*, his later work nevertheless has much in common with the Civil War novel. As James Colvert has pointed out, the quiet courage that Wilson, "the loud soldier," gains after his first experience of battle prefigures the stoicism of the regular soldiers in Crane's Spanish-American War writing.[56] Although the Spanish-American War writing's depiction of regular soldiers as stolid workmen contrasts with Henry Fleming's wild swings between courage and cowardice, Crane did not abandon entirely the comic studies of fear that had formed the basis of so much of his work. Instead, Crane assigned courage and cowardice, united in Henry Fleming, to two different groups of men.

Throughout his Spanish-American War journalism Crane directs his flair for creating a comedy of cowardice toward himself and the other correspondents. He writes that as he accompanied the Rough Riders toward their first engagement, "For my part, I declare that I was frightened almost into convulsions."[57] In "Marines Signaling Under Fire," he writes that when a sergeant stood on a ridge to signal, "we gave [him] sole possession of a particular part of the ridge. We didn't want it. He could have it and welcome. If the young sergeant had had the smallpox, the cholera, and the yellow fever, we could not have slid out with more celerity" (336). Early in the war, during the naval campaign, Crane wrote two dispatches that are small comic masterpieces of fear. "Narrow Escape of the Three Friends" and "Chased by a Big 'Spanish Man-O'-War'" describe with extravagant hyperbole the fear experienced by Crane and his colleagues aboard their newspaper dispatch boat as a seemingly hostile warship bears down on them. If Crane was indeed as terrified during the Cuban campaign as he claimed in his dispatches, he did not show it by his behavior. Numerous observers commented on his willingness to share the soldiers' danger and on his apparent lack of fear. Richard Harding Davis wrote, "Crane was the coolest man, whether army officer or civilian, that I saw under fire at any time during the war."[58] Whatever Crane's emotions in battle, his war correspondence repeatedly uses the figure of the frightened correspondent as a counter to the unfailingly impassive regular soldier.

None of Crane's dispatches celebrates the U.S. soldier more exuberantly than his account of the Battle of San Juan Hill, headlined "Stephen Crane's Vivid Story of the Battle of San Juan." This lengthy dispatch, published in the *World* almost two weeks after the battle, is a detailed account of the fighting on July 1 and 2 at the San Juan Heights, the war's most intense battle and a U.S. victory that effectively ended Spanish resistance. The dispatch opens by announcing Crane's focus on the individual soldier rather than on the sweeping perspective of the general officer. "No doubt when history begins to grind out her story we will find that many a thundering, fine, grand order was given," he writes, but he insists that the success of the battle was owing to "the splendid gallantry of the American private soldier."[59] Crane cannot assert that the soldiers of the regular army were solely responsible for the victory, because he was well aware that the First Volunteer Cavalry—the Rough Riders—played a prominent role. But he refuses to single out the volunteers, and his dispatch contains only one reference to the Rough Riders and none to Theodore Roosevelt.

Crane's description of the famous charge up San Juan Hill forms a fascinating contrast with Roosevelt's better-known account of the battle, which was published shortly after the war in *Scribner's* magazine and later included in Roosevelt's best-selling book *The Rough Riders* (1899). Perhaps the best summary of Roosevelt's account of the Battle of San Juan Hill is contained in the comment of Finley Peter Dunne's Mr. Dooley, who said that Roosevelt's book should have been titled *Alone in Cuba*.[60] According to Roosevelt, the Rough Riders and of course TR himself were at the center of the San Juan battle. In Crane's newspaper article the soldiers who take the hill, both regular and volunteer, are indistinguishable. Here is Crane's account of the charge:

> One saw a thin line of black figures moving across a field. They disappeared in the forest. The enemy was keeping up a terrific fire. Then suddenly somebody yelled: "By God, there go our boys up the hill!"

There is many a good American who would give an arm to get the thrill of patriotic insanity that coursed through us when we heard that yell.

Yes, they were going up the hill, up the hill. It was the best moment of anybody's life.

The distinctions, so important to Roosevelt, between hand-picked volunteers and regular soldiers are dissolved in the language of "black figures" and "our boys." And Crane turns the focus away from soldiers to spectators. He rewrites "The Open Boat" of the year before, in which he had said that "the best experience of his life" was "the subtle brotherhood of men that was here established on the seas."[61] In the midst of the noise, death, and victory at San Juan Crane abandons the pacific brotherhood of men at sea for the "patriotic insanity" of war.

Yet for all the celebratory jingoism of "Stephen Crane's Vivid Story," his handling of the charge up San Juan Hill is peculiarly muted. For immediately after the passage just quoted Crane shifts the scene from San Juan Hill to a road upon which wounded soldiers "were stringing back from the front, hundreds of them." Crane sets his soldiers in motion, "going up the hill, up the hill," then abruptly abandons them. Instead of offering the expected structure of a charge followed by victory, Crane forgoes narrative closure. He undercuts the "thrill of patriotic insanity" he has just described with a lengthy, graphic description of wounded men.

The article's disjointed structure and its descriptions of wounded men recall Crane's brilliant Greco-Turkish War dispatch, "A Fragment of Velestino." Like "Velestino" with its shards of narrative cobbled together, the jumbled structure of "Stephen Crane's Vivid Story" undercuts a simple, heroic reading of the Battle of San Juan Hill and conveys the complexity, confusion, and costs of battle.

In her perceptive reading of "Stephen Crane's Vivid Story" Amy Kaplan notes the article's disjointed structure and focuses on one lengthy digression, when Crane begins to describe the army's actions on the battle's second day and then abruptly writes, "It becomes necessary to speak of the men's opinion of the Cubans." What follows this sudden change of topic is chilling: "To put it shortly, both officers and privates have the most lively contempt for the Cubans. They despise them. They came down here expecting to fight side by side with an ally, but this ally has done little but stay in the rear and eat army rations, manifesting an indifference to the cause of Cuban liberty which could not be exceeded by some one who had never heard of it." The article continues in the same vein for six hundred words. Kaplan aptly summarizes the article's effect: it appropriates "the Cuban uprising as an American popular movement and [displaces] lazy, inefficient, hungry Cuban bodies with the spectacle of aggressive American manhood."[62]

However, it would be a mistake to judge Stephen Crane's attitude toward the Cuban insurgents solely on the basis of one article. Crane's view of the Cubans was variable and complex. Initially, his attitude was sympathetic, a stance that paralleled that of the broad American public. Gerald Linderman has traced the way that a romanticized image of the Cuban rebels gained currency in the United States between 1895, when the Cuban rebellion began, and 1898.[63] Thanks to the energetic efforts of Cuban representatives in the United States, aided by a sympathetic press, the Cuban rebels were seen as a noble and conventional fighting force akin to the Revolutionary heroes of 1776. In fact, the Cubans were desperately poor and outnumbered. Their survival between 1895 and 1898 depended on avoiding large-scale engagements with Spanish forces while engaging in guerrilla warfare. Small groups of poorly equipped men conducted raids that were intended not to defeat Spanish troops but to damage Spain's economic infrastructure: they stole Spanish supplies, burned sugar fields and mills, and destroyed railroad tracks, telegraph lines, and bridges.

Americans ignored the reality not only of the Cubans' mode of warfare but of their race. More than one-third of the Cuban population in 1898 was of African descent, and the proportion of blacks in the rebel forces was higher; by one estimate they made up four-fifths of the troops. Sympathizers with the Cuban cause, well aware of American racism, led the public to believe that Cubans were mostly white. For example, U.S. newspapers and magazines slighted the many high-ranking black officers in the rebel army and focused on General Maximo Gomez, who was said to be "of pure Spanish descent" and possessed of an "Anglo-Saxon tenacity of purpose."[64]

When the Americans landed in Cuba in June 1898, they expected to find contemporary versions of George Washington and his troops. Instead, they found a band of poverty-stricken, mostly black guerrilla fighters, and their surprise was almost instantly converted to contempt. Theodore Roosevelt's reaction was typical. After landing at Daiquiri, he wrote, "we found hundreds of Cuban insurgents, a crew of as utter taterdemalions as human eyes ever looked on. . . . It was evident, at a glance, that they would be no use in serious fighting."[65] We can see in the reactions of Roosevelt and other Americans a classic pattern of surprise and distaste that continues to play itself out when sheltered Americans suddenly find themselves in an underdeveloped country. British correspondent John Black Atkins perceptively recorded U.S. soldiers' encounters with Cuban insurgents. The Americans quickly became tired, Atkins wrote, "because the Cuban insurgent regarded every American as a kind of charitable institution, and expected him to disgorge on every occasion. The Cuban was continually pointing to the American's shirt, coat, or trousers, and then pointing to himself, meaning that he desired a transfer of property."[66]

Stephen Crane was well aware of U.S. soldiers' dislike of the Cubans. However, accustomed to extreme poverty from his experiences in the New York slums and his travels in Mexico, he initially served as a sympathetic interpreter of the Cubans' perspective for his U.S. audience. Crane compared the Cubans to New York slum dwellers. "Everybody knows that the kind of sympathetic charity which loves to be thanked is often grievously disappointed and wounded in tenement districts where people often accept gifts as if their own property had turned up after a short absence," he wrote in the *World*. "The Cubans accept our stores in something of this way." Observing U.S. soldiers' anger at Cubans' perceived ingratitude, described also by Atkins, Crane turned the tables and suggested that Americans might be at fault for their desire to be thanked. Crane noted the Cuban soldier's stoicism: "He starves and he makes no complaint. We feed him and he expresses no joy." He went on to offer his U.S. readers a sympathetic interpretation of this seeming indifference: "When you come to think of it, one follows the other naturally. If he had retained the emotional ability to make a fuss over nearly starving to death he would also have retained the emotional ability to faint with joy at sight of the festive canned beef, hard-tack and coffee."[67]

Elsewhere in his dispatches Crane contrasted the Cubans' mode of warfare with the Americans.' Roosevelt quickly concluded that the Cubans "would be of no use in serious fighting." In contrast, Crane sought to convey the Cubans' perspective. Crane had landed in Cuba with the marines, weeks ahead of Roosevelt and the army, and had an opportunity to observe the Cubans in combat. In a dispatch about a joint U.S. Marine-Cuban sortie against the Spanish, Crane offers a comic, sympathetic account of the Cubans' thoughts as they prepared for battle. With the "utter calm" of peasants, Crane writes, the men endured their officers' attempts to drill them in the manner of the marines. Shifting into interior monologue, Crane writes, "Order arms? Oh, very well. What does it matter?"[68] In writing about the Rough Riders' engagement at Las Guásimas, Crane notes that the Cubans, whose courage he praised, had different conceptions of warfare from the Americans. "The way our troops kept going, going," Crane writes, "never giving back a foot despite the losses, hanging on as if every battle was a life or death struggle—this seemed extraordinary to the Cuban."[69] In comments like these Crane shows his ability to adopt the Cubans' perspective and reveals an intuitive understanding of the Cubans' differing conception of warfare. As Linderman writes, "The Cubans were in no hurry. They had been battling Spaniards for more than three years. To employ haste implied a level of resources they had never achieved. They avoided decision because it could only go against them. A day well spent was one that prolonged the revolution."[70]

By the time Crane published his "Vivid Story of the Battle of San Juan," a month after his initial dispatches from Cuba, he had dropped his sympathetic stance for the more hostile attitude of the U.S. military and the majority of other correspondents. Yet this hostile attitude was not final. In the fall of 1898, after the war's conclusion, Crane wrote a short story, "The Clan of No-Name," that is unique among his Spanish-American War writing in having no American characters. The story's protagonist is a Cuban insurgent officer, and the tale takes place before the U.S. entry into the war. Its treatment of the insurgents is completely sympathetic, and the officer is a stoic hero in the mode of the regular soldiers of the U.S. Army.

In its varying attitudes toward the Cubans, Crane's Spanish-American War writing serves as a perfect representative of U.S. public opinion in 1898. Both are large; they contain multitudes. On the one hand, Americans saw the Spanish-American War as a crusade for justice and rejected any imperialist ambitions. On the other hand, Americans regarded the Cubans with contempt and believed they had an obligation to lift up the Cuban nation through firm but benevolent control. Amy Kaplan is correct that "Stephen Crane's Vivid Story" paves the way for U.S. imperialism. However, other Crane dispatches represent an attempt to comprehend sympathetically an alien culture and implicitly contain the caveat expressed in "The Mexican Lower Classes": "the most worthless literature of the world has been that which has been written by the men of one nation concerning the men of another."[71] What Edward Said writes of

Stephen Crane's brilliant and complex European friend could equally well be applied to the American writer: "It is no paradox . . . that [Joseph] Conrad was both anti-imperialist and imperialist."[72]

Certainly, Crane resisted the trend to interpret the U.S. victory in Cuba as a triumph for Anglo-Saxons, as did many of his contemporaries. According to the intricate tenets of late nineteenth-century racial theory, Anglo-Saxons constituted a "race" that was destined to play the leading role in world affairs. Josiah Strong's influential best-seller of 1885, *Our Country*, helped to spread the tenets of what Strong called "Anglo-Saxon Christian Imperialism." The world will soon "enter upon a new stage of its history—the final competition of races, for which the Anglo-Saxon is being schooled," Strong wrote. "Then this race of unequaled energy, . . . having developed peculiarly aggressive traits calculated to impress its institutions upon mankind, will spread itself over the earth."[73]

Strong's defense of Anglo-Saxon imperialism influenced U.S. policy toward Spain in the 1890s, as the United States confronted Spain with increasing belligerence. Many Americans viewed the Spanish people as an inferior "race," inherently cruel and barbarous. War with Spain, which could scarcely be justified in terms of U.S. political interests, was applauded as a means of asserting Anglo-Saxon superiority.[74] Numerous journalists and other writers interpreted the war against Spain in racial terms. George Bronson Rea, one of Crane's colleagues on the *New York World*, declared in his dispatch about the Battle of San Juan that the U.S. victory showed that "Spanish valor had to yield to the tenacity and courage of the Anglo-Saxons."[75] Theodore Roosevelt puffed both his erudition and his fiercely held racial theories when he noted in his book *The Rough Riders* that he was reading a French volume titled *Superiorité des Anglo-Saxons* as he headed toward Cuba.[76]

The participation of large numbers of African-American troops in the Spanish-American War posed difficulties for those who interpreted the war as an Anglo-Saxon victory. The U.S. Army in 1898 contained four regiments of black soldiers, who were famous as the Buffalo Soldiers for their exploits in the wars with the Plains Indians. Nearly one-quarter of the troops involved in the Spanish-American War's crucial Santiago campaign were African American, and the black troops' important role in the Battle of San Juan was widely acknowledged at the time.[77] Roosevelt, committed to white racial superiority, dealt with the awkward reality of black soldiers' contribution by attributing their success to their white officers. "No troops could have behaved better than the colored soldiers," he acknowledged, "but they are, of course, peculiarly dependent upon their white officers."[78]

In contrast, Stephen Crane is largely silent about U.S. soldiers' race in his Spanish-American War journalism. Like the other correspondents—all white—who covered the war, he fails to single out black troopers for praise or to celebrate their accomplishments as a group. However, he also fails to distinguish between white and black soldiers. The omission is striking in a context in which other writers always identify African American troops as "colored," an adjective which served to segregate the black soldiers and, in the eyes of white readers in 1898, to diminish their accomplishments. "Crane Tells the Story of the Disembarkment" is representative of Crane's work in this regard. At the disorganized disembarkation of the first army troops to reach Cuba, two soldiers drowned on their way to shore. Theodore Roosevelt in his book *The Rough Riders*, along with all the journalists who covered the scene, identifies the drowned men as "colored infantry soldiers."[79] Crane, alone among writers on the incident, never mentions the soldiers' race. He identifies them only as "men of the Tenth Cavalry," and he offers a somber and touching tribute. The two men, he writes, were "killed on the doorstep of Cuba, drowned a moment before they could set foot on that island which had been the subject of their soldierly dreams."[80] In the context of 1890s racism Crane's silence about race amounted to a progressive stand.

One other Crane dispatch is worth noting for its treatment of race. In his "Vivid Story of the Battle of San Juan," Crane writes of the charge up San Juan Hill, "One saw a thin line of black figures moving across a field." The sentence can be interpreted as purely visual impressionism: from a distance the figures are small, indistinct, and dark. On the other hand, the description of the soldiers as "black" is peculiar because, as Crane's readers would have known, the regular army soldiers wore blue uniforms, whereas the volunteers were in khaki. It is possible that Crane is rejecting the story of San Juan Hill as recorded by Roosevelt and embracing the version reported by African American soldiers in letters to their community newspapers: black troops played as crucial a role as the Rough Riders in the taking of San Juan Hill.[81]

Within days after the battle at San Juan Crane became critically ill with fever and returned to the United States. In New York in late July he left the *World* after a dispute with the business manager and signed on with Hearst's *Journal* to report the Puerto Rican campaign. Crane reached Puerto Rico in early August, staying for only a few days during the brief and almost bloodless campaign. Crane saw no combat in Puerto Rico; his three dispatches from the island report on the cultural clashes as U.S. soldiers met Puerto Rican civilians. A dispatch headlined "Grand Rapids and Ponce" is a humorous, deliberately neutral account of the encounter between disparate cultures. "You could not gauge the [encounter]," Crane writes; "you remained simply astounded." It was, he said, "as if a journal had announced: 'A Rochester trolley car has collided with an ox cart in Buenos Ayres.' "[82] The dispatch forgoes judgment of either Americans or Puerto Ricans in favor of a pose of astonishment at the sight of midwestern American soldiers patroling the dirty, dilapidated, but nevertheless romantic Caribbean city.

Crane's two other Puerto Rican dispatches abandon neutrality to champion the American cause. "The Porto Rican 'Straddle'" depicts the residents of one newly occupied town as dishonest and "shifty" natives who quickly change their allegiance from the Spanish to the Americans when it is to their advantage to do so. "A Soldier's Burial That Made a Native Holiday" is directly racist, perhaps the most unpleasant piece in the Crane canon. Describing the funeral of a U.S. soldier, Crane contrasts the Americans—twice characterized as "calm, stoical, superior"—with natives who observe the funeral as if it were a carnival, chattering and shrilling like parrots. He writes, "The little band of Americans seemed like beings of another world, with their gently mournful, impassive faces, during this display of monkeyish interest." The Puerto Ricans in "A Soldier's Burial" are childish and animalistic, clear inferiors of the physically large and impressively dignified Americans, who are described as "bronze men," as if they were heroic statues come to life.[83]

Crane left Puerto Rico in August for Havana, where he wrote a series of seventeen articles for the *Journal* during a four-month period. These dispatches are generally, as critics have called them, bland—disconnected assemblages of paragraphs on miscellaneous topics.[84] The *Journal* articles recall the "London Letters" by the pseudonymous Imogene Carter that Crane characterized as "rotten bad."[85] Crane was working furiously in Havana, desperately trying to write his way out of debts incurred by his lavish lifestyle in England. The *Journal* paid Crane only $20 a letter, and he presumably dashed the letters off quickly.[86] Most are random collections of observations about Havana; he wrote about courtship customs, pedestrian traffic, and church bells, among other topics. The various but mundane contents of the letters taxed the ingenuity of the *Journal*'s headline writers, who were reduced to a series of variations on the theme of "Stephen Crane's Views of Havana." Other headlines include "Stephen Crane in Havana," "Stephen Crane on Havana," and "Mr. Crane, of Havana."[87]

The other works that Crane produced during this period in Havana, the short stories collected in *Wounds in the Rain,* focus on the experience of U.S. soldiers and correspondents. The stories continue themes that Crane established in his dispatches: the stoicism and nobility of the regular army soldier, the regular's superiority to the volunteer, and correspondents' alternations between bravado and fear. The longest piece in *Wounds in the Rain* includes the same themes. However, it is not a short story but a nonfiction first-person memoir of Crane's war experiences. Seldom republished in subsequent collections of Crane's work and given little attention by critics, "War Memories" is a neglected masterpiece, Crane's best work of war journalism, and arguably one of our greatest nonfiction narratives about war.

"War Memories" had its origin in July 1899, when Lady Jennie Randolph Churchill, the glamorous American-born aristocrat, wrote to Crane asking him for a contribution to her recently established quarterly journal, the *Anglo-Saxon Review.* Lady Churchill suggested to Crane an article of six to ten thousand words on his experiences as a war correspondent. Seemingly dazzled by the invitation, Crane eagerly accepted, even though no payment was offered and he was at the time desperately short of money.[88] The prospect of writing for Lady Churchill's prestigious journal, combined with the noncommercial aspect of the assignment, seems to have liberated Crane artistically. He produced an autobiographical essay of nearly twenty thousand words—twice the suggested length—about his experiences in Cuba. "War Memories" is exceptional not only for its length but for its artistic daring. Crane used the piece as a stylistic testing ground; "War Memories" is an extended linguistic experiment, a technically daring text that marks a new phase in Crane's work.

One reason that "War Memories" is so little known, aside from its length, is that the work is difficult to classify. Caught awkwardly between story and book length, it falls with equal awkwardness between familiar genres. Is "War Memories" fiction or nonfiction? Story or autobiography? Journalism or memoir? The inability to pin down the work's genre seems to have caused critics and teachers to shy away from the text.[89] However, viewed within the fact-fiction discourse of 1890s journalism, "War Memories" appears less peculiar. Like Crane's New York City sketches, "War Memories" seems to combine observed incidents with the speculative and subjective. Although all the episodes described in "War Memories" are consistent with what we know from other sources about Crane's Spanish-American War experiences, in the opening paragraph the narrator refers in third person to "Vernall, the war correspondent"; later in the piece the narrator, speaking in first person, says that an officer addresses him as "Mr. Vernall."[90] Crane's use of this nom de guerre seems to add a fictional touch to the work. Or does it? "Vernall" may suggest the Latin word "veritas," truth. Does the name Vernall imply that the narrative is "all true"? Alternatively, the name may recall the word "vernal," suggesting that Vernall is a "green," untried young man plunged into a war that disorients him and renders him an unreliable narrator. Or is Crane simply being playful? For Vernall, it turns out, was the name of Crane's cook at his home in England.[91] "War Memories" self-consciously calls attention to its melding of factual and fictional discourses. In its self-reflexive playfulness with generic conventions "War Memories" is similar to Tim O'Brien's Vietnam War narrative *The Things They Carried* (1990), a work that features a character named Tim O'Brien, who may or may not be identical with the author, who may or may not have undergone the experiences described in the book.

If "War Memories" appears to us now to be a precursor of postmodern Vietnam War narratives, on its original publication it was read in the context of other summary accounts of the Spanish-American War. The most popular of these was Richard Harding Davis's *The Cuban and Porto Rican Campaigns* (1898), rushed into print soon after the war's end. Davis's book is a smoothly written overview of the war's major events. Davis follows the war in chronological order, from the declaration of war on April 22, 1898, to the August 12 cease-fire. He analyzes military strategy, singles out a few officers for praise, and offers an extended critique of commanding General William R. Shafter's shortcomings. He sums up the war, and his book, with an optimistic view of the future of U.S. imperialism: "Peace came with Porto Rico occupied by our troops and with the Porto Ricans blessing our flags, which must never leave the island. . . . The course of empire to-day takes its way to all points of the compass."[92]

"War Memories" can be seen as the direct antithesis of Davis's book. Where Davis is impersonal and analytic, Crane is personal and subjective.

In place of Davis's rational, chronological summary of major events Crane offers an assortment of anecdotes, their structure determined less by chronology than by the vagaries of memory, their content often trivial or absurd. Whereas Davis ends his book with a tribute to U.S. imperialism that justifies the war and summarizes its future significance, Crane rejects any totalizing interpretation, whether analysis of strategy or encomium to the benign paternal role that the United States will play in Spain's former colonies.

"War Memories" rejects not only conventional postwar analyses such as Davis's but also the jingoism of Crane's earlier Spanish-American War dispatches. "War Memories" displaces jingoism onto the U.S. public and onto an unnamed voiceless interlocutor who appears occasionally throughout the text. It is this interlocutor who, the text implies, initially calls the Spanish soldiers "enemies" in a passage describing Crane's first battle: "In this valley there was a thicket—a big thicket—and this thicket seemed to be crowded with a mysterious class of persons who were evidently trying to kill us. Our enemies? Yes—perhaps—I suppose so. Leave that to the people in the streets at home" (245). The narrator here, as in much of "War Memories," assumes the role of naïf absorbed by the mystery of war. When the interlocutor evidently calls the "mysterious" persons "enemies," the narrator agrees only reluctantly. Struggling to convey the existential reality of war, the narrator has no patience with the language of patriotism that must classify combatants as friends or enemies.

Throughout "War Memories" Crane avoids the patriotic, imperialistic discourse that Richard Harding Davis used to signify the meaning of the Spanish-American War. Instead, he offers one individual's recollections, and the structure of "War Memories" mimics the highly subjective sequence of memory. For example, in one tour-de-force sequence the interlocutor keeps asking to hear about the war's most famous battles— Las Guásimas, where Teddy Roosevelt's Rough Riders first came under fire, and the climactic Battle of San Juan Hill. But the narrator resists this pressure to deliver a straightforward narrative and veers off into one digression after another. Deferring his representation of the war's famous battles, Crane instead presents a narrative battle between the interlocutor, who wants to hear about the war's celebrated events, and the narrator, who finds the true significance of the war to lie not in objective summaries of dramatic engagements but in subjective anecdotes about seemingly mundane events. For example, after describing the landing of the U.S. Army troops in Cuba, the narrator tells how one morning he had breakfast with two officers, Greene and Exton of the 20th Infantry, and afterward, to his shame, saw the officers washing the breakfast dishes:

> I walked away, blushing. What? The battles? Yes, I saw something of all
> of them. I made up my mind that the next time I met Greene and Exton,
> I'd say: "Look here; why didn't you tell me you had to wash your own
> dishes that morning, so that I could have helped?" . . . But I never saw
> Captain Green again. . . . The next time I saw Exton—what? Yes, La
> Guasimas [sic]. That was the "rough-rider fight." . . . But if ever I meet
> Greene or Exton again—even if it should be twenty years—I am going
> to say, first thing: "Why—" What? Yes. Roosevelt's regiment and the
> First and Tenth Regular Cavalry. I'll say, first thing: "Say, why didn't you
> tell me you had to wash your own dishes, that morning, so that I could
> have helped?" My stupidity will be on my conscience until I die, if,
> before that, I do not meet either Greene or Exton. Oh yes, you are howl-
> ing for blood, but I tell you it is more emphatic that I lost my tooth-
> brush. Did I tell you that? Well, I lost it, you see, and I thought of it for
> ten hours at a stretch. (267–68)

Before the narrator obliges his interlocutor with an account of the Battle of San Juan Hill, he goes through numerous similar digressions. Crane's quirky narrative structure emphasizes that the reality of war is to be com-municated not through broad strategic analyses but through the minor details of one individual's experience.

The focus on individual experience in "War Memories" is, of course, also characteristic of *The Red Badge of Courage*. Countless critics have pointed out that *Red Badge* rejects the comprehensive perspective of the general officer in favor of Private Fleming's limited view. Thus "War Memories" can be seen as a continuation of the narrative techniques Crane first used in *Red Badge*. However, "War Memories" goes beyond *Red Badge* in both thematic and formal terms. For although both works attempt to convey to readers one person's experience of war, "War Memories" declares that to be an impossible goal. "War Memories" is only in part about war; its other subject is the inability of language to commu-nicate experience.

"War Memories" opens with an explicit announcement of its linguistic concerns. "But to get the real thing!" it begins. "It seems impossible! It is because war is neither magnificent nor squalid; it is simply life, and an expression of life can always evade us. We can never tell life, one to another, although sometimes we think we can" (229). In "War Memories" Crane uses an arsenal of innovative techniques that draw our attention to the limits of narrative and of language. Some techniques have already been mentioned: jumbled chronology, digressions, and the narrator's disputes with his interlocutor over what event he should cover next. Crane's opening exclamations about the impossibility of telling "the real thing" are followed by an episode that confirms his narrative despair. "War Memories" begins with a trivial incident that takes place aboard a newspaper dispatch boat as four correspondents leave Key West. When the boat hits heavy seas, a bunch of bananas hung in the correspondents' cabin starts swinging wildly and knocks the men out of their cabin. "You see?" the narrator asks at the end of the anecdote. "War! A bunch of bananas rampant because the ship rolled" (230).

From this point on "a bunch of bananas" becomes a tagline that concludes the narrator's accounts of his experiences, anecdotes that frequently mix violence and the commonplace in an absurd, incomprehensible brew. For example, after describing a dinner aboard a navy warship when a young officer played the piano while the ship shelled a column of Spanish cavalry, Crane concludes, "The piano's clattering of the popular air was often interrupted by the boom of a four-inch gun. A bunch of bananas!" (237). "A bunch of bananas," along with similar tag lines, recurs throughout "War Memories." These phrases serve as free-floating signifiers, their brevity and banality emphasizing the limits of language.

In its content as well as its form "War Memories" emphasizes the difficulties of communicating experience. The piece is filled with episodes of miscommunication. As described earlier, the narrator and his interlocutor are constantly at cross-purposes; while the interlocutor is howling for tales of blood, the narrator wants to talk about his lost toothbrush. The narrator has equally small success communicating with the other characters in his narrative. Repeatedly he describes his frustration when, after some dramatic life-threatening experience, he is unable to convey what he has just gone through. For example, after a battle in the Cuzco Hills, when two hundred marines engaged a Spanish force in the war's first U.S. victory, the narrator can find no one to whom he can tell his experience. Fresh from his "life's most fiery time," ready to shout out "with mingled awe and joy," he wants to recount his adventures to the other correspondents and their dispatch boat's crew but is met with indifference (252–53). Abashed, he retreats into silence.

Silence is a central motif of "War Memories." More than anything else, it is the piece's emphasis on silence that distinguishes it from *The Red Badge of Courage*. *Red Badge* consists in large part of Henry Fleming's voluble interior monologue, and the novel's power derives from its fluent transcription of a private soldier's stream of consciousness. In contrast, the narrator of "War Memories" repeatedly draws attention to the fact that he has no idea what goes on in the minds of the soldiers he observes. Walking among marines going into battle, he says, "As they trudged slowly in single file they were reflecting upon—what? I don't know" (242). "I don't know"; "I cannot imagine"—these repeated phrases serve as signifiers pointing to the inscrutable silence that, the narrator insists, is at the heart of war. The narrator repeats one story after another that has silence at its climax: the silence of men about to engage in battle; the terrible muteness of the wounded; the silence of civilians who observe wounded men filing off a ship; the hush with which a crowd of soldiers spontaneously salutes returning prisoners of war. Moved by these moments of silence, the narrator at times treats language as a betrayal; for example, he says that when the soldiers start cheering for the prisoners of war, "the whole scene went to rubbish" (298). In scenes of greatest emotional effect the text of "War Memories" fights against its linguistic limits and tries to achieve the unachievable condition of silence. Crane's account in "War Memories" of the famous Battle of San Juan, where U.S. soldiers charged into massive Spanish rifle fire and took a seemingly impregnable position, is terse in the extreme. He describes the battle with seeming reluctance, as if giving in to the pressure of the interlocutor's demands. And he ends his account of the soldiers' action by saying, "One cannot speak of it—the spectacle of the common man serenely doing his work. . . . One pays them the tribute of the toast of silence" (281).

"War Memories" concludes in taunting, puzzling fashion: "And you can depend upon it that I have told you nothing at all, nothing at all, nothing at all" (308). In his final sentence the narrator once again pushes up against the limits of language, directly addressing his reader, attempting to engage us in the construction of elusive meaning. But in his triply repeated negative he reminds us of the impossibility of comprehending the reality his words represent; war is finally unknowable, and the truest response is a reiterated phrase of denial that trails off into silence.

"Nothing at all." The conclusion of "War Memories" may suggest that Crane had reached an artistic dead end—as if, eighty years ahead of his time, he had become the most pessimistic of deconstructionists, conscious of language's inherent unreferentiality but unable to take any pleasure in the free play of signifiers. But Crane continued writing after "War Memories," and he thought enough of the piece to republish it in *Wounds in the Rain*. His twenty-thousand-word narrative is more than a tale full of sound and fury, signifying nothing at all. "War Memories" has much to tell us about both art and war.

Artistically, "War Memories" leapfrogs modernism, landing on post-modernist ground. It is as if Crane knew already the project of his most prominent artistic successor and set out to undermine it. That successor is Ernest Hemingway, Crane's self-acknowledged literary offspring, who wrote that his artistic intention was to get "the real thing" in writing.[93] The opening sentence of "War Memories" suggests that Hemingway's project is naive. To get "the real thing," Vernall/Crane cries, is "impossible," because language is always inadequate to communicate experience: "We can never tell life, one to another, although sometimes we think we can."

Crane rejects Hemingway's positivist view of language, yet the two writers share a commitment to the representation of war as a central artistic goal. In many ways "War Memories" prefigures *A Farewell to Arms* (1929). Crane's narrative can be seen as an extended gloss on the famous passage in *A Farewell to Arms* that rejects abstract words—"honor," "courage"—in favor of the concrete names of villages and rivers.[94] Crane repudiates the Richard Harding Davis honor-and-courage approach to the Spanish-American War and remains silent about the topics that absorb Davis's attention: strategies, victories, the glories of U.S. imperialism. Within the text of "War Memories" Crane portrays the interlocutor as an avid reader of Davis-like accounts who wants to hear romantic stories about the celebrated battles, whereas his narrator insists on recounting seemingly trivial but personally significant events. Like *A Farewell to Arms*, "War Memories" rejects the abstract, manipulative rhetoric of general officers, politicians, and newspapers in favor of concrete, subjective narrative.

However, "War Memories" is not, one needs to add, an antiwar work. Although Crane shows war to be a brutal process whose product is injured bodies, he never questions the necessity or justice of the Spanish-American War, and he regards the private soldiers of the regular army as heroes.

Although the narrator of "War Memories" says that war is "death, and a plague of the lack of small things, and toil," at the same time he is always conscious of the glamour of war (254). Immediately after the passage just quoted Crane cannot resist telling an anecdote in which he figures as a comic yet romantic figure: when he goes straight from the battlefield to a cable station in Jamaica and from there to a swank hotel, he overhears a woman in the hotel lobby ask, "Who *is* that chap in the very dirty jack-boots?" (254). Michael Herr could be speaking of Stephen Crane when he says that he never knew anyone who was insensible to the glamour that resulted "when the words 'war' and 'correspondent' got joined."[95]

In its frank acknowledgment of war's linked brutality and glamour, in its postmodern foregrounding of the limitations of language, "War Memories" is closer to Herr's *Dispatches* (1977) than it is to Hemingway's work. The two works have hauntingly similar endings. Crane's "I have told you nothing at all, nothing at all, nothing at all" is echoed in Herr's "Vietnam Vietnam Vietnam, we've all been there."[96] Both endings move beyond rationality, beyond referentiality in an effort to invoke the hallucinatory, incantatory powers of language. Both Crane and Herr establish a personalist epistemology, rejecting abstract analysis in favor of an intensely subjective recording of their experience. Philip Biedler could be referring to "War Memories" when he writes that a text's "real terrain . . . is the terrain of consciousness itself"; the comment is actually about *Dispatches*.[97]

Although "War Memories" has received scant critical comment, critics have lavished commentary on *Dispatches*. Along with much praise for its postmodern brilliance *Dispatches* has received significant criticism. Some of that criticism can be applied to "War Memories" as well. For example, John Carlos Rowe has argued that the personalist epistemology privileged in *Dispatches* and other Vietnam War literature reflects American mythologizing of the special value of direct experience and displaces the serious political and historical analysis necessary to understand the Vietnam War.[98] "War Memories" is unquestionably limited to a personalist epistemology that neglects political analysis. However, it also neglects the rationales for imperialism that dominate other contemporary narratives of the Spanish-American War—including Crane's war correspondence. In her essay dealing with Crane's newspaper dispatch about the Battle of San Juan, Amy Kaplan concludes that the dispatch inscribes not only the U.S. victory at San Juan but the racist, imperialist postwar American agenda.[99] The same cannot be said of "War Memories." In its intense subjectivity and commitment to experiential immediacy the text of "War Memories" conspicuously refuses to contribute to the discourse of imperialism. The narrator is so wary of abstract conclusions that he rejects even his interlocutor's attempt to label Spanish soldiers as "enemies."

"War Memories" represents a departure not only from Crane's war correspondence but also from his earlier work. Ever since Crane's death at twenty-eight of tuberculosis, a favorite game among his readers has been to speculate about the works he might have written had he lived. "War Memories" points to some fascinating new directions. This lengthy memoir—the only significant autobiographical writing Crane ever did outside his letters—suggests new authorial stances for a writer who, before this point, had fiercely adhered to Flaubert's dictum that the artist should be as invisible within his work as God within his creation. "War Memories" shows Crane experimenting with an autobiographical technique as rich and complex as that of Michael Herr. It shows Crane experimenting also with a variety of other stylistic techniques, mentioned earlier: a structure based on the vagaries of memory, the interweaving of absurdist tag lines in complex motifs, the use of an interlocutor, and self-reflexive foregrounding of the text's linguistic limitations. Had Crane lived, would "War Memories" have marked the initiation of Crane's "experimental phase," equivalent in its daring and significance to the artistic experiments that his fellow expatriate and friend, Henry James, was conducting in the late 1890s? Would "War Memories" have prepared the way for Crane's own "major phase"?

The questions are unanswerable. However, it is important to note that the text that prompts the questions arose from Stephen Crane's journalism. "War Memories," although it was not published in a newspaper, can be seen as part of the fact-fiction discourse of 1890s journalism. The work's blurring of genres and self-reflexive attention to its truth status have their origins in the journalistic conventions that Stephen Crane turned to his own ends throughout his career.

"I came near being swamped by journalism," Crane supposedly said.[100] He was expressing a view that would be echoed by the many twentieth-century reporter-novelists who experienced a conflict between journalism and fiction, between writing that offered immediate payment and work with a long-delayed financial reward, between assignments that needed immediate attention and the uninterrupted time necessary to complete a novel.[101] Numerous writers have testified to those conflicts; Stephen Crane surely felt them. However, 1890s journalism also provided Crane with the opportunity to develop a distinctively ironic authorial voice as a teenaged reporter on the New Jersey shore; to experiment with urban modes of life radically different from his middle-class upbringing and to publish his complex accounts of his experiences; to travel across North America and Europe, exploring points of view as various as a Mexican peasant's and an English constable's; and to write additional masterpieces on the experience of war. The example of Stephen Crane's career and work would heavily influence writers of the next generation, particularly two reporter-novelists who had an enormous influence on modern American literature: Theodore Dreiser and Ernest Hemingway.

CHAPTER 6

Journalism and the Making of Modern American Literature

THEODORE DREISER AND ERNEST HEMINGWAY

Although he died childless at twenty-eight, Stephen Crane helped to father a revolution in American literary life. During Crane's youth in the 1880s, William Dean Howells and Henry James tried to defend literature's elite cultural status by denigrating mass-circulation journalism and attacking reporters. Crane's easy alternations between the roles of reporter and novelist and his blurring of distinctions between journalism and fiction undermined the cultural hierarchy that Howells and James worked so vigorously to defend. In the years following Crane's death in 1900, the relations between journalism and literature altered radically. Thousands of would-be novelists went to work for newspapers, hoping to reproduce the career of Crane and other reporter-artists. A surprising number succeeded.

Theodore Dreiser and Ernest Hemingway were among those who did. Like Crane, Dreiser and Hemingway started their careers as newspaper reporters. However, the newspaper experience of each shaped his work in unique ways. Dreiser, born within a few weeks of Crane in 1871, could not be influenced in his early career by Crane's example. When Dreiser decided at twenty to become a reporter, Crane was still writing anonymous articles for the New Jersey Coast News Bureau. However, Dreiser became aware of his talented contemporary with the publication of *The Red Badge of Courage* in 1895. He expressed his admiration in his newly founded magazine *Ev'ry Month*, calling Crane "brilliant." [1] Dreiser never matched Crane's journalistic brilliance during the 1890s; Dreiser's early journalism is pedestrian. However, late in the decade he revealed his regard for Crane by the sincerest form of flattery: he plagiarized from one of Crane's articles.[2]

If Dreiser never rivaled Crane's success as a writer of literary journalism, as a novelist he had a powerful influence on modern American literature, and his greatest novels were strongly influenced by journalism. His fiction's debt to journalism is evident in *An American Tragedy* (1925), which is based on a 1906 murder case. Dreiser's principal source for the novel was the *New York World*, a debt he did little to conceal. Dreiser drew attention to his novel's newspaper-reported origins, modeling the name of his protagonist Clyde Griffiths on that of convicted murderer Chester Gillette, hewing closely to the facts of the Gillette case, and even quoting extensively from newspaper summaries of the trial and of the murdered woman's letters to her lover.[3] Although Dreiser's debt to journalism is most obvious in *An American Tragedy*, all his novels can be seen as newspaper-derived. In autobiographical writings Dreiser frequently recounted how his reporting exposed him to realities of poverty, crime, and sexual misconduct that the popular fiction of the 1890s ignored. His avowed aim was to bring those realities into modern literature, to become the Balzac of the front page, incorporating the newspaper's most sordid and sensationalistic subject matter into the modern American novel.

Hemingway shared Dreiser's admiration for Crane, including Crane in his radically brief honor roll of American writers. "The good writers are Henry James, Stephen Crane, and Mark Twain," he wrote in *The Green Hills of Africa*. "That's not the order they're good in. There is no order for good writers."[4] Hemingway's earliest career choice would have been unthinkable without Crane's example. The Hemingway family had a long association with Oberlin College—Ernest's father, his older sister, and all his Hemingway aunts and uncles studied there—and in his senior year of high school the only departure from family tradition that Ernest imagined was to attend the University of Illinois instead.[5] But after his high school graduation in 1917 Hemingway decided to turn from his family's expectation of college attendance to take a job as a reporter on the *Kansas City Star*. He told his friends that the way to his dream of becoming a fiction writer lay not through college but through newspaper work—an idea made possible by the careers of Stephen Crane and other reporter-novelists of the 1890s.[6]

Like Crane, Hemingway went on to write distinguished literary journalism. Like Dreiser, he turned to the newspaper for subject matter for his fiction. However, the most profound effect of his newspaper experience was on his style. Hemingway entered journalism twenty-five years after Dreiser. During that period newspapers' front pages shifted from a Victorian emphasis on writing deemed colorful—Dreiser said the style could also be characterized as discursive and long winded—to the terse prose characteristic of twentieth-century journalism.[7] When Hemingway landed his first reporting job on the *Kansas City Star* in 1917, the editor handed him the newspaper's style sheet, which began, "Use short sentences. Use short first paragraphs. Use vigorous English."[8] Hemingway's famous style, which appeared full blown in his first American publication, *In Our Time* (1925), was not shaped solely by his newspaper experience; critics have traced a variety of influences. However, the terse prose of modern journalism contributed to Hemingway's immensely influential modernist style. For Hemingway, as for Dreiser, the newspaper played a crucial role in his contributions to the making of modern American literature.

Although Crane and Dreiser both worked for newspapers and magazines throughout the 1890s, the two writers' journalism differed dramatically, and journalism played a very different role in their careers. From the age of twenty Crane turned the fact-fiction discourse of 1890s journalism to his own ends, publishing polished gems that gleamed with his distinctively ironic prose style. He turned the mundane genre of the vacation resort news article into a vehicle for sharply comic observations on the middle class at play. He used the common form of the journalistic experiment to convey the realities of urban poverty to his readers and to conduct profound naturalistic investigations into the social construction of human identity. He wrote travel journalism that moves far beyond the touristic to consider subtleties of perception, economic and political oppression, and humanity's struggle against nature. He published an account of his experience in an open boat that is regarded as one of the greatest short works in American literature. He wrote dazzling war correspondence that conveys the complexity, confusion, and inconsequentiality of battle. Crane also took advantage of his role as reporter for mass-circulation newspapers to gather experiences that might otherwise have been inaccessible to the son of a Methodist minister. As Alfred Kazin has noted, journalism "opened up to [Crane] places and people, from the Bowery in New York to the Balkans at war, that many other Americans of 'good family' missed."[9]

Crane used his role as a newspaper reporter to descend on the social scale, to sleep in Bowery flophouses and crouch in trenches alongside private soldiers. To the young Theodore Dreiser newspaper reporting represented an opportunity to move *up* the social ladder, to escape from the poverty and disreputability of his immigrant Catholic family. When Dreiser landed his first reporting job, he had been working for two years as a laundry truck driver and as a bill collector for cheap furniture stores. Dreiser did not need newspaper experience to introduce him to the slums; he had been living and working in them.[10] Dreiser saw newspaper reporting as a way out of poorly paid, dead-end jobs. Journalists, he naively believed, were uniformly "prosperous and happy." In his autobiography of his years in journalism, *Newspaper Days* (1922), Dreiser describes his fantasies about the newspaper business:

> I painted reporters and newspaper men generally as receiving fabulous salaries, being sent on the most urgent and interesting missions. I think I confused, inextricably, reporters with ambassadors and prominent men generally. Their lives were laid among great people, the rich, the famous, the powerful; and because of their position and facility of expression and mental force they were received everywhere as equals. Think of me, new, young, poor, being received in that way![11]

Dreiser's dreams of affluence were checked as soon as he was hired by the *Globe*, one of Chicago's smallest newspapers; his salary was only $15 a week.[12] However, his vision of circulating among the great and powerful was answered to some extent; Dreiser's first assignment was to cover the Democratic Party's national convention, held in Chicago in June 1892. Once the convention was over, though, Dreiser found that his role of reporter was as likely to take him into the slums as into the haunts of the elite.

The first two *Globe* articles that can reliably be identified as Dreiser's illustrate both the range of his reporting duties and the limitations of his journalism. His article on the Democratic convention—heavily edited, Dreiser reveals in his autobiography, by a copy editor sympathetic to the inept but promising beginner—is a purely factual account. Its headline, "Cleveland and Gray the Ticket," is fully representative of both the article's content and its pedestrian style.[13] Dreiser's second identifiable article, published one month later, is at the opposite end of the journalistic spectrum. "Cheyenne, Haunt of Misery and Crime" is a feature article on a Chicago slum district. Although Dreiser's convention article is packed with names of politicians, the slum feature has no proper names. Like Crane's New York City sketches, Dreiser's feature is part of the 1890s fact-fiction discourse. However, whereas Crane pushed the limits of newspaper writing in his technically daring experiments, Dreiser fell into conventional Victorian sentimentality. His article on the Cheyenne slum district opens by noting that at night its streets are walked by sick men, drunkards, thieves, "and other characters lost to all semblance of manhood." Appealing in his opening to Victorian gender stereotypes, Dreiser concludes with grandiose, sentimental rhetoric: "What can be done for [the slum dwellers]? How can they be uplifted? They nestle in the very arms of free education and are not aroused. Let the wise of the world ponder. Let human pity extend a helping hand."[14] The article's sentimentality would be often repeated in Dreiser's 1890s journalism.

Stephen Crane used the freedom inherent in the fact-fiction discourse of 1890s newspapers to write brilliantly original ironic features. However, the fact-fiction discourse included the freedom to be sentimental, and it was this discursive strategy that Theodore Dreiser, like most reporters, seized. The sentimentality of his Cheyenne slum district article in the *Chicago Globe* is characteristic of much of his journalism. Many of the 234 newspaper articles that scholars have been able to identify as Dreiser's are features that use the fact-fiction discourse to take a humorous and sentimental perspective. For example, "Hospital Violet Day," one of the few clippings from his newspaper days that Dreiser saved, describes a spring day at an unnamed Pittsburgh hospital. The opening paragraph concludes, "the morning awakened to the patients most pleasantly, and caused many a weary sufferer to turn, blink and bless the great Creator for another May Day of life, reviving beauty and delicious warmth."[15] Similar sentimentality suffuses the rest of the article and can be found throughout Dreiser's newspaper journalism.

Critics and biographers have mined Dreiser's newspaper writing for its connections to his later work. They have found articles that describe real-life counterparts of *Sister Carrie*'s Hurstwood, the sex criminal Isadore Berchansky in *The Hand of the Potter*, and the title character in "Nigger Jeff." In addition, they have found in his newspaper writing a detailed treatment of everyday life, an "awe of the world of fact" in the words of one critic, that, they argue, helps to explain Dreiser's practice as a literary realist.[16] Although these critical analyses have been illuminating, I intend to take a different approach to Dreiser's newspaper journalism. Rather than analyze the articles themselves—which, compared to Crane's journalism, are formulaic and thin—I want to look at the statements Dreiser made later in his career about his newspaper work. In interviews, letters, and autobiographical writings Dreiser offered narratives about his newspaper experience that illuminate his self-construction of roles as both 1890s reporter and twentieth-century novelist.

Intriguingly, Dreiser crafted two quite different narratives about his newspaper experience. One narrative, which appears only in an essay published near the end of his career, is a simple tale about journalism's inferiority to literature. "Lessons I Learned from an Old Man" (1938) describes an interview that Dreiser, as a young reporter, conducted with a retired manufacturer in order to gather the wealthy businessman's opinions on a new railroad terminal project. Dreiser says that when he was escorted into the presence of this powerful figure, he was astonished to find a small feeble old man, listless and indifferent. "Yes, my boy, I will answer all your questions," Dreiser reports the old man saying, "only my interest in all these things is now so slight that it seems scarcely worth while. I do not know why they trouble to ask me."[17] Dreiser recorded the man's replies in his reporter's notebook, but what truly interested him was the spectacle of this wizened old man ensconced in a great house, the contrast between the manufacturer's former power and his current feeble indifference. In his essay Dreiser says that he asked himself, "*Why was it that a newspaper must entirely ignore that which interested me now?* . . . What did one, or could one, do with such facts, such pictures, if not publish them in a newspaper?" (302). The essay ends with Dreiser's answer to his youthful questions, reached, he says, only "after several years of meditation": "Literature, as I now saw, and art in all its forms, was this other realm. . . . There, if anywhere, were to be reported or painted such conditions and scenes as this about which I had meditated and which could find no place in the rush and hurry of our daily press. Then it was, and not until then, that the real difference between journalism and literature became plain" (304). In "Lessons" Dreiser constructs a simple dichotomy between journalism and literature. The artist is the antithesis of the reporter. Literature consists of the reality that cannot be told in journalism.

In this 1938 essay, written when he was in his late sixties, Dreiser treats journalism as a sort of antidiscourse, serving to define by contrast the more valuable discourse of literature. However, "Lessons" represents an exception to the rule of Dreiser's statements about journalism. Earlier in his career, in letters, interviews, and an autobiographical volume, Dreiser offered a more complex treatment of the relation between journalism and literature, depicting literature not as journalism's discursive opposite but as a discourse dependent upon journalism in order to reach its full potential. And it is this model of literature's dependence upon journalism that, as we shall see, Dreiser relied upon in writing his greatest novels.

The primary value of his three years' experience as a newspaper reporter, Dreiser said repeatedly during the decades between 1910 and 1930, was the range of experience to which he was exposed. His "real contact with life," Dreiser wrote in a 1916 letter to H. L. Mencken, began with his entry into newspaper work. He encountered "murders, arson, rape, sodomy, bribery, corruption, trickery and false witness in every conceivable form."[18] Dreiser's collected newspaper articles reveal that he was not exaggerating. Assigned to St. Louis's crime-ridden third police district, Dreiser wrote articles on infanticide, adultery, murders, murder-suicides, and sexual assaults on children.

However, Dreiser was also sent to cover lavish balls given by St. Louis socialites. Dreiser repeatedly comments in *Newspaper Days* on the extraordinary social and economic contrasts he experienced in his rounds as a reporter. "Regularly it would be a murder, a suicide, a failure, a defalcation which I would be assigned to cover, and on the same day there would be an important wedding, a business or political banquet, a ball or a club entertainment of some kind," he writes in a representative passage.[19] Stephen Crane, freelance features writer, went undercover in order to experience the contrasts of misery and luxury that could be found in the city. Dreiser, as a beginning reporter on a daily newspaper, had no need to seek out such contrasts; he was forced to encounter them in the daily rounds of his work. Hurled between the social heights and depths, Dreiser felt that he was seeing and reporting in his articles the harsh truths of U.S. society.

In *Newspaper Days* Dreiser repeatedly portrays the metropolitan paper's news columns as a truthful record of their society. He places the news columns in opposition to the discourses of the editorial page, religion, and fiction. The first and most vivid example of opposing discourses in *Newspaper Days* occurs in Dreiser's description of the bohemian circle of reporters and illustrators he encountered in St. Louis. A reporter in that circle, Robert Hazard, had written a novel that dealt frankly with vice and sexuality. Handing Dreiser the manuscript to read, Hazard told him, "Of course a thing like this could never be published over here. We'd have to get it done abroad" (131–32). Dreiser devotes a lengthy section of *Newspaper Days* to Hazard's novel, using it as an occasion to decry the timidity of American art in the 1890s and to contrast America's various public discourses with the newspaper's realism. The fiction writer "couldn't write about life as it was," Dreiser claims. "The publishers wouldn't stand for it." He continues:

> You had to write about [life] as somebody else thought it was, the ministers and farmers and dullards of the home. Yet here [Hazard] was, as was I, busy in a profession that was hourly revealing the fact that this sweetness and light code, this idea of a perfect world which contained neither sin nor shame for any save vile outcasts, criminals and vagrants, was the trashiest lie that was ever foisted upon an all too human world. Not a day, not an hour, but the pages of the very newspaper we were helping to fill with our scribbled observations were full of the most incisive pictures of the lack of virtue, honesty, kindness, even average human intelligence, not on the part of a few but of nearly everybody. . . . If a man like Hazard or myself had ventured to transpose a true picture of facts from the news columns of the paper, from our own reportorial experiences, into a story or novel, what a howl! (132–33)

Newspaper Days asserts that in the 1890s the daily newspaper was the only truthful discursive form. Dreiser made the same point in a 1911 interview:

> Great American novels can't be written while we refuse to countenance the true expression of the American temperament; while we refuse to hear of what goes on in the cities to-day—except by reading in the newspapers and the magazines. And let me say that for real worth in what literature is supposed to stand for, to-day's newspapers and magazines are so far ahead of all the novels that have been published that there is no comparison.[20]

In this interview and throughout *Newspaper Days* Dreiser portrays the news article as his literary ideal—a contradiction of the view he espoused in "Lessons I Learned from an Old Man."

However, after a few years as a newspaper reporter Dreiser became disgusted by the low pay and insecurity of the journalist's profession. At that point he shifted the vision of wealth and glamour he had once associated with reporters onto fiction writers. He imagined, despite his friend Hazard's cautionary example, that his role would be to bring the realities he witnessed as a reporter into American fiction. Working as a reporter in Pittsburgh in 1894, Dreiser discovered Balzac; the experience was for him a "literary revolution." "I saw for the first time how a book should be written," he later told an interviewer.[21] Dreiser did not attempt to write fiction for a full five years after first reading Balzac. However, in *Newspaper Days* and in interviews he located his genesis as a novelist in Pittsburgh, where he simultaneously reported city news and worked his way through *La comédie humaine*. In Dreiser's self-creation myth his artistic destiny was to become a Balzac of the front page, to write novels of American life that applied Balzac's "epic" vision to events such as those he covered as a reporter.[22] In the years to come Dreiser would deliberately inscribe within his greatest novels their origins in the daily newspaper.

Sister Carrie's first readers commented on the novel's newspaper origins. A reader for Harper & Brothers, the publishing firm to which Dreiser initially submitted his manuscript, began his report, "This is a superior piece of reportorial realism—of highclass newspaper work."[23] The comment was not intended as a compliment; the reader went on to recommend that the firm reject the manuscript. Reviewers of the novel's first edition, published by Doubleday, Page in 1900, were generally more sympathetic, but they too noted the book's links to journalism. It "tells of a common experience, as too often the daily newspapers witness," one reviewer wrote in a typical comment.[24] These readers' observations cannot have come as a surprise to Dreiser, because he took pains to bring the newspaper into his novel in a variety of ways. One can call *Sister Carrie* "reportorial," as did the Harper & Brothers reader, but that term scarcely gives a sense of how thoroughly the newspaper permeates the novel.

In obvious ways *Sister Carrie* shares its subject matter with the newspaper. As is well known, the model for *Sister Carrie*'s title character was Dreiser's sister Emma, who fled from Chicago to New York with her married lover after he stole money from the saloon where he worked. Dreiser based *Sister Carrie* on family experience, but the novel's origins are journalistic as well as personal. As reviewers noted in 1900, "too often the daily newspapers witness" stories like Carrie's, and Emma Dreiser's experience was extensively documented by the Chicago press in 1886.[25] Moreover, men similar to Hurstwood in his period of decline could be easily found in the newspapers. Dreiser may have written an 1895 *New York World* article about a tramp who, like Hurstwood, committed suicide in his flophouse room by turning on the gas; certainly Dreiser, who was reporting for the *World* at the time, would have read the piece.[26] The entire New York City section of *Carrie*, with its dual emphases on the glamorous world of the theater and the miserable existence of the tramp, mirrors 1890s New York newspapers' obsessions with both Broadway and the Bowery.

Sister Carrie's style is in important ways as journalistic as its subject matter. The novel's opening sentences reveal Dreiser's newspaper training:

> When Caroline Meeber boarded the afternoon train for Chicago, her total outfit consisted of a small trunk, a cheap imitation alligator-skin satchel, a small lunch in a paper box, and a yellow leather snap purse, containing her ticket, a scrap of paper with her sister's address in Van Buren Street, and four dollars in money. It was in August, 1889. She was eighteen years of age, bright, timid, and full of the illusions of ignorance and youth. (1)

Like a good lead, the novel's opening paragraph briskly and concretely answers the classic journalistic questions: Who? What? Where? When? Why?[27] Moreover, the use of historically and geographically accurate proper nouns, such as Chicago's Van Buren Street, continues throughout the book. *Sister Carrie* is filled with names of actual hotels, restaurants, department stores, theaters, actors, and producers in both Chicago and New York. Dreiser's manuscript contains dozens more proper names that were cut from the published novel.[28] In its density of reference to actual people and places *Sister Carrie* resembles a newspaper.

It is not only in subject matter and style that *Sister Carrie* can be called journalistic; Dreiser went further in his efforts to bring the newspaper into his novel. At several points in his manuscript he literally pasted in journalistic material, so that the manuscript of *Sister Carrie* resembles a collage. The most obvious example occurs in chapter 38 of the manuscript, when Hurstwood is job hunting in New York City. Dreiser clipped actual Help Wanted ads from the *New York Journal* and pasted them into his manu-

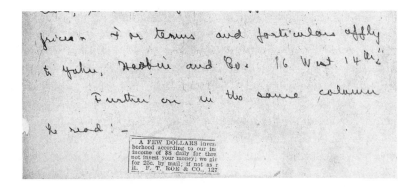

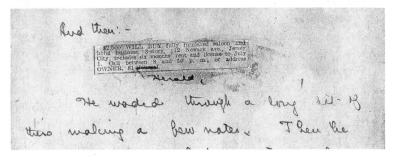

FIGURE 6.1 Manuscript pages from Dreiser's *Sister Carrie*, 1900. Rare Books and Manuscripts Division, The New York Public Library, Astor, Lenox and Tilden Foundation.

script. Studying the original manuscript, one has the eerie feeling of looking over Hurstwood's shoulder as he peruses the newspaper.

Dreiser performed a similar cut-and-paste operation in his initial description of traveling salesman Charles Drouet. An admirer of popular Chicago newspaper columnist George Ade, Dreiser was struck by Ade's column of October 7, 1899, which described the amatory techniques of the "masher." As he created the masher Drouet, Dreiser copied out portions of Ade's sketch and pasted them into his manuscript.[29] If Dreiser perhaps saw his copying as an homage to Ade, two reviewers of *Sister Carrie*'s first edition saw it as plagiarism.[30] Evidently stung by the charge, Dreiser altered the passage in the second (1907) edition, the only change he made.[31] It is somewhat surprising that Dreiser bothered to eliminate the few sentences taken from Ade, because *Sister Carrie* contains more blatant borrowings, notably in chapters 40 and 41, devoted to a Brooklyn streetcar strike.

Dreiser's account of the strike relies on two newspaper sources. In January 1895, when Dreiser was working as a reporter for the *New York World*, streetcar workers in Brooklyn walked off the job for what turned out to be a long and violent strike. Dreiser was not assigned to cover the strike, but he presumably read about it in the *World*. In *Sister Carrie* Hurstwood similarly reads about the strike in the *World*, and Dreiser copied headlines and other material from the newspaper into his manuscript (297–98, 313). In addition, Dreiser incorporated elements from articles he wrote for the *Toledo* (Ohio) *Blade* in 1894. Assigned to cover a Toledo streetcar strike, Dreiser rode on a nearly deserted car and applied for a job as a scab motorman—experiences he would draw on in his depiction of Hurstwood.[32]

Furthermore, in his chapters on the strike Dreiser emphasized the newspaper's dual status as referential guide to events and as self-contained narrative. As two of *Sister Carrie*'s most astute recent critics have observed, the newspaper plays as important a role for Hurstwood in his decline as the theater does for Carrie in her ascent.[33] Out of work after the saloon he managed in New York for three years has folded, Hurstwood only half-heartedly looks for employment. After days spent loafing in hotels, he returns in the evenings to the flat he shares with Carrie and buries himself in the newspapers. The newspapers serve Hurstwood as a narcotic, insulating him from the economically and socially chaotic city that he has come to fear. Each day Hurstwood buys the *World* and the *Sun*, the two premier examples of the new journalism in New York City during the early 1890s, papers filled with lively "human interest" articles cast in the fact-fiction discourse of the era. Hurstwood's difficulties seem to "vanish in the items he so well loved to read" (255); he maintains his daily dose of journalistic narcotic for nearly a year after becoming unemployed.

Finally, stung by Carrie's accusations, Hurstwood decides to apply for a job as a scab motorman in Brooklyn after he reads a notice in the *World*. In that moment he puts aside the newspaper as self-contained narrative and uses it as referential guide to the world outside his comfortable flat. It is as if Hurstwood decides to step into a newspaper article—and when he does so, he is literally struck by reality. Running a streetcar, deserted except for two police guards, along the streets of Brooklyn, Hurstwood is pelted first with curses, then, in ascending order of violence, with mud, rocks, fists, and a bullet. Grazed by a pistol shot, Hurstwood exclaims weakly, "George! this is too much for me," and walks off the job (313). He heads for home, back to his comfortable chair and his newspapers. He picks up the *World* and is soon engrossed in narratives about the strike.

In the strike episode Dreiser weaves a complex tapestry of autobiographical, journalistic, and fictional discourses. An invented character, based on a man who was covered in front-page newspaper articles and whom Dreiser knew personally, reads actual material from a newspaper for which Dreiser worked. He then experiences events that Dreiser had reported as a journalist, and finally he reads in the newspaper about the events he has just experienced. As the novel progresses, Hurstwood will undergo curiouser and curiouser journeys, at one point stepping through the looking glass into a text of Dreiser's journalism.

The text is "Curious Shifts of the Poor," an article by Dreiser originally published in *Demorest's* magazine in 1899.[34] Tracing the complicated textual history of this article is like entering a hall of mirrors, so frequent are the repetitions. The article had its origin in meteorological and economic reality: during the 1890s New York City suffered a series of severe winters. At the same time, New York, like the rest of the country, experienced the after-effects of the financial panic of 1893. The panic ushered in an economic depression, the worst the country had ever experienced, which lasted for several years. As a result of massive unemployment, the number of tramps in New York City increased enormously during the 1890s.

Dreiser's "Curious Shifts" documents tramp life in New York during the harsh winters of the 1890s. The article consists of four vignettes: a former soldier, identified only as "the Captain," stands on Broadway in the theater district collecting money that he uses to buy lodging house beds for any tramps who care to wait beside him; tramps line up to enter a free lunch mission conducted by the Sisters of Mercy; during a snow storm a crowd of men waits to enter a Bowery lodging house; and men line up at midnight outside Fleischman's restaurant, where anyone can receive a free loaf of bread.

Although Dreiser's article is based on actual scenes—three of the four vignettes contain verifiable details, such as the exact location of the charity—it is also mediated through other representations of New York City, notably works by Alfred Stieglitz and Stephen Crane. Ellen Moers has traced in detail Dreiser's borrowings from both artists.[35] His debt to Stieglitz is a general one; Stieglitz's photograph "Winter on Fifth Avenue," also known as "The Storm," served to establish the blizzard as a defining trope of urban experience in the 1890s. Dreiser's debt to Crane is more specific. One of his four vignettes, the description of men waiting to enter an unnamed Bowery lodging house, is closely based on Crane's 1894 sketch "The Men in the Storm." Although Dreiser copies only one sentence from Crane (Crane: "There was an absolute expression of hot dinners in the pace of the people." Dreiser: "There was supper in every hurrying pedestrian's face."), he borrows both his subject matter and its treatment from Crane's sketch.

Soon after publishing "Curious Shifts," a work of journalism based on other journalism, Dreiser incorporated his article in the text of *Sister Carrie*. With an admirable economy Dreiser used all four vignettes in chapters 45 and 47, which describe Hurstwood's downward slide into poverty and homelessness. For the former chapter Dreiser even used his *Demorest's* magazine title, "Curious Shifts of the Poor." Writing—or, rather, constructing—these chapters, Dreiser simply interleaved with the *Sister Carrie* manuscript the original manuscript pages of his *Demorest's* article. All he had to do was change verb tenses and identify Hurstwood as one of the previously unnamed men seeking charity.[36] With this deft inter-weaving of journalistic and novelistic texts, Hurstwood became a charac-ter in Dreiser's journalism, a trick later used in film by Woody Allen with the appearance of his character Zelig in newsreel footage. Thus Dreiser inserted one more journalistic fragment in *Sister Carrie*'s collage. In his first novel Dreiser, the newspaperman who had determined to become a Balzac of the front page, constructed a dense intertextual collage that draws readers' attention to his novel's newspaper origins. He was to repeat this tactic frequently in the years to come.

Jennie Gerhardt (1911), Dreiser's second novel, was, like *Sister Carrie*, inspired by a member of his family. Like *Carrie*, *Jennie Gerhardt* has links to the newspaper. In its tales of the scandalous private life of public figures *Jennie Gerhardt* follows the sensationalistic agenda of the new journalism of Dreiser's newspaper days. His next two published novels, *The Financier* (1912) and *The Titan* (1914), are almost entirely newspaper derived. These two novels about the ruthless capitalist Frank Cowperwood are based with extraordinary closeness on the career of Chicago millionaire Charles T. Yerkes (1837–1905). Dreiser did extensive newspaper research for the novels, and he gathered thousands of clippings and notes about Yerkes. As Robert Penn Warren observed, Cowperwood "is not a fictional creation based on Yerkes; he is, insofar as Dreiser could make him, the image of Yerkes."[37]

After his venture into autobiographical fiction in *The "Genius"* (1915), Dreiser returned to newspaper sources for *An American Tragedy* (1925), based on the 1906 Chester Gillette murder case. In many ways Dreiser fundamentally altered Gillette's character and motives. Yet at the same time Dreiser used a wealth of details from the original case that emphasize his novel's newspaper origins. And he took the collage technique of *Sister Carrie* to much greater lengths, using long passages of verbatim newspaper material in his novel. The published novel includes approximately thirty full pages of material taken directly from newspaper sources. Unsurprisingly, Dreiser was charged with "cold-blooded plagiarism"; the implication was that he lacked imagination.[38] However, the more than eight hundred pages of original prose in *An American Tragedy* seem more than enough to vindicate Dreiser's imagination; his thirty pages of transcribed material are not the result of a failure of inventiveness. Putting aside hostile critics' charges of plagiarism, we can more fruitfully ask why Dreiser kept so close to his newspaper sources.

The models for Clyde Griffiths and Roberta Alden of *An American Tragedy* were Chester Gillette and Grace "Billie" Brown. Gillette and Brown met in Cortland, New York, at a shirt factory owned by Gillette's uncle, where both were employed. A romance ensued and Brown became pregnant. Gillette resisted her pleas that they marry. Instead, on July 11, 1906, Gillette took Brown out in a rowboat on Big Moose, a remote lake in the Adirondacks. There, he beat her unconscious with a tennis racket, overturned the boat, and swam to shore. Brown's body was soon recovered, and Gillette immediately became a suspect. Authorities found Brown's beseeching letters to Gillette in his room and used them against him at his trial. He was convicted of murder and was executed in the electric chair on March 30, 1908.[39]

A recent study of the sources of *An American Tragedy* concludes that Dreiser "borrowed the details of the Gillette murder to provide realism for his story, but he created the whole apparatus of motivation in *An American Tragedy*."[40] However, Dreiser's use of the Gillette case goes far beyond efforts to "provide realism." Rather, Dreiser adheres with an obsessive closeness to the case's minute details.[41] Clyde Griffiths's name obviously mimics Chester Gillette's; Roberta Alden's nicknames of "Bert" and "Bobbie" echo Grace Brown's "Billie"; the Big Bittern Lake where Roberta dies recalls the Gillette case's Big Moose Lake. Dreiser went beyond such mimicry, adding details unaltered from the Gillette case; for example, both Gillette and Clyde Griffiths assumed the alias Carl Graham at one point. And although Clyde strikes Roberta in the rowboat with a camera, not a tennis racket, Dreiser nevertheless mentions that Clyde has a tennis racket strapped to his luggage, as if wishing, even when departing from his source material, to remind readers of it.

The dense network of allusions to the Gillette case in *An American Tragedy* has little to do with literary realism; other names and details would have worked as well in establishing verisimilitude. Rather, Dreiser draws our attention to his novel's dependence upon newspaper-reported events. Dreiser's debt to the newspaper is even more obvious in the thirty pages of transcribed material, almost all of it taken from the pages of the *New York World*. Most of Dreiser's transcriptions occur in book 3 of *An American Tragedy*, the section detailing Clyde's trial. The prosecutor's and defense lawyer's statements to the jury, the examination and cross-examination of Clyde, the judge's instructions to jurors—all are based closely on the *World*'s extensive coverage of the case. Furthermore, Dreiser quotes liberally from Grace Brown's lengthy letters to Gillette, which were read in court, summarized in the *World*, and published in pamphlet form.

Most critics who have explored Dreiser's use of his newspaper sources in *An American Tragedy* emphasize the transformations he made and conclude by celebrating his originality.[42] The originality of *An American Tragedy* is indisputable. However, the novel's unoriginality is just as striking. Constantly, whether through small details of names and objects or through lengthy verbatim borrowings, Dreiser reminds readers of his novel's newspaper origins. Moreover, one of his relatively few major departures from the facts of the Gillette case serves to emphasize the importance of the newspaper in Dreiser's fictional practice and its centrality in American culture.

Dreiser locates the genesis of Clyde's murder plot in an article that Clyde reads in the newspaper. Skimming the *Albany Times-Union*, an actual newspaper, Clyde comes across a Dreiser-invented story: an account of a presumed double drowning at Pass Lake in the Adirondacks. According to the article Clyde reads, a man and a woman took a rowboat out on the lake and were not seen again. The rowboat was found floating upside down; the man's and woman's hats were nearby. The woman's body was recovered, but searchers were unable to find the man's body in the thirty-foot-deep lake. Neither the man nor the woman could be identified. After reading this article, Clyde for the first time considers solving his dilemma by murdering Roberta, and in the rest of book 2 he sets out to reproduce, with great fidelity, this newspaper article. He searches out a remote, deep Adirondacks lake, uses aliases to conceal his and Roberta's identities, and buys a straw hat that he can leave floating on the water.

In making Clyde "author" his crime based on a newspaper article, Dreiser draws an uncanny parallel between himself and his fictional creation. Both Theodore Dreiser and Clyde Griffiths are inspired by a newspaper article to invent a crime. But as if to emphasize his authorial control, Dreiser depicts Clyde as an inept author. Clyde imagines that his actions on Big Bittern Lake will be read as an accident like the one at Pass Lake. However, virtually from the moment the overturned rowboat and Roberta's body are discovered, everyone involved in the Big Bittern case suspects that she has been murdered, and they quickly establish her identity and arrest Clyde. Clyde intends to write an imitation of the Pass Lake newspaper story, but he swiftly passes from being the author of an event to being the subject of others' stories. In book 3 of *An American Tragedy*, the sequel to Roberta's drowning, Clyde Griffiths virtually loses his identity, becoming a character in stories authored by journalists or lawyers and a mouthpiece for others' narratives.

Book 3 opens with the county coroner receiving a telephone call about a drowning at Big Bittern Lake. Almost immediately, before heading off to the scene of the drowning, the coroner orders his assistant to contact the two local newspapers. From this point on Clyde will be the subject of numerous newspaper stories. Reporters from around the nation come to cover his trial, and they widely disseminate the district attorney's damning portrait of Clyde as a calculating murderer. Even when Clyde is called as a witness in his defense, the story he tells on the stand is no more accurate than the accusatory narratives printed in the newspapers. Clyde's attorneys have determined that what he tells them about Roberta's death is too implausible to convince a jury, and they script a new narrative for him, a self-exculpatory tale that Clyde delivers unconvincingly.

Convicted and sentenced to the electric chair, Clyde makes one final public statement to the newspapers, at the suggestion of the Reverend Duncan McMillan, a vigorous young clergyman who has become Clyde's spiritual adviser. Dreiser prints Clyde's entire statement. It begins, "In the shadow of the Valley of Death, it is my desire to do everything that would remove any doubt as to my having found Jesus Christ, the personal Savior and unfailing friend. My one regret at this time is that I have not given Him the preëminence in my life while I had the opportunity to work for Him."[43] After writing this statement, Clyde is "not a little impressed" by its difference from anything he has said before. A careful follower of the Chester Gillette case would be not a little impressed by its similarity to Gillette's final statement; Dreiser copied verbatim Gillette's words as reported in the *World*.[44] Clyde's last statement serves as a final example of Dreiser's collage technique and as one more reminder of his novel's newspaper origins.

The statement also serves as a critique of journalistic and religious discourses. For as soon as the Reverend McMillan pockets the statement, Clyde begins to doubt its truth. Questions flicker through his mind: "Was he truly saved? . . . Could he rely on God with that absolute security which he had just announced now characterized him? Could he?" (868). Clyde's final statement emphasizes Dreiser's debt to his newspaper sources. At the same time, Clyde's reactions to his words suggest that the newspaper text is at best inadequate, at worst fundamentally misleading.

An American Tragedy reveals Dreiser to be torn between the two positions expressed in his autobiographical writings. Clyde's final statement, like the glibly denunciatory newspaper articles that appear throughout his trial, suggests that journalism provides an inadequate false discourse in contrast to the truth of Dreiser's fictional discourse—the position Dreiser took in his late essay, "Lessons I Learned from an Old Man." Yet the novel also supports Dreiser's earlier statements about newspapers as a crucial source for fiction: "They are vital, dramatic, true presentations of the life that is being lived today," he had said in 1911. In *An American Tragedy* Dreiser denounces newspapers and asserts his fiction's superiority. Yet at the same time he draws our attention to his novel's dependence on newspaper sources, inscribing the newspaper-reported details and language of the Chester Gillette case in his work. Like *Sister Carrie*, *An American Tragedy* insists on the newspaper's central role in its creation.

Ernest Hemingway, already determined to be a writer by the time he graduated from high school in 1917, followed the career pattern set two decades earlier by Stephen Crane and other celebrity journalists of the 1890s: he rejected college in favor of newspaper work. Shortly after his eighteenth birthday Hemingway became a reporter for the *Kansas City Star*, which he proudly regarded as "the best paper in the U.S."[45] If the young reporter was indulging in hyperbole, still the *Kansas City Star* was one of the most widely respected newspapers in the Midwest, distinguished since its creation in 1880 for its conservative layout and lively writing.[46] The paper's editors promoted their version of good prose through the *Star*'s style sheet. After its terse opening ("Use short sentences. Use short first paragraphs. Use vigorous English. Be positive, not negative.") the style sheet went on to advise, "Avoid the use of adjectives, especially such extravagant ones as *splendid, gorgeous, grand, magnificent*, etc."[47] The style sheet was a virtual declaration of war on Victorian diction. And, as countless critics have observed since, the *Star*'s rules can also serve nicely as a description of the modernist prose pioneered by Ernest Hemingway.

Hemingway gave the critics their lead when, on a visit to Kansas City in 1940, he began reminiscing to a reporter about the *Star*'s style sheet. "Those were the best rules I ever learned for the business of writing," Hemingway told the reporter. "I've never forgotten them. No man with any talent, who feels and writes truly about the thing he is trying to say, can fail to write well if he abides with them."[48] Taking Hemingway at his word, a Yale graduate student named Charles Fenton set out ten years later to revolutionize Hemingway criticism by overturning the conventional wisdom that Hemingway's style was, as Fenton put it, "one part Pound, two parts Gertrude Stein."[49] The crucial influence on Hemingway's style, Fenton argued in his dissertation, was the apprenticeship in journalism. In 1954 Fenton published his revised dissertation as *The Apprenticeship of Ernest Hemingway*. If Fenton's book did not completely turn critics' attention away from Pound's and Stein's influence on Hemingway, still it had an enormous effect on Hemingway criticism. Since the publication of Fenton's book virtually every discussion of Hemingway's style has made a nod toward the influence of his newspaper work, and several major analyses of his journalism have appeared.[50]

Fenton's revisionist view became so widely accepted that it was only a matter of time until a new revisionist argument appeared to challenge Fenton. It came in 1990, with Ronald Weber's *Hemingway's Art of Nonfiction*. Weber argued that Fenton had overestimated journalism's influence on Hemingway's fictional style, and in support of his argument he collected a barrage of Hemingway statements to counter the 1940 tribute to the *Kansas City Star* style sheet. Weber noted that Hemingway's complaints about journalism's negative influence on a fiction writer began early in his career: "This goddamn newspaper stuff is gradually ruining me," Hemingway wrote to Sherwood Anderson in 1922, before he had published a word of fiction.[51] The complaints continued. In 1934 he told an aspiring writer, "Forget about newspaper work. Do anything else to make a living, but not that. Newspaper work is the antithesis of writing and it keeps writers pooped out so they can't write." When the acolyte protested, "But you used to be a newspaper man and you became a writer," Hemingway replied, "In spite of it."[52] Weber titles his chapter on Hemingway's newspaper work "In Spite of It."

Weber's argument for the insignificance of Hemingway's newspaper work relies largely on the derogatory statements about journalism that Hemingway made throughout his career. Fenton and other critics who regard the journalism as an important influence cite Hemingway's many tributes to his newspaper experience. But any effort to use Hemingway's statements about journalism to evaluate its significance in his career and work is doomed to failure, because his statements are unabashedly contradictory. Reversing the approach I used to analyze Theodore Dreiser, in the remainder of this chapter I ignore Hemingway's comments about journalism in favor of an examination of the journalism and fiction he wrote early in his career, between his debut on the *Kansas City Star* in 1917 and the publication of *In Our Time* in 1925. That examination reveals that although journalism played an important role in Ernest Hemingway's development as a writer, its role was more complex than has conventionally been argued.

~

Because the *Kansas City Star* carried no bylines, it is difficult to identify the stories written by Hemingway during his six-month stint on the newspaper from October 1917 to April 1918. Matthew Bruccoli located a dozen articles that can with certainty be attributed to Hemingway, but these articles are generally uncharacteristic of Hemingway's work for the *Star*. Identified as Hemingway's because he thought enough of them to send them to his parents or because colleagues on the paper remembered their distinctive subject matter and treatment, most articles collected by Bruccoli in *Ernest Hemingway, Cub Reporter* are features rather than news stories.[53]

One can get a better sense of Hemingway's standard output on the *Star* from his recollection of his daily beat—he said he covered the 15th Street police station, Union Station, and General Hospital—and from the single *Kansas City Star* assignment sheet that survives from the period of Hemingway's tenure.[54] The sheet for January 3, 1918, lists seven assignments for the eighteen-year-old Hemingway: undertakers, hospitals, General Hospital, Union Station, "Dr. Tiffany—St Luke's," a shooting incident, and meningitis cases.[55] Although it is difficult to be sure which articles resulted from these assignments, it seems fairly certain that the following front-page story from that afternoon's *Star* is by Hemingway. It reads in its entirety: "Dr. Flavel B. Tiffany is not expected to live through the day. Since being taken to St. Luke's Hospital last Friday his condition has gradually grown worse."[56] Each day's *Star* contained dozens of similar short items; Hemingway presumably ground out hundreds of them during his time there. A young man of enormous energy, he boasted to his father that he was averaging a full column a day of material for the *Star*, given the newspaper's small type and long columns, that was an impressive output.[57]

The brevity encouraged on the *Star* may well have shaped the mature Hemingway's famously terse style. However, reading through the *Star* during the months Hemingway wrote for the paper, one finds that relatively few stories were as dry as Hemingway's notice of Dr. Tiffany's condition. The *Star* had a reputation for entertaining as well as informing readers, and even relatively straightforward news stories frequently used colorful language that appealed to readers' humor or sentiment. For example, a *Star* business-news article on the closing of a local brewery, published soon after Hemingway joined the staff, began, "Booze is due to lose another friend in Kansas City within the month when the Rochester Brewing Company . . . closes its doors."[58] Hemingway used similarly colorful language to enliven a series of armed forces recruiting stories that he was assigned to write. An article on the army's new tank corps calls this branch of the service "thrilling work" and contains a heavily romanticized description of these "great steel monsters" in action.[59]

The longest of the articles identified as Hemingway's is a feature that appeared in the *Star*'s Sunday edition. Titled "At the End of the Ambulance Run," the article contains a series of short, disconnected vignettes describing various hospital emergency room scenes.[60] Critics have argued that these vignettes look forward to the brief "chapters" that make up the 1924 Paris edition of *in our time* and that are interleafed with the short stories of the 1925 *In Our Time*.[61] However, "At the End of the Ambulance Run" can equally well be described as looking backward—to the fact-fiction discourse of 1890s journalism and to the formulaic commercial fiction that Hemingway initially took as his model.

"At the End of the Ambulance Run" appeared in the third of the Sunday *Star*'s three sections, a section filled with serialized novels, fashion and society notes, a children's page, and illustrated poems. The article's physical appearance—it has a hand-drawn headline and accompanying captioned illustrations—links it to the serialized fiction in the same section rather than to the unillustrated, typographically sober articles on the front page. With its almost complete avoidance of proper nouns and its storytelling narrative conventions, "At the End of the Ambulance Run" could fit easily into the fact-fiction discourse of 1890s Sunday newspapers, where almost all of Stephen Crane's work appeared. However, Hemingway's work is suffused with a sentimentality that Crane rigorously avoided. For example, Hemingway's first vignette concludes,

> It was merely one of the many cases that come to the city dispensary from night to night—and from day to day for that matter; but the night shift, perhaps, has a wider range of the life and death tragedy—and even comedy, of the city. When "George" comes in on the soiled, bloody stretcher and the rags are stripped off and his naked, broken body lies on the white table in the glare of the surgeon's light, and he dangles on a little thread of life, while the physicians struggle grimly, it is all in the night's work, whether the thread snaps or whether it holds so that George can fight on and work and pay.

The hackneyed metaphor of the "thread of life" recalls Victorian mourning sentiments; it also anticipates the clichés that fill the unpublished short stories Hemingway wrote one year later when, home from World War I, he attempted to sell formulaic stories to the *Saturday Evening Post*.[62]

Back in Kansas City twenty-two years after he had left the *Star*, reminiscing to a young reporter from the paper, Hemingway generously praised the *Star* and extolled the importance of the lessons he learned there. However, it is clear that the *Star*'s style sheet did not by itself shape Hemingway's prose style. If it had, Hemingway's first short stories, written in 1919 after his work on the *Star*, could not be so genuinely dreadful. It is likely that the *Star*'s style sheet had some delayed influence on Hemingway's later fiction, but the *Star*'s influences were negative as well as positive. The newspaper encouraged a terse style, but it also permitted sentimentality of the sort Dreiser had used in his 1890s journalism. Hemingway's next regular newspaper experience, which began in 1920 and lasted almost four years, was similarly double edged. However, during the course of it Hemingway turned himself from a conventional journalist and writer of third-rate formula fiction into America's most influential modern prose writer.

Early in 1920, a year after he had returned from his World War I experience in Italy, Ernest Hemingway found himself in Toronto in the improbable role of nanny to the frail teenage son of a wealthy Toronto couple. The position, unsurprisingly, did not last long, but while he was in Toronto Hemingway managed to sign on as a freelance contributor to the *Toronto Star Weekly*. The *Star Weekly*, the Saturday supplement to the *Toronto Daily Star*, was a general interest magazine delivered by mail to households across Canada and the northern United States, a potpourri of news, feature articles, fiction, and humor. Hemingway was free to contribute virtually anything he pleased to the magazine. The discursive freedom Hemingway enjoyed on the *Star Weekly* was equivalent to that which Stephen Crane experienced in his journalism. Like 1890s Sunday newspapers, the *Star Weekly* was the site of a fact-fiction discourse; the qualities of verifiability, impersonality, and objectivity that we associate with newspaper journalism today had little importance in the *Star Weekly*. The *Star Weekly* ignored distinctions between fiction and nonfiction in favor of an emphasis on lively, entertaining writing.[63]

Hemingway began by providing the *Star Weekly* with humorous articles. Infatuated with Ring Lardner, he had published Lardner imitations in his high school newspaper and in his Italian Red Cross ambulance unit's newsletter in 1918. ("Well Al we are here in this old Italy and now that I am here I am not going to leave it. Not at all if any. And that is no New Years revolution Al but the truth," the latter began.[64]) A year and a half later he was still writing Lardner-derived humor. One of his first articles for the *Star Weekly* was a Crane-like "experiment": Hemingway joined the down-and-out men of Toronto who got free shaves at a barber college. But whereas Crane used his experiments as explorations in class distinctions and individual consciousness, Hemingway turned his experiment into a purely—and wonderfully successful—humorous sketch. He depicts his terror as he subjects himself to the noticeably inept hands of a beginning barber armed with a straight razor:

Just then I noticed that my barber had his left hand bandaged.
"How did you do that?" I asked.

"Darn near sliced my thumb off with the razor this morning," he replied amiably.[65]

The twenty-year-old writer's "Taking a Chance for a Free Shave" is perhaps the funniest thing Hemingway ever wrote, although he published a number of other humorous sketches during his four years on the *Star Weekly*. Of the three dozen features he published in the *Star Weekly* during his initial two years as a freelancer, nearly half are humorous pieces. Of the remainder, most give the "true gen"—Hemingway's phrase for insider's knowledge—on fishing, boxing, or crime. These invariably competent and frequently clever articles reveal Hemingway's lifelong interests in the outdoors, violence, and violent sports, but they give little indication of the mature Hemingway style. That style would evolve with surprising rapidity during the early months of 1922, when the twenty-two-year-old Hemingway moved to Paris with his new wife, Hadley Richardson, armed with letters of introduction to Ezra Pound and Gertrude Stein.

Newspaper work made it possible for Hemingway to go to Paris. He had arranged with the *Toronto Star* to serve as European correspondent for both the daily and weekly editions. Because the *Star* took its European spot news from the wire services, Hemingway was expected to send features on European life, signed "letters" similar to those Henry James and Stephen Crane wrote as European correspondents for U.S. newspapers. Initially, Hemingway sent to the *Star* the lightweight feature articles one would expect of a new arrival in Paris. His first two articles from Europe are headlined, "Tourists Are Scarce at the Swiss Resorts" and "A Canadian with One Thousand a Year Can Live Very Comfortably and Enjoyably in Paris." However, within a few weeks he was sending the *Star* "true gen" articles that contrast the tourist's superficial view of Paris with the writer's insider knowledge. For example:

[The tourist] wants to see the nightlife of Paris and what he does see is a special performance by a number of bored but well-paid people of a drama that has run many thousands of nights and is entitled "Fooling the Tourist." While he is buying champagne and listening to a jazz band, around the corner somewhere there is a little Bal Musette where the apaches, the people he thinks he is seeing, hang out with their girls, sit at long benches in the little smoky room, and dance to the music of a man with an accordion who keeps time with the stamping of his boots.[66]

Only three months after completing a string of similar "true gen" articles on Paris, Hemingway published an extraordinary article that dispenses with both the tourist's perspective and satire of tourists. Instead, Hemingway produced an article on fishing that can stand alongside his 1925 masterpiece, "Big Two-Hearted River."

The twenty-two-year-old Hemingway published "There Are Great Fish in the Rhône Canal" in the *Toronto Daily Star* of June 10, 1922. Two years earlier, soon after he began writing for the *Toronto Star*, he had published his first fishing article. The earlier article, "Are You All Set for the Trout?" is a how-to piece enlivened with cutely humorous touches. "I can't write any more just now," it concludes. "I'm going trout fishing."[67] In contrast, "The Rhône Canal" is a lyrical description of one day's fishing, filled with the sensuous details that mark the mature Hemingway style. Here are the opening paragraphs:

> In the afternoon a breeze blows up the Rhone valley from Lake Geneva. Then you fish upstream with the breeze at your back, the sun on the back of your neck, the tall white mountains on both sides of the green valley and the fly dropping very fine and far off on the surface and under the edge of the banks of the little stream, called the Rhone canal, that is barely a yard wide, and flows swiftly and still.
>
> Once I caught a trout that way. He must have been surprised at the strange fly and probably struck from bravado, but the hook set and he jumped into the air twice and zigged nobly back and forth and towards every patch of weed at the current bottom until I slid him up the side of the bank.
>
> He was such a fine trout that I had to keep unwrapping him to take a look and finally the day got so hot that I sat under a pine tree on the bank of the stream and unwrapped the trout entirely and ate a paper-bag full of cherries I had and read the trout-dampened *Daily Mail*. It was a hot day, but I could look out across the green, slow valley past the line of trees that marked the course of the Rhone and watch a waterfall coming down the brown face of the mountain. The fall came out of a glacier that reached down toward a little town with four gray houses and three gray churches that was planted on the side of the mountain and looked solid, the waterfall, that is, until you saw it was moving. Then it looked cool and flickering, and I wondered who lived in the four houses and went to the three churches with the sharp stone spires.[68]

This beautifully evocative passage shares the features of Hemingway's fully developed mature prose style, soon to be displayed in *In Our Time* (1925) and *The Sun Also Rises* (1926): a simple vocabulary, restrained use of adjectives, frequent repetition, and a syntax marked by compound phrases and clauses strung together with "and." Most of all, the passage reveals Hemingway's gift for sensuous details, his emphasis not only on sight but on the feel of breeze and sun, the touch of a trout-dampened newspaper, the taste of cherries.

In its simple, repetitive language "Rhône Canal" recalls the prose of Sherwood Anderson, whom Hemingway had met in Chicago the previous year, and Gertrude Stein, whom he met in Paris. She and Anderson together formed Hemingway, Stein claimed, and their examples clearly had much to do with Hemingway's transformation in the two-year period between his humorous how-to article on trout fishing of 1920 and his piece on the Rhône canal.[69] However, the critics who have emphasized the importance of Hemingway's training on the *Kansas City Star* would draw our attention to the closeness with which the article follows the rules of the *Star*'s style sheet, such as "Avoid the use of adjectives, especially . . . extravagant ones." It is impossible to determine if the mature Hemingway style owes more to Anderson, Stein, or the *Kansas City Star*. However, it is important to note that this style first received publication in a daily newspaper. A year before Hemingway published his first fiction, he developed his distinctive prose style in pieces he wrote for the *Toronto Star*.[70] Later in his career, concerned about his stature as a fiction writer, Hemingway claimed that his "newspaper stuff" had "nothing to do with the other writing which is entirely apart and starts with the first IN OUR TIME."[71] Creating his own genesis myth, Hemingway wanted to locate his origins in the garden of avant-garde Paris. But "The Rhône Canal" and other pieces of equal distinction show that Hemingway's mature writing style was forged in the undistinguished crucible of a Canadian newspaper.

Hemingway continued writing for the *Toronto Star* for a year and a half after his breakthrough feature articles of 1922. Some of the one hundred articles he wrote during this period are sensually evocative pieces as fine as "The Rhône Canal"; some are hurriedly produced hack work; most are news articles resulting from assignments he was given in Switzerland, Germany, and Turkey. Hemingway's output for the *Star* was prodigious during these eighteen months, but it ceased entirely early in 1924, when he returned to Paris with his wife and newborn son after a brief and unhappy interlude in Toronto. Hemingway quit the *Star* in order to devote himself to his other writing; his initial task was to oversee the publication in Paris of his first book of fiction, *in our time* (1924).

Yet is it accurate to label *in our time* fiction? That label has become conventional among Hemingway critics, but the book stubbornly resists facile generic classification. *in our time* lacks the straightforward declaration of contents provided by Hemingway's other Parisian avant-garde publication, helpfully titled *Three Stories and Ten Poems* (1923). The only sign of *in our time*'s genre is the statement on an endpaper that it is part of a series of "contemporary English prose." The book consists of eighteen extremely brief chapters, most of them fewer than two hundred words, each isolated in a sea of white space on an oversized page. Rearranged and slightly revised, the *in our time* chapters reappeared as the "interchapters" separating the stories of *In Our Time* (1925), Hemingway's first American publication.

Shelley Fisher Fishkin has described the *in our time* chapters as "apparently documentary vignettes."[72] The uncertainty of the description is apt. The chapters appear to be documentary in their frequent references to actual people and places. Twelve of the book's eighteen chapters deal with either World War I or bullfighting, and these are peppered with the names of famous battles (the Champagne, Mons, Fossalta) and bullfighters (Villalta, Maera). Three treat events resulting from the Greco-Turkish conflict of 1920–22, and another two feature violent episodes set in the United States, one involving a well-known Chicago gangster. In their topicality and their frequent references to actual public figures the *in our time* chapters deliberately foster uncertainty about their generic status. Are they factual or fictional? Documentary or short story? Like Dreiser's *An American Tragedy*, *in our time* blends the factual and the invented, insisting on its journalistic origins.

The World War I and bullfighting chapters treat events that might have been reported in a newspaper, but many are narrated in a distinctive first-person voice that links them to oral storytelling tradition as much as to any written genre. The book's final chapter, about the Greek king, had its origins in a feature article Hemingway published in the *Toronto Star*, but the chapter's first-person narration gives it an anecdotal rather than journalistic flavor.[73] However, four chapters, taken directly from newspaper accounts, retain third-person narration and resemble, as Charles Fenton pointed out, the brief "items" with which the *Kansas City Star* filled its pages.[74]

One chapter comes directly from the pages of the *Star*. Chapter 9 describes two Hungarians who rob a cigar store and are shot by a police officer "from the Fifteenth Street police station." The chapter includes dialogue that could never have been printed in a newspaper, even if a reporter had been present to hear it: "Hell Jimmy, you oughtn't to have done it," the policeman's partner tells him. "There's liable to be a hell of a lot of trouble." The cop replies coolly, "They're wops ain't they? Who the hell is going to make any trouble?"[75] This chilling exchange is Hemingway's invention, but the episode had its origins in an incident reported in the *Kansas City Star* on November 19, 1917, soon after Hemingway began working on the paper.[76] Although we cannot be certain that Hemingway wrote the report in the *Star* of two men shot by police after robbing a cigar store, we know that the Fifteenth Street police station was part of his beat. And as Fenton pointed out, Hemingway seems to emphasize his text's journalistic origins by assiduously following the *Star*'s style sheet in his spelling and capitalization of the chapter's Kansas City place names.[77]

Hemingway took another *in our time* chapter from an event reported in Chicago newspapers on April 15, 1921, when he was living in the city. Chapter 17, which begins, "They hanged Sam Cardinella at six o'clock in the morning in the corridor of the county jail" (28), describes the execution of an actual gangster, imaginatively embroidering the accounts that Hemingway read in Chicago newspapers.[78] Hemingway took from the newspapers the image of Cardinella's physical helplessness at his execution; the prisoner had to be carried to the scaffold. However, as in the chapter on the Hungarian robbers, Hemingway added details unprintable in a newspaper of the time, such as having Cardinella lose control of his bowels as the guards place the hood over his head.

Hemingway followed the same procedure of adding to newspaper articles in his chapter 6 account of another execution. "They shot the six cabinet ministers at half-past six in the morning against the wall of a hospital," the piece begins (14). Hemingway's chapter derives from a newspaper article on the execution of six Greek ministers following the debacle of the Greek army's defeat by Turkish troops.[79] Both chapter 6 and the Sam Cardinella chapter combine journalistic specificity (the setting of a hospital or a county jail at a precise time) with generalizing vagueness (the chapters do not mention Greece or Chicago).

The brief, violent episodes from Europe and the United States described in these *in our time* chapters combine events made familiar in newspaper pages with details unreportable in the journalism of the era. However, one of the book's most powerful vignettes achieves its effect largely through omitting details reported in the newspaper. Chapter 3, which describes a procession of refugees, is closely adapted from one of Hemingway's *Toronto Star* articles. In transforming the piece from newspaper article to *in our time* chapter, Hemingway cut an already terse cabled dispatch by almost two-thirds.

Hemingway's original dispatch resulted from a *Toronto Star* assignment to cover the final weeks of the Greco-Turkish conflict of 1920–22. The sporadic warfare of those years represented an extension of the battles between Greece and Turkey that Stephen Crane had witnessed in 1897, although by 1922 the fighting had shifted eastward to Anatolia and Thrace.[80] Three weeks after he arrived in Constantinople in the fall of 1922 Hemingway witnessed the evacuation from eastern Thrace of refugees fleeing the approaching Turkish army. The misery of the rain-soaked civilians affected Hemingway deeply, and he covered the exodus in two articles for the *Star*, one a brief cable that appeared on October 20 and the other a long mailed feature published a month later. The first three paragraphs of the five-paragraph cable read as follows:

Adrianople.—In a never-ending, staggering march, the Christian population of Eastern Thrace is jamming the roads toward Macedonia. The main column crossing the Maritza River at Adrianople is twenty miles long. Twenty miles of carts drawn by cows, bullocks and muddy-flanked water buffalo, with exhausted, staggering men, women and children, blankets over their heads, walking blindly along in the rain beside their worldly goods.

This main stream is being swelled from the back country. They don't know where they are going. They left their farms, villages and ripe, brown fields and joined the main stream of refugees when they heard the Turk was coming. Now they can only keep their places in the ghastly procession while mud-splashed Greek cavalry herd them along like cowpunchers driving steers.

It is a silent procession. Nobody even grunts. It is all they can do to keep moving. Their brilliant peasant costumes are soaked and draggled. Chickens dangle by their feet from the carts. Calves nuzzle at the draught cattle wherever a jam halts the stream. An old man marches under a young pig, a scythe and a gun, with a chicken tied to his scythe.

A husband spreads a blanket over a woman in labor in one of the carts to keep off the driving rain. She is the only person making a sound. Her little daughter looks at her in horror and begins to cry. And the procession keeps moving.[81]

For the *in our time* chapter Hemingway condensed his 343-word cable to a single brief paragraph:

Minarets stuck up in the rain out of Adrianople across the mud flats. The carts were jammed for thirty miles along the Karagatch road. Water buffalo and cattle were hauling carts through the mud. No end and no beginning. Just carts loaded with everything they owned. The old men and women, soaked through, walked along keeping the cattle moving. The Maritza was running yellow almost up to the bridge. Carts were jammed solid on the bridge with camels bobbing along through them. Greek cavalry herded along the procession. Women and kids were in the carts, crouched with mattresses, mirrors, sewing machines, bundles. There was a woman having a kid with a young girl holding a blanket over her and crying. Scared sick looking at it. It rained all through the evacuation. (11)

Charles Fenton devotes more than six pages to analyzing Hemingway's transformation of his newspaper article into one of the most powerful paragraphs he ever published.[82] Following Fenton, several other critics have also written lengthy explications of these two passages, exploring how Hemingway used his "aesthetic theory of omission" to turn a well-written newspaper article into a dazzling sketch.[83] Without once again repeating those explications, I can note that the *in our time* chapter could be described as more journalistic than the journalism—that is, it is terser, more impersonal, seemingly more "objective."[84] The original dispatch had ended with two paragraphs of commentary on the problems of relief work, concluding, "Nearly half a million refugees are in Macedonia now. How they are to be fed nobody knows, but in the next month all the Christian world will hear the cry: 'Come over into Macedonia and help us!' "[85] The *in our time* chapter rigorously avoids this sort of analysis and appeal for sympathy. The seemingly dry factuality of Hemingway's early work led one of the few reviewers of his Parisian publications to link his writing to journalism. "What Mr. Hemingway has added" to his stories, an anonymous reviewer for the *Kansas City Star* wrote in 1924, "is a certain superior objectivity. He has taken hold of the best quality that modern journalism has, and he has carried [journalistic objectivity] forward to a new point."[86] Writing at the commencement of Ernest Hemingway's career, the *Star*'s reviewer was the first critic to link Hemingway's innovative prose style to the objective prose of modern journalism.

Hemingway provided critics with reasons to search for the roots of his work in journalistic prose. Shortly after returning from Turkey, Hemingway showed his *Toronto Star* dispatch on the refugees at Adrianople to Lincoln Steffens. Steffens, recalling the event in his *Autobiography*, wrote that he had been impressed by the dispatch's "vivid, detailed picture of . . . that miserable stream of hungry, frightened, uprooted people," and he told Hemingway that he could envision the scene. "No," Hemingway corrected him, "read the cabelese, only the cabelese. Isn't it a great language?"[87] Charged by the word for cables, newspaper correspondents had to write their spot news reports in extremely taut prose. Critics have suggested that the influence of "cabelese," combined with the dicta of the *Kansas City Star* style sheet, significantly shaped the mature Hemingway style. John Dos Passos wittily and acutely characterized Hemingway's style as a combination of "cablese and the King James Bible."[88] The *in our time* chapter on the refugees at Adrianople serves to illustrate how Hemingway's art can be even more telegraphic in its extreme terseness than were his journalistic telegrams.

With its prose a heightened version of newspaper style and its subject matter drawn from recent events and actual newspaper stories, *in our time* foregrounds its connections to journalism. Bill Bird, the book's publisher, was struck by its journalistic qualities, and he determined to highlight those qualities in his design for the book. His original concept was to frame each of the book's eighteen chapters in a border of newsprint; when that idea proved infeasible, Bird designed a collage of newspaper clippings as a cover.[89] The articles on *in our time*'s cover—which deal with war, crime, and bullfighting, among other topics—accurately reflect the book's frequently journalistic subject matter. At the same time, they suggest Hemingway's partly newspaper-derived style. Within two years, after the publication of *In Our Time* (1925) and *The Sun Also Rises* (1926), the Hemingway subject matter and style would be internationally acclaimed, and his fiction widely imitated.

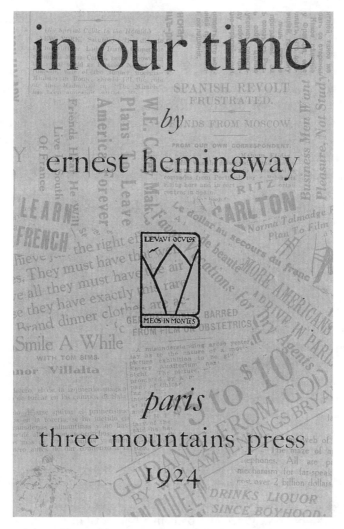

FIGURE 6.2 Cover of Hemingway's *in our time*, 1924. Princeton University Library.

What role did the newspaper play in the making of that fiction? Hemingway's statements are contradictory, and critics are divided. However, it seems possible to make a few assertions: Hemingway's mature style has a strong resemblance to the style encouraged on the *Kansas City Star*, even if that newspaper was not as dryly objective as has generally been assumed; like Stephen Crane, Hemingway used the discursive freedom available to him as a newspaper feature writer to develop a distinctive prose style; like Theodore Dreiser's novels, Hemingway's *in our time* draws attention to its newspaper origins, offering densely intertextual collages that combine journalism and fiction. Moreover, like Crane and Dreiser, Hemingway continued to write journalism throughout his career, serving as a correspondent in the Spanish Civil War and World War II, writing a column for *Esquire* magazine, and reporting on bullfighting for *Life*.

Hemingway frequently acknowledged the benefits of his apprenticeship in journalism, but he generally added a caveat, as in his statement that newspaper work is valuable to a writer "up until the point that it forcibly begins to destroy your memory. A writer must leave it before that point. But he will always have scars from it."[90] Stephen Crane and Theodore Dreiser both made similar statements. Ronald Weber has used these and other writers' warnings against journalism to argue that American writers' experience in newspaper work had no influence on modern American literature, that journalism served principally as an antitype against which writers reacted.[91] But, to quote D. H. Lawrence again, one must trust the tale, not the teller.[92] Such modern masterpieces as "The Open Boat," *An American Tragedy*, and *in our time* all draw readers' attentions to their journalistic origins.

In addition, Crane's, Dreiser's, and Hemingway's careers as newspaper reporters-turned-novelists have influenced the career choices of countless young men and women. By the time Ernest Hemingway joined the staff of the *Kansas City Star* in 1917, just two decades after the publication of *The Red Badge of Courage* made Stephen Crane the idol of newspaper offices across the United States, virtually every reporter in the *Star* newsroom was secretly working on a novel.[93] The myth of the reporter-artist continues today. After former *Albany Times-Union* reporter William Kennedy won the Pulitzer prize for his novel *Ironweed* in 1984, an Albany newsman said enviously, "Bill has done what every reporter fantasizes about."[94]

Moreover, Crane's and Hemingway's literary journalism served as precursor to the nonfiction renaissance of the last thirty years. Although Tom Wolfe claimed that the New Journalism sprang full grown, like Athena, from the brow of Wolfe and his colleagues on the *New York Herald Tribune*, numerous critics have refuted that contention.[95] They have traced a genealogy of American literary journalism running from Crane and other writers of the late nineteenth century through Ernest Hemingway, James

Agee, and their midcentury peers and on to literary journalists of today such as Michael Herr, Norman Mailer, Joan Didion, and Wolfe himself.

Starting in the 1880s, William Dean Howells and Henry James depicted the newspaper as the enemy of the novel. James went further, creating a myth of the artist destroyed by journalism. However, the example of Stephen Crane and the reporter-novelists who followed him established a competing myth of the artist nurtured by journalism, a narrative that has taken a much stronger hold on the national imagination. The careers and work of Crane, Dreiser, Hemingway, and their successors in fiction and nonfiction, the critical practice of writers in and out of the academy, and this study all attest to journalism's powerful role in the making of modern American literature.

NOTES

Introduction

1. William D. Howells, *A Modern Instance* (1882; Boston: Houghton Mifflin, 1957), 136.

2. The concept of cultural sacralization comes from Lawrence Levine, *Highbrow/Lowbrow: The Emergence of Cultural Hierarchy in America* (Cambridge, Mass.: Harvard University Press, 1988), 85–168.

3. My descriptions of nineteenth-century newspapers are based on extensive reading of numerous newspapers from the period. Most newspapers I have examined were published in New York City, which has served as the acknowledged leader in newspaper publishing since the antebellum era; I also read newspapers published in Boston, Philadelphia, and Washington, D.C. I have relied on the collections of Firestone Library, Princeton University; Skillman Library, Lafayette College; and the New York Public Library. I have also relied on the following overviews of U.S. journalism history: Gerald J. Baldasty, *The Commercialization of News in the Nineteenth Century* (Madison: University of Wisconsin Press, 1992); Michael Emery and Edwin Emery, *The Press and America: An Interpretive History of the Mass Media*, 7th ed. (Englewood Cliffs, N.J.: Prentice-Hall, 1992); Alfred McClung Lee, *The Daily Newspaper in America: The Evolution of a Social Instrument* (1937; New York: Octagon Books, 1973); Frank Luther Mott, *American Journalism*, 3d ed. (New York: Macmillan, 1962); Michael Schudson, *Discovering the News: A Social History of American Newspapers* (New York: Basic Books, 1978); and Michael Schudson, *The Power of News* (Cambridge, Mass.: Harvard University Press, 1995).

4. Emery and Emery, *Press and America*, 100, 178; Lee, *Daily Newspaper*, 728.

John C. Nerone offers an important analysis of the penny press in "The Mythology of the Penny Press," *Critical Studies in Mass Communication* 4 (1987); reprinted in Jean Folkerts, ed., *Media Voices: An Historical Perspective* (New York: Macmillan, 1992), 157–82.

5. Emery and Emery, *Press and America*, 174.

6. So many studies since the mid-1970s have complicated the notion of literary "realism" that it has become, as Michael Davitt Bell says, one of those words "which mean nothing without quotes." However, Bell goes on to use the term in *The Problem of American Realism: Studies in the Cultural History of a Literary Idea* (Chicago: University of Chicago Press, 1993). His introduction provides an excellent brief summary of recent critical work on realism and offers a convincing argument for continued use of the term. Like Bell, I find the term useful, not as a way to describe texts' mimetic fidelity—it is not clear that *The Bostonians* is any closer to "reality" than is *The House of the Seven Gables*—but as a means of talking about what writers in a particular historical period saw themselves as doing.

7. H. L. Mencken, "Introduction," *Major Conflicts*, vol. 10 of *The Work of Stephen Crane* (New York: Knopf, 1926), x–xi.

8. Richard H. Brodhead, *Cultures of Letters: Scenes of Reading and Writing in Nineteenth-Century America* (Chicago: University of Chicago Press, 1993).

9. Bell, *Problem of American Realism*, 17–38, 131–48.

10. Bernard Weinstein is a notable exception; see "Stephen Crane: Journalist," in Joseph Katz, ed., *Stephen Crane in Transition: Centenary Essays* (DeKalb: Northern Illinois University Press, 1972), 3–34. A few book-length studies treat Crane's journalism as seriously as his fiction: Patrick K. Dooley, *The Pluralistic Philosophy of Stephen Crane* (Urbana: University of Illinois Press, 1993); Milne Holton, *Cylinder of Vision: The Fiction and Journalistic Writings of Stephen Crane* (Baton Rouge: Louisiana State University Press, 1972); Marston LaFrance, *A Reading of Stephen Crane* (Oxford, England: Oxford University Press, 1971).

11. See Thomas B. Connery, ed., *A Sourcebook of American Literary Journalism* (Westport, Conn.: Greenwood, 1992).

12. Thomas A. Gullason, "The 'Lost' Newspaper Writings of Stephen Crane," *Syracuse University Library Associates Courier* 21 (1986): 68.

13. Lennard Davis, *Factual Fictions: The Origins of the English Novel* (New York: Columbia University Press, 1983). Thomas B. Connery applies Davis's concept to late nineteenth-century literary journalism in "Hutchins Hapgood and the Search for a 'New Form of Literature,'" *Journalism History* 13 (Spring 1986): 2–9; and in "A Third Way to Tell the Story: American Literary Journalism at the Turn of the Century," in Norman Sims, ed., *Literary Journalism in the Twentieth Century* (New York: Oxford University Press, 1990), 3–20. See also Barbara Lounsberry, *The Art of Fact: Contemporary Artists of Nonfiction* (Westport, Conn.: Greenwood, 1990), xvii.

14. On the rise of objectivity see Schudson, *Discovering the News*, 121–59.

15. Ellen Moers, *Two Dreisers* (New York: Viking, 1969), 3–69; Larzer Ziff, *The*

American 1890s: Life and Times of a Lost Generation (New York: Viking, 1966), 146–65; Christopher P. Wilson, *The Labor of Words: Literary Professionalism in the Progressive Era* (Athens: University of Georgia Press, 1985); Amy Kaplan, *The Social Construction of American Realism* (Chicago: University of Chicago Press, 1988); Thomas Strychacz, *Modernism, Mass Culture, and Professionalism* (New York: Cambridge University Press, 1993).

16. Shelley Fisher Fishkin, *From Fact to Fiction: Journalism and Imaginative Writing in America* (Baltimore: Johns Hopkins University Press, 1985).

17. Phyllis Frus, *The Politics and Poetics of Journalistic Narrative* (New York: Cambridge University Press, 1994), xviii, 5.

1. Journalism as Threat: William Dean Howells and Henry James

1. For the developing conflict between forms of cultural production during the nineteenth century see Lawrence Levine, *Highbrow/Lowbrow: The Emergence of Cultural Hierarchy in America* (Cambridge, Mass.: Harvard University Press, 1988).

2. Ralph Waldo Emerson, *The Journals and Miscellaneous Notebooks*, vol. 5, ed. Merton M. Sealts Jr. (Cambridge, Mass.: Harvard University Press, 1965), 462. Hans Bergmann notes the hostility of many antebellum writers to the penny press in *God in the Streets: New York Writing from the Penny Press to Melville* (Philadelphia: Temple University Press, 1995), 30.

3. Henry David Thoreau, *Walden* (1854; Princeton, N.J.: Princeton University Press, 1971), 52.

4. Henry David Thoreau, "Slavery in Massachusetts," *Reform Papers* (Princeton, N.J.: Princeton University Press, 1973), 100.

5. The *Evening Post* did not disappear. It survived, evolving over the years into today's *New York Post*, a tabloid owned by Rupert Murdoch. One can only imagine what William Cullen Bryant would think.

6. Henry James, "The Question of Our Speech," *French Writers and American Women*, (Branford, Conn.: Compass, 1960), 28–29.

7. W. D. Howells, *Years of My Youth* (1916; Bloomington: Indiana University Press, 1975), 15.

8. W. D. Howells, "The Country Printer," *Impressions and Experiences* (New York: Harper, 1896), 1–44. Edwin Harrison Cady confirms Howells's description of the newspaper in "William Dean Howells and the *Ashtabula Sentinel*," *Ohio State Archaeological and Historical Quarterly* 53 (1944): 39–51. The Howellses' emphasis on poetry in the *Sentinel* was not unusual. William Charvat points out that in the early nineteenth century, poetry "was used widely in newspapers and magazines. . . . Editors never paid for it because the supply was unlimited" (*Literary Publishing in America, 1790–1850* [Philadelphia: University of Pennsylvania Press, 1959], 65).

9. The extent to which Howells romanticized antebellum Jefferson in "The Country Printer" can be gauged by comparing the essay with letters he wrote while he lived in Jefferson and shortly afterward. He wrote to his cousin Dune Dean on September 9, 1857: "I pass up and down the streets of this not-to-be-sufficently-detested village and consider that there is not one in it (saving my own kin) for whom I care a hands turning, and . . . all in it are about that much interested in me" (George Arms and Christoph K. Lohmann, eds., *Selected Letters of W. D. Howells*, vol. 1 [Boston: Twayne, 1979], 11). To his father he wrote on August 25, 1864, "I have not yet . . . shaken off my old morbid horror of going back to live in a place where I have been so wretched. If you did not live in J[efferson] . . . I never should enter the town again. It cannot change so much but I shall always hate it" (Arms and Lohmann, *Selected Letters* 1:197).

10. Rodney D. Olsen, *Dancing in Chains: The Youth of William Dean Howells* (New York: New York University Press, 1991), 105. Olsen provides the most thorough account of Howells's early years. I have also relied on two other biographies, Edwin H. Cady, *The Road to Realism* (Syracuse: Syracuse University Press, 1956), and Kenneth Lynn, *William Dean Howells: An American Life* (New York: Harcourt Brace, 1971).

11. Howells, *Years of My Youth*, 122–23.

12. Henry James, *Parisian Sketches*, ed. Leon Edel and Ilse Dusoir Lind (New York: New York University Press, 1957), 210. For information on James and the *Tribune* I have also relied on Leon Edel, *Henry James: The Conquest of London: 1870–1881* (1962; New York: Avon, 1978), 197–245; and on Ilse Dusoir Lind, "The Inadequate Vulgarity of Henry James," *Publications of the Modern Language Association* 66 (1951): 886–910.

13. James, *Parisian Sketches*, 3–13.

14. Ibid., xvi.

15. Edel, *Conquest of London*, 238.

16. James, *Parisian Sketches*, xvi.

17. Ibid., 217–20.

18. Henry James, "The Next Time," in F. O. Matthiessen, ed., *Stories of Artists and Writers* (New York: New Directions, n.d.), 272.

19. Frank Luther Mott, *American Journalism*, 3d ed. (New York: Macmillan, 1962), 411.

20. Emery and Emery, *The Press and America*, 172, 203.

21. William Charvat, *The Profession of Authorship in America, 1800–1870* (1968; New York: Columbia University Press, 1992), 5–28; Cathy N. Davidson, *Revolution and the Word: The Rise of the Novel in America* (New York: Oxford University Press, 1986), 15–37.

22. For sources on journalism history see Introduction, note 2.

23. On the post–Civil War book publishing industry see Daniel H. Borus, *Writing Realism: Howells, James, and Norris in the Mass Market* (Chapel Hill: University of North Carolina Press), 37–39; and Donald Sheehan, *This Was*

Publishing: A Chronicle of the Book Trade in the Gilded Age (Bloomington: Indiana University Press, 1952).

24. "Howells's 'A Modern Instance,'" *Century* 25 (1883): 463–65.

25. Borus, *Writing Realism*, 148.

26. Michael Anesko, *"Friction with the Market": Henry James and the Profession of Authorship* (New York: Oxford University Press, 1986), 113–14; Nelson Lichtenstein, "Authorial Professionalism and the Literary Marketplace, 1885–1900," *American Studies* 19 (1978): 35–53.

27. F. O. Matthiessen, *The James Family* (1947; New York: Random House, 1980), 320. On the belles-lettres "coterie" audience, see Borus, *Writing Realism*, 27–34.

28. Anesko, *"Friction with the Market,"* 122.

29. W. D. Howells, "The Man of Letters as a Man of Business," *Literature and Life* (New York: Harper, 1902), 1.

30. On Howells's business acumen see Borus, *Writing Realism*, 49–57; Lynn, *William Dean Howells*, 4–5; and Christopher P. Wilson, "Markets and Fictions: Howells' Infernal Juggle," *American Literary Realism* 20 (1988): 2–22.

31. Leon Edel, ed., *Henry James Letters*, vol. 2 (Cambridge, Mass.: Harvard University Press, 1975), 156.

32. Alfred R. Ferguson, "The Triple Quest of Henry James: Fame, Art, and Fortune," *American Literature* 27 (1956): 483. Michael Anesko writes that James "was among the first men of letters to deal effectively with publishers in both England and America" (*"Friction with the Market,"* 36). See also Anne T. Margolis, *Henry James and the Problem of Audience: An International Act* (Ann Arbor, Mich.: UMI Research Press, 1985), 20–23.

33. William Dean Howells, "Emile Zola," in Clara Marburg Kirk and Rudolf Kirk, eds., *William Dean Howells: Representative Selections* (New York: Hill and Wang, 1961), 382.

34. Arms and Lohmann, *Selected Letters of W. D. Howells*, 2:295.

35. Charles F. Wingate, ed., *Views and Interviews on Journalism* (New York: F. B. Patterson, 1875), 92–93, 318.

36. Amy Kaplan, *The Social Construction of American Realism* (Chicago: University of Chicago Press, 1988), 27. My discussion of *A Modern Instance* builds on Kaplan's interpretation of the novel.

37. Alan Trachtenberg, *The Incorporation of America: Culture and Society in the Gilded Age* (New York: Hill and Wang, 1982), 194.

38. William D. Howells, *A Modern Instance* (1882; Boston: Houghton-Mifflin, 1957), 89. Subsequent quotations are cited parenthetically.

39. William D. Howells, *The Rise of Silas Lapham* (1885; Boston: Houghton-Mifflin, 1957), 17.

40. Although Howells's unadorned prose style conveys greater sincerity than Bartley's orotund writing, it is no more "natural" and no less the result of artifice. See Hugh Kenner's incisive analysis of the "plain style" written by George Orwell

(and by Howells), "The Politics of the Plain Style," *New York Times Book Review*, September 15, 1985, reprinted in Norman Sims, ed., *Literary Journalism in the Twentieth Century* (New York: Oxford University Press, 1990), 183–90.

41. Kaplan (*Social Construction*, 39) and Philip Fisher draw attention to the similarities between literary realism and newspaper publicity in *Silas Lapham*: Philip Fisher, "Appearing and Disappearing in Public: Social Space in Late-Nineteenth-Century Literature and Culture," in Sacvan Bercovitch, ed., *Reconstructing American Literary History* (Cambridge, Mass.: Harvard University Press, 1986), 174–75.

42. W. D. Howells, *The Quality of Mercy* (New York: Harper, 1891), 151. Subsequent quotations are cited parenthetically.

43. Other writers of the era, notably Dion Boucicault in "The Decline and Fall of the Press," *North American Review* 145 (July 1887): 32–39, echoed Howells's complaints against the profit motive in journalism. For a brief survey of such complaints see Hazel Dicken-Garcia, *Journalistic Standards in Nineteenth-Century America* (Madison: University of Wisconsin Press, 1989), 186–88.

44. Quoted in Trachtenberg, *Incorporation of America*, 186.

45. Howells, *Years of My Youth*, 176.

46. Richard Brodhead gives an excellent brief account of nineteenth-century literary culture in "Literature and Culture," in Emory Elliott, ed., *Columbia Literary History of the United States* (New York: Columbia University Press, 1988), 467–81.

47. Trachtenberg, *Incorporation of America*, 185.

48. Howells, "Man of Letters," 21; Howells, *The Altrurian Romances*, vol. 20 of Clara Kirk and Rudolf Kirk, eds., *A Selected Edition of W. D. Howells* (Bloomington: Indiana University Press), 27; and Howells, "Novel-Writing and Novel-Reading: An Impersonal Explanation," *Bulletin of the New York Public Library* 62 (1958): 30.

49. Howells, "Man of Letters," 21; *Heroines of Fiction*, vol. 1 (New York: Harper, 1901), 190. See Elise Miller, "The Feminization of American Realist Theory," *American Literary Realism* 23 (1990): 20–41.

50. W. D. Howells, *My Literary Passions* (New York: Harper, 1895), 12–13.

51. Michael Davitt Bell, *The Problem of American Realism: Studies in the Cultural History of a Literary Idea* (Chicago: University of Chicago Press, 1993), 17–38.

52. Howells, *My Literary Passions*, 124; *Years of My Youth*, 122.

53. Henry James, *The Tragic Muse*, vol. 2 (New York: Scribner's, 1908), 197.

54. James, "Question of Our Speech," 28–29.

55. Henry James, *The Bostonians* (1886; New York: New American Library, 1980). Subsequent parenthetical citations are to this edition.

56. Critics Michael Anesko, Ian F. A. Bell, and Jennifer Wicke have analyzed the importance of Pardon and publicity in *The Bostonians*, and my discussion builds on their interpretations: Anesko, *"Friction with the Market,"* 79–100; Bell, *Henry James and the Past* (London: Macmillan, 1991), 61–144; Wicke, *Advertising*

Fictions: Literature, Advertisement, and Social Reading (New York: Columbia University Press, 1988), 90–102. Sara Blair's analysis of journalism's function in *The Princess Casamassima* is also relevant: *Henry James and the Writing of Race and Nation* (New York: Cambridge University Press, 1996), 98–103.

57. Henry James, *The Complete Notebooks of Henry James*, ed. Leon Edel and Lyall H. Powers (New York: Oxford University Press, 1987), 19. James was not the only writer who wished to *bafouer* the prying reporter. See Dicken-Garcia, *Journalistic Standards*, 190–200.

58. Mott, *American Journalism*, 386; Michael Schudson, *The Power of News* (Cambridge, Mass.: Harvard University Press, 1995), 72–93.

59. Alfred Habegger, *Henry James and the "Woman Business"* (New York: Cambridge University Press, 1989), 225.

60. Ibid., 6.

61. In *Gender, Fantasy, and American Realism* (New York: Columbia University Press, 1982) Alfred Habegger devotes a chapter to the topic, "Henry James and W. D. Howells as Sissies."

62. Leon Edel, *Henry James: The Middle Years, 1882–1895* (1962; New York: Avon, 1978), 148.

63. For background on the Peabody-Birdseye affair see Matthiessen, *James Family*, 325–27; and Mary Frew Moldstad, "Elizabeth Peabody Revisited," *Henry James Review* 9 (1988): 209–11. Alfred Habegger suggests that James's "outraged" description of Pardon's journalistic practice ("He poured contumely on their private life, on their personal appearance, with the best conscience in the world") "describes James's own performance more accurately than it describes Pardon's bland journalistic intrusions" (*Henry James*, 211–12).

64. Anesko, *"Friction with the Market,"* 79–85.

65. Quoted in Anesko, *"Friction with the Market,"* 79.

66. Ibid., 86.

67. Ibid., 87.

68. Quoted in Leon Edel, ed., *Henry James Letters*, vol. 3 (Cambridge, Mass.: Harvard University Press, 1980), 25.

69. Ibid., 209.

70. In his preface to the New York edition of *"The Lesson of the Master" and Other Tales*—a volume that contains tales of the literary life—James informs his readers that the stories came partly from his experiences: the "personal states . . . of my hapless friends in the present volume . . . , the embarassments and predicaments studied, the tragedies and comedies recorded, can be intelligibly fathered but on [the author's] own intimate experience" (James, *The Art of the Novel* [New York: Scribner's, 1934], 221).

71. On the use of "myth" in this sense see Richard Slotkin's trilogy on the American West: *Regeneration Through Violence: The Mythology of the American Frontier* (Middletown, Conn.: Wesleyan University Press, 1973); *The Fatal Environment: The Myth of the Frontier in the Age of Industrialization, 1800–1890* (New

York: Atheneum, 1985); *Gunfighter Nation: The Myth of the Frontier in Twentieth-Century America* (New York: Atheneum, 1992).

72. James, *Complete Notebooks*, 123, 109. These entries are for June 4, 1895, and January 26, 1895. James also referred to Reid and the *Tribune* in his entry for November 25, 1881 (216).

73. Henry James, "The Next Time," *Stories of Writers and Artists*, 252. Subsequent quotations are cited parenthetically.

74. Henry James, "Broken Wings," *Stories of Writers and Artists*, 325.

75. Henry James, "The Death of the Lion," *Stories of Writers and Artists*, 218.

76. James, *Complete Notebooks*, 86.

77. Ibid.

78. Henry James, "John Delavoy," in vol. 4 of *The Complete Tales of Henry James*, ed. Leon Edel (London: Rupert Hart-Davis, 1964), 424, 428.

79. I have found the following treatments of late nineteenth-century magazines particularly helpful: Brodhead, "Literature and Culture"; Margolis, *Henry James*; Richard Ohmann, *Selling Culture: Magazines, Markets, and Class at the Turn of the Century* (New York: Verso, 1996); Ohmann, "Where Did Mass Culture Come From?: The Case of Magazines," *Berkshire Review* 16 (1981): 85–101; and Matthew Schneirov, *The Dream of a New Social Order: Popular Magazines in America, 1893–1914* (New York: Columbia University Press, 1994).

80. Margolis, *Henry James*, 81.

81. See Richard H. Brodhead's analysis of James's late style in *The School of Hawthorne* (New York: Oxford University Press, 1986), 166–200. See also Thomas Strychacz, *Modernism, Mass Culture, and Professionalism* (New York: Cambridge University Press, 1993), 62–83.

82. Allon White, *The Uses of Obscurity: The Fiction of Early Modernism* (London: Routledge and Kegan Paul, 1981), 134.

83. James, *Henry James Letters*, 4:250.

84. W. H. Auden, "The American Scene," *The Dyer's Hand and Other Essays* (New York: Random House, 1962), 314. See also Tony Tanner, *Henry James and the Art of Nonfiction* (Athens: University of Georgia Press, 1995), 3–24.

85. Henry James, *The American Scene* (1907; Bloomington: Indiana University Press, 1968), 35. Subsequent quotations are cited parenthetically.

86. My interpretation of *The American Scene* builds on that of Richard S. Lyons, "'In Supreme Command': The Crisis of the Imagination in James's *The American Scene*," *New England Quarterly* 55 (1982): 517–39.

87. Lionel Trilling, "The Bostonians," *The Opposing Self* (1955; New York: Harcourt Brace, 1979), 96.

88. Henry James, "The Point of View," *Complete Tales*, 4:506–507, 509.

89. Henry James, *The Reverberator* (1888; New York: Grove Press, 1979), 42. Subsequent quotations are cited parenthetically.

90. James, *Complete Notebooks*, 40.

91. James, *Art of the Novel*, 186–87, 188.

92. In his interpretation of *The Reverberator* Strychacz notes that the novel's treatment of journalism is more complex than James's initial notebook entry would suggest. See Strychacz, *Modernism, Mass Culture, and Professionalism*, 45–61.

93. Henry James, *The Portrait of a Lady*, vol. 1 (New York: Scribner's, 1908), 121. Subsequent quotations are cited parenthetically.

2. The Launching of Stephen Crane: Early Journalism

1. Henry James, *The Bostonians* (1886; New York: New American Library, 1980), 100.

2. Biographical information on Crane comes from several sources. The most important and reliable are Stanley Wertheim and Paul Sorrentino, eds., *The Correspondence of Stephen Crane* (New York: Columbia University Press, 1988); and Wertheim and Sorrentino, *The Crane Log: A Documentary Life of Stephen Crane, 1871–1900* (New York: G. K. Hall, 1994). Biographies of Crane include Christopher Benfey, *The Double Life of Stephen Crane* (New York: Knopf, 1992); John Berryman, *Stephen Crane: A Critical Biography*, rev. ed. (New York: Farrar Straus Giroux, 1962); James B. Colvert, *Stephen Crane* (New York: Harcourt Brace Jovanovich, 1984); and R. W. Stallman, *Stephen Crane* (New York: Braziller, 1968). The Berryman, Colvert, and Stallman biographies must be used with caution, because they rely on the now discredited biography by Thomas Beer, *Stephen Crane: A Study in American Letters* (New York: Knopf, 1923). On Beer see John Clendenning, "Thomas Beer's *Stephen Crane*: The Eye of His Imagination," *Prose Studies* 14 (1991): 68–80; and Stanley Wertheim and Paul Sorrentino, "Thomas Beer: The Clay Feet of Stephen Crane Biography," *American Literary Realism* 22 (1990): 2–16.

3. Shelley Fisher Fishkin, *From Fact to Fiction: Journalism and Imaginative Writing in America* (Baltimore: Johns Hopkins University Press, 1985); Larzer Ziff, *The American 1890s: Life and Times of a Lost Generation* (New York: Viking, 1966), 146–55; Ellen Moers, *Two Dreisers* (New York: Viking, 1969), 21; Tom Wolfe, *The New Journalism* (New York: Harper & Row, 1973), 45; Christopher Benfey, *The Double Life of Stephen Crane* (New York: Knopf, 1992).

4. [Stephen Crane] "Avon's School by the Sea," *New-York Tribune*, August 4, 1890, p. 5. All quotations in this chapter from Crane's journalism come from the original newspaper publication. Because none of his articles occupies more than one page in its original appearance, I cite the source only once. All of Crane's sketches cited in this chapter are reprinted in *Tales, Sketches, and Reports*, vol. 8 of *The Works of Stephen Crane*, ed. Fredson Bowers (Charlottesville: University Press of Virginia, 1973). Most are also available in Stephen Crane, *Prose and Poetry* (New York: Library of America, 1984).

5. "On the New-Jersey Coast," *New-York Tribune*, August 21, 1892, p. 22.

6. "Saratoga Weather Fine," *New-York Tribune*, July 10, 1892, p. 22.

7. [Crane] "Avon's School by the Sea." In *Tales, Sketches, and Reports* editor

Fredson Bowers has attributed one other article from 1890 to Crane and has reprinted one article from 1888 and one from 1889 as "possible attributions." All three attributions seem highly conjectural. The articles are worth reading as typical contributions from Townley Crane's news bureau, but their links to Stephen Crane are tenuous. In "The 'Lost' Newspaper Writings of Stephen Crane," *Syracuse University Library Associates Courier* 21 (1986): 57–87, Thomas A. Gullason attributes an 1887 New Jersey shore report to Crane. Again, the attribution seems highly conjectural.

8. Harold F. Wilson, *The Jersey Shore*, vol. 1 (New York: Lewis Historical Publishing, 1953), 507. On Asbury Park see also John T. Cunningham, *The New Jersey Shore* (New Brunswick, N.J.: Rutgers University Press, 1958), 53–56.

9. [Crane] "Avon's School by the Sea"; [Stephen Crane] "Crowding into Asbury Park," *New-York Tribune*, July 3, 1892, p. 28.

10. [Stephen Crane] "Howells Discussed at Avon-by-the-Sea," *New-York Tribune*, August 18, 1891, p. 5.

11. In *Tales, Sketches, and Reports* Bowers attributes one other article from 1891 to Crane and reprints eleven more articles as possible attributions.

12. Stephen Crane, "Henry M. Stanley," *Vidette* [Claverack College and Hudson River Institute], February 1890, pp. 8–9, reprinted in *Tales, Sketches, and Reports*, 565–67.

13. For information on the Cranes and Sullivan County see Stallman, *Stephen Crane*, 37–44. See also Stallman's introduction to Stephen Crane, *Sullivan County Tales and Sketches*, ed. R. W. Stallman (Ames: Iowa State University Press, 1968). Melvin Schoberlin edited the first collection of the Sullivan County sketches, *The Sullivan County Sketches of Stephen Crane* (Syracuse, N.Y.: Syracuse University Press, 1949). The complete sketches are also available in *Tales, Sketches, and Reports*.

14. [Stephen Crane] "The Octopush," *New-York Tribune*, July 10, 1892, p. 17.

15. [Stephen Crane] "The Last of the Mohicans," *New-York Tribune*, February 21, 1892, p. 12.

16. [Stephen Crane] "Not Much of a Hero," *New-York Tribune*, May 1, 1892, p. 15.

17. See, for example, Dee Brown, *Bury My Heart at Wounded Knee: An Indian History of the American West* (1971; New York: Bantam, 1972), 413–18.

18. Front-page headlines in the *Tribune* on December 31, 1890, include these two: "The Battle on Wounded Knee / Treachery of the Indians in Attacking the Troops" and "Another Indian Fight / Over Thirty Savages Shot, But No Soldiers Killed."

19. [Stephen Crane] "The Way in Sullivan County," *New-York Tribune*, May 8, 1892, p. 15.

20. [Stephen Crane] "Bear and Panther," *New-York Tribune*, July 17, 1892. p. 18.

21. [Stephen Crane] "Hunting Wild Hogs," *New-York Tribune*, February 28, 1892, p. 17.

22. Michael Fried, *Realism, Writing, Disfiguration: On Thomas Eakins and Stephen Crane* (Chicago: University of Chicago Press, 1987). For a metafictional interpretation of a Sullivan County tale see Joseph Church, "Reading, Writing, and the Risk of Entanglement in Crane's 'Octopush,'" *Studies in Short Fiction* 29 (1992): 341–46.

23. Willis Fletcher Johnson, "The Launching of Stephen Crane," *Literary Digest International Book Review* 4 (1926): 288.

24. [Stephen Crane] "Meetings Begun at Ocean Grove," *New-York Tribune*, July 2, 1892, p. 4.

25. [Crane] "Crowding into Asbury Park."

26. [Stephen Crane] "On the Board Walk," *New-York Tribune*, August 14, 1892, p. 17.

27. [Stephen Crane] "Joys of Seaside Life," *New-York Tribune*, July 17, 1892, p. 18.

28. This passage by Crane bears a remarkable linguistic resemblance to a passage from Mark Twain's preface to "Those Extraordinary Twins," published in the same volume with *Pudd'nhead Wilson* in 1894. Mark Twain writes, "I had seen a picture of a youthful Italian 'freak'—or 'freaks'—which was—or which were—on exhibition in our cities—a combination consisting of two heads and four arms joined to a single body and a single pair of legs—and I thought I would write an extravagantly fantastic little story with this freak of nature for hero—or heroes" (*Pudd'nhead Wilson and Those Extraordinary Twins* [1894; New York: Norton, 1980], 119.) Did Mark Twain read the anonymous description of the fakir in the *New-York Tribune* in 1892?

29. [Stephen Crane] "The Seaside Hotel Hop," *New-York Tribune*, September 11, 1892, p. 15.

30. "Round About New Jersey," *Philadelphia Press*, August 18, 1892, p. 6.

31. [Stephen Crane] "On the New-Jersey Coast," *New-York Tribune*, August 21, 1892, p. 22.

32. Letter to the Editor, "Selections from the Mail," *New-York Tribune*, August 24, 1892, p. 9.

33. *Asbury Park Journal*, quoted in Schoberlin, *Sullivan County Sketches*, 8.

34. *Tribune* editor Johnson insists in "Launching of Stephen Crane" that Crane was not fired (290). In his introduction to *Sullivan County Sketches* Schoberlin lists all the friends and family members—eleven people—who wrote or testified that both Stephen and Townley Crane were fired (5n).

3. Reporting the City: New York Journalism

1. James L. Ford, *The Literary Shop and Other Tales* (New York: Geo. H. Richmond, 1894), 154.

2. Isaac F. Marcosson, *David Graham Phillips and His Times* (New York: Dodd, Mead, 1932), 219.

3. Lincoln Steffens, *The Autobiography of Lincoln Steffens* (New York: Harcourt Brace, 1931), 314, 339.

4. Charles A. Dana, *The Art of Newspaper Making* (New York: Appleton, 1895), 27.

5. H. L. Mencken, "Introduction," *Major Conflicts*, vol. 10 of *The Work of Stephen Crane* (New York: Knopf, 1926), x–xi. Although Mencken, Lincoln Steffens, James L. Ford, and their contemporaries articulated the myth of the reporter-artist, numerous later critics have written about the nineteenth-century origins of the reporter-artist. See Shelley Fisher Fishkin, *From Fact to Fiction: Journalism and Imaginative Writing in America* (Baltimore: Johns Hopkins University Press, 1985); Ellen Moers, *Two Dreisers* (New York: Viking, 1969), 3–69; Ronald Weber, "Journalism, Writing, and American Literature," Occasional Paper no. 5, Gannett Center for Media Studies, New York, 1987; Christopher P. Wilson, *The Labor of Words: Literary Professionalism in the Progressive Era* (Athens: University of Georgia Press, 1985); and Larzer Ziff, *The American 1890s: Life and Times of a Lost Generation* (New York: Viking, 1966), 146–65. Phyllis Frus and Thomas Strychacz critique these writers' accounts: Frus, *The Politics and Poetics of Journalistic Narrative* (New York: Cambridge University Press, 1994), xviii; Strychacz, *Modernism, Mass Culture, and Professionalism* (New York: Cambridge University Press, 1993), 1–44. Howard Good analyzes how novels written by journalists contributed to the myth in *Acquainted with the Night: The Image of Journalists in American Fiction, 1890–1930* (Metuchen, N.J.: Scarecrow Press, 1986).

My use of the term "myth" relies on Richard Slotkin's in his trilogy of the American West; see chap. 1, note 71.

6. Richard M. Weatherford, ed., *Stephen Crane: The Critical Heritage* (London: Routledge & Kegan Paul, 1973), 18, 42.

7. "Holland" [Elisha Jay Edwards], quoted in Marston LaFrance, *A Reading of Stephen Crane* (Oxford, England: Oxford University Press, 1971), 52.

8. Tom Wolfe, *The New Journalism* (New York: Harper & Row, 1973), 45.

9. James B. Colvert, "Introduction," *Bowery Tales*, vol. 1 of *The Works of Stephen Crane*, ed. Fredson Bowers (Charlottesville: University Press of Virginia, 1969), xxxiii–xxxvii; Stanley Wertheim and Paul Sorrentino, *The Crane Log: A Documentary Life of Stephen Crane, 1871–1900* (New York: G. K. Hall, 1994), 62, 80.

10. Donald Pizer, ed., *Literary Criticism of Frank Norris* (Austin: University of Texas Press, 1964), 164.

11. James B. Colvert, *Stephen Crane* (New York: Harcourt Brace Jovanovich, 1984), 47–50; Marcus Cunliffe, "Stephen Crane and the American Background of *Maggie*," *American Quarterly* 7 (1955): 31–44; Laura Hapke, *Girls Who Went Wrong: Prostitutes in American Fiction, 1885–1917* (Bowling Green, Ohio:

Bowling Green State University Popular Press, 1989), 45–67; Giorgio Mariani, *Spectacular Narratives: Representations of Class and War in Stephen Crane and the American 1890s* (New York: Peter Lang, 1992), 35–67.

12. Stanley Wertheim and Paul Sorrentino, eds., *The Correspondence of Stephen Crane*, vol. 1 (New York: Columbia University Press, 1988), 52–53.

13. D. H. Lawrence, *Studies in Classic American Literature* (1923; New York: Penguin, 1977), 8.

14. Stephen Crane, *Maggie: A Girl of the Streets (A Story of New York)* (1893), in *Stephen Crane: Poetry and Prose* (New York: Library of America, 1984), 24. Subsequent quotations are cited parenthetically.

15. Thomas Beer, *Stephen Crane: A Study in American Letters* (New York: Knopf, 1924), 85.

16. [Stephen Crane] "Meetings Begun at Ocean Grove," *New-York Tribune*, July 2, 1892, p. 4.

17. Joseph J. Kwiat, "The Newspaper Experience: Crane, Norris, and Dreiser," *Nineteenth-Century Fiction* 8 (1953): 103, 117.

18. Thomas A. Gullason, "The 'Lost' Newspaper Writings of Stephen Crane," *Syracuse University Library Associates Courier* 21 (1986): 68.

19. Walter Benjamin, "The Storyteller," *Illuminations* (New York: Schocken, 1969), 89. Subsequent quotations are cited parenthetically.

20. Michael Schudson, "Why News Is the Way It Is," *Raritan* 2 (1983): 109–25. See also Robert Darnton, "Writing News and Telling Stories," *Daedalus* 104 (Spring 1975): 175–94; Frus, *Politics and Poetics*; and the work of Hayden White, particularly "The Fictions of Factual Representation," *Tropics of Discourse: Essays in Cultural Criticism* (Baltimore: Johns Hopkins University Press, 1978), 121–34; and "The Value of Narrativity in the Representation of Reality," *The Content of the Form: Narrative Discourse and Historical Representation* (Baltimore: Johns Hopkins University Press, 1987), 1–25.

21. Melvin H. Schoberlin, "Flagon of Despair: Stephen Crane," unfinished Crane biography, Syracuse University Library.

22. Gullason, "'Lost' Newspaper Writings," 60.

23. "Typical Scenes in a Summer Garden," *New York Herald*, July 5, 1891, p. 21. Alan Trachtenberg notes Jacob Riis's use of the tour guide stance in *How the Other Half Lives*; see Trachtenberg, "Experiments in Another Country: Stephen Crane's City Sketches," *Southern Review* 10 (1974): 271–72.

24. "Where 'De Gang' Hears the Band Play," *New York Herald*, July 5, 1891, p. 21.

25. [Stephen Crane] "The Broken-Down Van," *New-York Tribune*, July 10, 1892, p. 8. Because Crane's New York City newspaper sketches occupy no more than one page in their original appearance, the source for each is cited only once. Although I have used the original newspaper appearance as my source, all the sketches I discuss are reprinted in R. W. Stallman and E. R. Hagemann, eds., *The New York City Sketches of Stephen Crane* (New York: New York University Press,

1966) and in Stephen Crane, *Tales, Sketches, and Reports*, vol. 8 of *The Works of Stephen Crane*, ed. Fredson Bowers (Charlottesville: University Press of Virginia, 1973). Most, although not all, sketches are reprinted in Stephen Crane, *Prose and Poetry* (New York: Library of America, 1984).

26. "Sharks That Search New York for Prey," *New York Press*, April 22, 1894, sec. 2, p. 2.

27. "Good Samaritans Are Often Duped," *New York Press* April 29, 1894, sec. 3, p. 1.

28. John F. Kasson offers other examples of monitory literature in his discussion of "social counterfeits" in *Rudeness and Civility: Manners in Nineteenth-Century Urban America* (New York: Hill and Wang, 1990), 100–11.

29. The crusades mentioned appeared in the *Press* in November 1894, the *Herald* in August 1892, and the *World* in February 1894.

30. "Heard on the Street Election Night" is preserved in an undated clipping in a Stephen Crane scrapbook in the Columbia University Library. Although the article was obviously printed in the *New York Press* sometime after the November 1894 municipal election, no researcher has found the edition. Presumably, the article appeared in some edition of the newspaper that has not been preserved. Stallman and Hagemann, *New York City Sketches*, pp. 103–107, and Crane, *Tales, Sketches, and Reports*, pp. 333–37, reprint the article.

31. Stephen Crane, "Coney Island's Failing Days," *New York Press*, October 14, 1894, sec. 5, p. 2.

32. Stephen Crane, "In a Park Row Restaurant," *New York Press*, October 28, 1894, sec. 5, p. 3.

33. Stallman and Hagemann, *New York City Sketches*, 97n.

34. Stephen Crane, "When Every One Is Panic Stricken," *New York Press*, November 25, 1894, sec. 4, p. 6.

35. Stephen Crane, "When Man Falls a Crowd Gathers," *New York Press*, December 2, 1894, sec. 3, p. 5.

36. The letter to the editor is contained in a Crane scrapbook in the Columbia University Library.

37. Quoted in Paul Boyer, *Urban Masses and Moral Order in America, 1820–1920* (Cambridge, Mass.: Harvard University Press, 1978), 127.

38. On nineteenth-century attitudes toward poverty see Robert H. Bremner, *From the Depths: The Discovery of Poverty in the United States* (New York: New York University Press, 1956).

39. "Poverty's Sunny Side," *New York Press*, May 27, 1894, sec. 3, p. 2.

40. Christopher Benfey, *The Double Life of Stephen Crane* (New York: Knopf, 1992), 79. Painter John Sloan described Crane as "human rather than socially conscious" (Van Wyck Brooks, *John Sloan: A Painter's Life* [New York: Dutton, 1955], 56n).

41. My reading of "The Men in the Storm" builds on Alan Trachtenberg's interpretation in "Experiments in Another Country."

42. Stephen Crane, "The Men in the Storm," *Arena*, October 1894, p. 662. Subsequent quotations are cited parenthetically.

43. [Jacob Riis] "Police Lodgings," *New York World*, February 12, 1893, p. 25. This unsigned article is included in Riis's scrapbooks, Jacob A. Riis Papers, Library of Congress.

44. The three articles mentioned appeared in Sunday editions of the *New York World*, April 1, 1894, p. 20; April 29, 1894, p. 25, and March 25, p. 19, 1894.

45. Barbara Belford, *Brilliant Bylines: A Biographical Anthology of Notable Newspaperwomen in America* (New York: Columbia University Press, 1986), 114–29, describes Nellie Bly and reprints one of her *World* articles about the lunatic asylum. See also Brooke Kroeger, *Nellie Bly: Daredevil, Reporter, Feminist* (New York: Times Books, 1994), 79–99.

46. James Greenwood, "A Night in a Workhouse," in Peter Keating, ed., *Into Unknown England, 1866–1913: Selections from the Social Explorers* (Manchester, England: Manchester University Press, 1976).

47. "A Tour of the Charities: Experiences of a Press Reporter Who Applied for Aid," *New York Press*, January 14, 1894, sec. 2, p. 2; and "A Night with Outcasts," *New York Press*, March 11, 1894, sec. 2, p. 2.

48. "The Demon Realism," cartoon in *New York World*, April 22, 1894: color supplement, n.p.

49. One example of the misery/luxury contrast from the thousands available during the 1890s is found in the widely circulated Populist Party platform of 1892, which includes a reference to "the two great [American] classes—tramps and millionaires." Quoted in Robert Dallek, *The American Style of Foreign Policy: Cultural Politics and Foreign Affairs* (New York: Knopf, 1983), 4.

50. See Carlos A. Schwantes, *Coxey's Army: An American Odyssey* (Lincoln: University of Nebraska Press, 1985). Denunciations of Coxey's Army in the *New York Press* and other newspapers are too numerous to cite; Schwantes gives numerous examples of the press coverage.

51. Francis Wayland, quoted in John Seelye, "The American Tramp: A Version of the Picaresque," *American Quarterly* 15 (1963): 541. For further background on tramps see Michael Denning, *Mechanic Accents: Dime Novels and Working-Class Culture in America* (New York: Verso, 1987), 149–57; Kenneth L. Kusmer, "The Underclass in Historical Perspective: Tramps and Vagrants in Urban America, 1870–1930," in Rick Beard, ed., *On Being Homeless: Historical Perspectives* (New York: Museum of the City of New York, 1987), 20–31; and Paul T. Ringenbach, *Tramps and Reformers, 1873–1916: The Discovery of Unemployment in New York* (Westport, Conn.: Greenwood, 1973).

52. For examples, see Jacob A. Riis, *How the Other Half Lives* (1890; New York: Dover, 1971), 61–67; Police Lodgings," *New York World*, February 12, 1893, p. 25. and the following articles in the Riis Papers, Library of Congress: "The Tramps Marching," *New York World*, June 25, 1883; "The Station House Lodgers," *New-*

York Tribune, January 31, 1892; and "New York's Wayfarers' Lodge," *Christian Union*, December 2, 1895.

53. Stephen Crane, "An Experiment in Misery," *New York Press*, April 22, 1894, sec. 3, p. 2. This opening is absent from Crane's revised version of the sketch, which he published in *The Open Boat and Other Stories* (London: Heinemann, 1898).

54. Benedict Giamo, *On the Bowery: Confronting Homelessness in American Society* (Iowa City: University of Iowa Press, 1989), 93–100.

55. Stephen Crane, "An Experiment in Luxury," *New York Press* , April 29, 1894, sec. 3, p. 2.

56. Stephen Crane, "In the Depths of a Coal Mine," *McClure's*, August 1894, p. 205. Subsequent quotations are cited parenthetically.

57. Stephen Crane, draft of "In the Depths of a Coal Mine," *Tales, Sketches, and Reports*, 605. Subsequent quotations are cited parenthetically.

58. Corwin Linson, *My Stephen Crane*, ed. Edwin H. Cady (Syracuse, N.Y.: Syracuse University Press, 1958), 69.

59. Edwin H. Cady, "Introduction," in Stephen Crane, *Tales, Sketches, and Reports*, xxxvi–xxxvii.

60. Howells's 1890s essays on New York City are collected in *Impressions and Experiences* (New York: Harper's, 1896) and *Literature and Life* (New York: Harper's, 1902). The three subjects mentioned are found, respectively, in "The Midnight Platoon," *Literature and Life*; "An East-Side Ramble," *Impressions and Experiences*; and "Tribulations of a Cheerful Giver, *Impressions and Experiences*.

61. Stephen Crane, "In the Broadway Cars," *New York Sun*, July 26, 1896, sec. 2, p. 3. This article was syndicated nationally by McClure.

62. Stephen Crane, "What Life Was Like in Bloody Days Gone by in Minetta Lane," *New York Herald*, December 20, 1896, sec. 5, p. 5. The article was syndicated nationally in a number of newspapers under different headlines. I have used the title "Stephen Crane in Minetta Lane" because that title is used in Stallman and Hagemann, *New York City Sketches* and Crane, *Tales, Sketches, and Reports*.

63. Lewis A. Erenberg, *Steppin' Out: New York Nightlife and the Transformation of American Culture, 1890–1930* (Chicago: University of Chicago Press, 1981), 18–20.

64. On racial attitudes among turn-of-the-century progressives see Lawrence J. Oliver, *Brander Matthews, Theodore Roosevelt, and the Politics of American Literature, 1880–1920* (Knoxville: University of Tennessee Press, 1992), 33–81.

65. B. A. Botkin, ed., *New York City Folklore* (New York: Random House, 1956), 331.

66. The headline quoted comes from Stephen Crane, "The 'Tenderloin' as It Really Is," *New York Journal*, October 25, 1896, pp. 13–14. The other two articles in the series are Stephen Crane, "In the 'Tenderloin,'" November 1, 1896, p. 25; and Stephen Crane, "Yen-Nock Bill and His Sweetheart," November 29, 1896, p. 35.

67. See Dean Latimer and Jeff Goldberg, *Flowers in the Blood: The Story of Opium* (New York: Franklin Watts, 1981), 201–15.

68. Helen Campbell et al., *Darkness and Daylight; or Lights and Shadows of New York Life* (Hartford, Conn.: Hartford Publishing, 1891), 573.

69. Riis, *How the Other Half Lives*, 78, 83.

70. [Stephen Crane] "Opium's Varied Dreams," *New York Sun*, May 17, 1896, sec. 3, p. 3.

71. Crane, *Tales, Sketches, and Reports*, 873.

72. Information on the Dora Clark episode is taken from Olov W. Fryckstedt, "Stephen Crane in the Tenderloin," *Studia Neophilologica* 34 (1962): 136–63; and from the newspaper articles and other documents reprinted in Stallman and Hagemann, *New York City Sketches*, 217–60. Christopher P. Wilson provides a complex reinterpretation of the episode in "Stephen Crane and the Police," *American Quarterly* 48 (1996): 273–315.

73. Stephen Crane, "Adventures of a Novelist," *New York Journal*, September 20, 1896, pp. 17–18.

74. Stallman and Hagemann, *New York City Sketches*, 219, 222; Fryckstedt, "Stephen Crane in the Tenderloin," 148.

75. "Crane Had a Gay Night," *New York World*, October 16, 1896, reprinted in Stallman and Hagemann, *New York City Sketches*, 248.

76. Stallman and Hagemann, *New York City Sketches*, 245, 249.

4. *The Shape of a Cloak and a Point of View: Travel Journalism*

1.Stanley Wertheim and Paul Sorrentino, eds., *The Correspondence of Stephen Crane*, vol. 1 (New York: Columbia University Press, 1988), 45.

2. On newspaper syndicates, see Charles Johanningsmeier, *Fiction and the American Literary Marketplace: The Role of Newspaper Syndicates, 1860–1900* (Cambridge, England: Cambridge University Press, 1997).

3. Stephen Crane, "Queenstown," *Tales, Sketches, and Reports*, vol. 8 of *The Works of Stephen Crane*, ed. Fredson Bowers (Charlottesville: University Press of Virginia, 1973), 485. I have relied on *Tales, Sketches, and Reports* as my source for Crane's travel journalism because of the pieces' complex textual history. Most were syndicated and appeared in several different newspapers in slightly varying versions. Most works discussed in this chapter are also reprinted in Stephen Crane, *Prose and Poetry* (New York: Library of America, 1984).

4. Henry Nash Smith, *Virgin Land: The American West as Symbol and Myth* (Cambridge, Mass.: Harvard University Press, 1950).

5. Stephen Crane, "Nebraska's Bitter Fight for Life," *Tales, Sketches, and Reports*, 409. Subsequent quotations are cited parenthetically.

6. Smith, *Virgin Land*, 182.

7. Dorothy Weyer Creigh, *Nebraska: A Bicentennial History* (New York:

Norton, 1977), 176. See also Gilbert C. Fite, *The Farmers' Frontier, 1865–1900* (New York: Holt, Rinehart & Winston, 1966), 113–36; and James C. Olson, *History of Nebraska*, 2d ed. (Lincoln: University of Nebraska Press, 1966), 220–31.

8. Stephen Crane, *The Black Riders* (1895), in Crane, *Prose and Poetry* (New York: Library of America, 1984), 1318, 1304, 1302.

9. Stephen Crane, "Stephen Crane in Texas," *Tales, Sketches, and Reports*, 468; Stephen Crane, "Galveston, Texas, in 1895," *Tales, Sketches, and Reports*, 474.

10. Richard Slotkin, *Gunfighter Nation: The Myth of the Frontier in Twentieth-Century America* (New York: HarperCollins, 1992), 60–61.

11. John Cawelti, *Adventure, Mystery, and Romance: Formula Stories as Art and Popular Culture* (Chicago: University of Chicago Press, 1976), 216–19.

12. Richard White, "Frederick Jackson Turner and Buffalo Bill," in James R. Grossman, ed., *The Frontier in American Culture* (Berkeley: University of California Press, 1994), 27.

13. See Slotkin, *Gunfighter Nation*, 156–93, on the "red-blooded" school of western fiction; and White, "Turner and Buffalo Bill," 47–52, on the West as a field for the reconstruction of Anglo-Saxon manhood.

14. Raymund A. Paredes, "Stephen Crane and the Mexican," *Western American Literature* 6 (1971): 38.

15. Jamie Robertson, "Stephen Crane, Eastern Outsider in the West and Mexico," *Western American Literature* 13 (1978): 243–57.

16. Stephen Crane, "Free Silver Down in Mexico," *Tales, Sketches, and Reports*, 446.

17. Stephen Crane, "The Mexican Lower Classes," *Tales, Sketches, and Reports*, 435. Subsequent quotations are cited parenthetically.

18. David Spurr offers a provocative interpretation of Crane's Mexican journalism, quite different from mine, in *The Rhetoric of Empire: Colonial Discourse in Journalism, Travel Writing, and Imperial Administration* (Durham, N.C.: Duke University Press, 1993), 55–57. See also Giorgio Mariani, *Spectacular Narratives: Representations of Class and War in Stephen Crane and the American 1890s* (New York: Peter Lang, 1992), 69–72.

19. Richard H. Brodhead, *Cultures of Letters: Scenes of Reading and Writing in Nineteenth-Century America* (Chicago: University of Chicago Press, 1993), 126.

20. Stephen Crane, "London Impressions," in *Tales, Sketches, and Reports*, 683. Subsequent quotations are cited parenthetically. Milne Holton is one of the few critics to have analyzed "London Impressions," and he uses a phrase from it as the title of his book on Crane: *Cylinder of Vision: The Fiction and Journalistic Writings of Stephen Crane* (Baton Rouge: Louisiana State University Press, 1972).

21. Justin Sturgis, "Crane in London: The American Novelist Investigating English with a Microscope," *Wave*, September 18, 1897, quoted in R. W. Stallman, *Stephen Crane: A Biography* (New York: George Braziller, 1968), 307–308. On the question of whether Frank Norris was "Justin Sturgis," see Stanley

Wertheim and Paul Sorrentino, *The Crane Log: A Documentary Life of Stephen Crane, 1871–1900* (New York: G. K. Hall, 1994), 273.

22. Stephen Crane, *Tales, Sketches, and Reports,* 734.

23. Stephen Crane, "The European Letters," *Tales, Sketches, and Reports,* 693–726.

24. Wertheim and Sorrentino, *Correspondence of Stephen Crane,* 1:306. The "friend" was Cora Howorth Stewart, who lived with Crane in England as his common-law wife. Cora Crane, as she called herself from 1897 on, was an intelligent, complex woman whom Crane had met the previous year in Jacksonville, Florida, where she supported herself as the madam of a high-class brothel. Although she had never been published before meeting Crane, under his tutelage she began writing for newspapers.

25. Lillian Barnard Gilkes, "The London Newsletters of Stephen and Cora Crane: A Collaboration," *Studies in American Fiction* 4 (1976): 186.

26. Stephen Crane, "The Scotch Express," *Tales, Sketches, and Reports,* 743. Subsequent quotations are cited parenthetically.

27. Harold Frederic, one of Crane's traveling companions, would almost certainly have drawn Crane's attention to the name change. Frederic had written about it a few years earlier in his novel *The Return of the O'Mahoney* (1892). This information comes from Donald Vanouse, "Stephen Crane's Reports from Occupied Ireland," paper presented at the American Literature Association, Baltimore, May 28, 1995).

28. Stephen Crane, "Queenstown," *Tales, Sketches, and Reports,* 483. Subsequent quotations are cited parenthetically.

29. A good brief survey of this period of Irish history can be found in John O'Beirne Ranelagh, *A Short History of Ireland* (Cambridge, England: Cambridge University Press, 1983), 129–51.

30. Stephen Crane, "Ballydehob," *Tales, Sketches, and Reports,* 487. Subsequent quotations are cited parenthetically.

31. Ranelagh, *Short History of Ireland,* 149.

32. Stephen Crane, "The Royal Irish Constabulary," *Tales, Sketches, and Reports,* 489. Subsequent quotations are cited parenthetically.

33. "Stephen Crane's Own Story" has a complicated textual history, because the article was syndicated by both Bacheller and the *New York Press;* see Fredson Bowers's textual note in *Reports of War,* vol. 9 of *The Works of Stephen Crane,* ed. Fredson Bowers (Charlottesville: University Press of Virginia, 1971), 466–75. I have taken quotations, cited parenthetically, from this volume. Quotations from "The Open Boat" are taken from the original publication in *Scribner's,* June 1897, pp. 728–40.

34. Eric Solomon, *Stephen Crane: From Parody to Realism* (Cambridge, Mass.: Harvard University Press, 1966), 152–53.

35. Edwin H. Cady, *Stephen Crane,* rev. ed. (Boston: Twayne, 1980), 151.

36. Christopher Benfey makes this point in his analysis of "Stephen Crane's

Own Story" and "The Open Boat," in *The Double Life of Stephen Crane* (New York: Knopf, 1992), 189–98. I have also benefited greatly from Phyllis Frus's analyses of these two works: "Two Tales 'Intended to Be After the Fact,'" in Chris Anderson, ed., *Literary Nonfiction: Theory, Criticism, Pedagogy* (Carbondale: Southern Illinois University Press, 1989), 125–51; and Frus, *The Politics and Poetics of Journalistic Narrative* (New York: Cambridge University Press, 1994), 13–52.

5. *After* The Red Badge: *War Journalism*

1. Stanley Wertheim and Paul Sorrentino, eds., *The Correspondence of Stephen Crane*, vol. 1(New York: Columbia University Press, 1988), 294–96, 302.

2. Joseph Conrad, "Introduction," in Thomas Beer, *Stephen Crane: A Study in American Letters* (New York: Knopf, 1923), 32.

3. Ibid., 32–33.

4. H. G. Wells, "Stephen Crane: From an English Standpoint," *North American Review* 171 (1900), reprinted in Richard M. Weatherford, ed., *Stephen Crane: The Critical Heritage* (London: Routledge & Kegan Paul, 1973), 270–71. For a recent retelling of the Wellsian narrative of Crane's life see Philip Gerard Holthaus, "Preface," in Stanley Wertheim and Paul Sorrentino, *The Crane Log: A Documentary Life of Stephen Crane, 1871–1900* (New York: G. K. Hall, 1994), ix.

5. For example, James B. Colvert writes, "The value . . . of the war correspondence is that it confirms our understanding of that long metaphor of man in face of ultimate crisis which his fiction brilliantly elaborates" ("Introduction," in *Reports of War*, vol. 9 of *The Works of Stephen Crane*, ed. Fredson Bowers [Charlottesville: University Press of Virginia, 1971], xxix).

6. Stephen Crane, "The Red Badge of Courage Was His Wig-Wag Flag," *New York World*, July 1, 1898, p. 3.

7. John Berryman, *Stephen Crane: A Critical Biography*, rev. ed. (New York: Farrar, Straus, & Giroux, 1962), 297–325; Christopher Benfey, *The Double Life of Stephen Crane* (New York: Knopf, 1992).

8. Philip Rahv, "The Cult of Experience in American Writing," *Essays on Literature and Politics, 1932–1972* (Boston: Houghton Mifflin, 1978), 21.

9. T. J. Jackson Lears, *No Place of Grace: Antimodernism and the Transformation of American Culture, 1880–1920* (New York: Pantheon, 1981), 123, 124. See also John Higham, "The Reorientation of American Culture in the 1890s," *Writing American History: Essays on Modern Scholarship* (Bloomington: Indiana University Press, 1970), 73–102.

10. Lears, *No Place of Grace*, 98.

11. Carl Sandburg, *Always the Young Strangers* (New York: Harcourt, Brace, 1952), 409.

12. James D. Hart, *The Popular Book: A History of America's Literary Taste* (Berkeley: University of California Press, 1963), 151–52.

13. Conrad, "Introduction," 11.

14. Arthur Waugh, quoted in Wertheim and Sorrentino, *Crane Log*, 247.

15. On the history of war correspondence see Philip Knightley, *The First Casualty* (New York: Harcourt Brace Jovanovich, 1975).

16. Richard Clogg, *A Short History of Modern Greece* (Cambridge, England: Cambridge University Press, 1979), 93–94. See also R. W. Stallman and E. R. Hagemann, eds., *The War Dispatches of Stephen Crane* (New York: New York University Press, 1964), 3–11.

17. Wertheim and Sorrentino, *Correspondence of Stephen Crane*, 1:281.

18. Robert H. Davis, "Introduction," *Tales of Two Wars*, vol. 2 of *The Work of Stephen Crane* (New York: Knopf, 1925), xiv.

19. Stephen Crane, "An Impression of the 'Concert,'" *Reports of War*, 7, 11. Subsequent quotations from this article are cited parenthetically. Although I prefer to quote from the original newspaper sources, the publication history of Crane's Greco-Turkish war dispatches makes this difficult. Virtually all the dispatches received multiple publication. For instance, "An Impression of the 'Concert'" was published in the *Westminster Gazette* and syndicated by McClure, for a total of nine printings, each slightly different. Therefore, all quotations from Crane's Greco-Turkish war dispatches are taken from *Reports of War*. Editor Fredson Bowers's lengthy notes in this volume explain the dispatches' complicated textual history. All of Crane's war correspondence can also be found in Stallman and Hagemann, *War Dispatches*. Most articles I discuss are collected in Stephen Crane, *Poetry and Prose* (New York: Library of America, 1984).

20. *New-York Tribune*, May 18, 1897, p. 6.

21. Stephen Crane, *Reports of War*, 426. Notes by volume editor Fredson Bowers provide the information about the headline and portrait.

22. Stephen Crane, "Crane at Velestino," *Reports of War*, 19–20.

23. Stephen Crane, "Stephen Crane Tells of War's Horrors," *Reports of War*, 54.

24. John Bass, "How Novelist Crane Acts on the Battlefield," *New York Journal*, May 23, 1897, p. 35, reprinted in Stallman and Hagemann, *War Dispatches*, 43.

25. Stallman and Hagemann, *War Dispatches*, 10.

26. Crane, "A Fragment of Velestino," *New York Journal,* June 13, 1897, pp. 24–25.

27. Crane, "A Fragment of Velestino," *Reports of War,* 27–28. Further quotations from "A Fragment of Velestino" are cited parenthetically.

28. See, for example, Donald Pease, "Fear, Rage, and the Mistrials of Representation in *The Red Badge of Courage*," in Eric J. Sundquist, ed., *American Realism: New Essays* (Baltimore: Johns Hopkins University Press, 1982), 155–75.

29. Elaine Scarry, *The Body in Pain* (New York: Oxford University Press, 1985),

72–73. Benfey quotes Scarry in his analysis of "A Fragment of Velestino" in *Double Life of Stephen Crane*, 210–11.

30. Crane, "Crane at Velestino," *Reports of War*, 20.

31. David F. Trask, *The War with Spain in 1898* (New York: Macmillan, 1981), xiii. Numerous earlier works promoted the popular view of yellow journalism's responsibility for the war. Two works focusing on the topic are Marcus M. Wilkerson, *Public Opinion and the Spanish-American War* (Baton Rouge: Louisiana State University Press, 1932); and Joseph E. Wisan, *The Cuban Crisis as Reflected in the New York Press* (New York: Columbia University Press, 1934). Walter LaFeber anticipated Trask's dismissal of yellow journalism's influence in *The New Empire* (Ithaca, N.Y.: Cornell University Press, 1963), 401.

32. On Spanish-American War correspondents see Charles H. Brown, *The Correspondents' War* (New York: Scribner's, 1967); and Joyce Milton, *The Yellow Kids: Foreign Correspondents in the Heyday of Yellow Journalism* (New York: Harper & Row, 1989).

33. Richard Harding Davis, "Our War Correspondents in Cuba and Puerto Rico," *Harper's New Monthly Magazine* 98 (1899): 941. See also Scott C. Osborn, "The 'Rivalry-Chivalry' of Richard Harding Davis and Stephen Crane," *American Literature* 28 (1956): 50–61.

34. Milton, *Yellow Kids*, xiv. See also Gerald F. Linderman, *The Mirror of War: American Society and the Spanish-American War* (Ann Arbor: University of Michigan Press, 1974), 148–73.

35. Wertheim and Sorrentino, *Correspondence of Stephen Crane*, 2: 364.

36. Roosevelt praises Davis in *The Rough Riders* (New York: Scribner's, 1899), 90–91. *New York Journal* reporter James Creelman gives his account of leading a charge in *On the Great Highway: The Wanderings and Adventures of a Special Correspondent* (Boston: Lothrop, 1901), 203–209. Crane's *World* colleague Sylvester Scovel is treated at length in Milton, *Yellow Kids*, 306–308, 322.

37. Stephen Crane, "The Terrible Captain of the Captured Panama," *New York World*, April 28, 1898, p. 3.

38. Stephen Crane, "Inaction Deteriorates the Key West Fleet," *New York World*, May 6, 1898, p. 3.

39. Stephen Crane, "In the First Land Fight Four of Our Men Are Killed," *New York World*, June 13, 1898, p. 1.

40. F. H. Nichols, "Mutilation of Our Marines," *New York World*, June 15, 1898, p. 1.

41. Stephen Crane, "Only Mutilated by Bullets," *Reports of War*, 131.

42. Trask, *War with Spain*, 190.

43. Walter Millis, *The Martial Spirit* (New York: Houghton Mifflin, 1931), 151–60; Trask, *War with Spain*, 145–62; Linderman, *Mirror of War*, 60–72.

44. "Rough Riders Will Play Polo in Cuba," *New York World*, June 7, 1878, p. 3; "How the Rough Rider Looks in His Uniform," *New York World*, June 7, 1898, p. 4.

45. "John Jacob Astor, Richest Soldier in the U.S. Army," *New York World Sunday Magazine*, June 12, 1898, n.p.

46. "Young 'Ham' Fish Died Like a Hero," *New York World*, June 26, 1898, p. 2. See also "Hamilton Fish, Jr. Was Big, Brave and Well-Liked," *New York World*, June 25, 1898, p. 1; and Harriet Hubbard Ayer, "Hero Hamilton Fish Through His Mother's Eyes," *New York World*, July 3, 1898, p. 17.

47. Stephen Crane, "Roosevelt's Rough Riders' Loss Due to a Gallant Blunder," *New York World*, June 26, 1898, p. 2.

48. Crane, "Stephen Crane at the Front for the World," *New York World*, July 7, 1898, p. 8.

49. Roosevelt, *Rough Riders*, 107–108; Richard Harding Davis, *The Cuban and Porto Rican Campaigns* (New York: Scribner's, 1898), 132–34.

50. Stephen Crane, "Hunger Has Made Cubans Fatalists," *New York World*, July 12, 1898, p. 4.

51. Stephen Crane, "Regulars Get No Glory," *New York World*, July 20, 1898, p. 6.

52. Stephen Crane, "Marines Signaling Under Fire at Guantanamo," *McClure's*, February 1899, pp. 332–36.

53. Wertheim and Sorrentino, *Correspondence of Stephen Crane*, 2: 438–39.

54. Stephen Crane, "The Price of the Harness," *Wounds in the Rain* (New York: Frederick A. Stokes, 1900), 2–3. Subsequent quotations are cited parenthetically.

55. Susan Jeffords, *The Remasculinization of America: Gender and the Vietnam War* (Bloomington: Indiana University Press, 1989), 13.

56. James B. Colvert, "Stephen Crane: Style as Invention," in Joseph Katz, ed., *Stephen Crane in Transition: Centenary Essays* (DeKalb: Northern Illinois University Press, 1972), 150.

57. Crane, "Stephen Crane at the Front."

58. Davis, "Our War Correspondents," 942. See Wertheim and Sorrentino, *Correspondence of Stephen Crane*, for three letters from marines remarking on Crane's coolness under fire (2:426, 478, 563). See also an unpublished letter from *New York Herald* correspondent E. W. McCready to B. J. R. Stolper, January 22, 1934, Columbia University Library.

59. Stephen Crane, "Stephen Crane's Vivid Story of the Battle of San Juan," *New York World*, July 14, 1898, p. 3.

60. Finley Peter Dunne, quoted in Oliver Jensen, ed., *The Nineties* (New York: American Heritage, 1967), 108.

61. Stephen Crane, "The Open Boat," *Scribner's*, June 1897, pp. 730–31.

62. Amy Kaplan, "Black and Blue on San Juan Hill," in Amy Kaplan and Donald Pease, eds., *Cultures of United States Imperialism*, (Durham, N.C.: Duke University Press, 1993), 225.

63. Linderman, *Mirror of War*, 114–47.

64. Ibid., 132.

65. Roosevelt, *Rough Riders*, 75.

66. Frank Freidel, *The Splendid Little War* (Boston: Little, Brown, 1958), 94–95.

67. Crane, "Hunger Has Made Cubans Fatalists."

68. Crane, "The Red Badge of Courage Was His Wig-Wag Flag."

69. Crane, "Hunger Has Made Cubans Fatalists."

70. Linderman, *Mirror of War*, 141.

71. Stephen Crane, "The Mexican Lower Classes," *Tales, Sketches, and Reports*, vol. 8 of *The Works of Stephen Crane*, ed. Fredson Bowers (Charlottesville: University Press of Virginia, 1973), 436.

72. Edward Said, *Culture and Imperialism* (New York: Knopf, 1993), xviii.

73. Josiah Strong, *Our Country* (1885; Cambridge, Mass.: Harvard University Press, 1963), 213–14.

74. Linderman, *Mirror of War*, 119–27.

75. George Bronson Rea, "San Juan, Spain's Strongest Outpost, Taken by Assault," *New York World*, July 3, 1898, p. 3.

76. Roosevelt, *Rough Riders*, 47. See Thomas G. Dyer, *Theodore Roosevelt and the Idea of Race* (Baton Rouge: Louisiana State University Press, 1980).

77. William B. Gatewood Jr., *Black Americans and the White Man's Burden, 1898–1903* (Urbana: University of Illinois Press, 1975), 58–59; Gatewood, *"Smoked Yankees" and the Struggle for Empire* (Urbana: University of Illinois Press, 1971), 41–46.

78. Roosevelt, *Rough Riders*, 146.

79. Ibid., 71.

80. Stephen Crane, "Crane Tells the Story of the Disembarkment," *New York World*, July 7, 1898, p. 8.

81. Gatewood, *"Smoked Yankees"*, 69–70, 92–97, 201.

82. Stephen Crane, "Grand Rapids and Ponce," *New York Journal*, August 17, 1898, p. 4.

83. Stephen Crane, "The Porto Rican 'Straddle,'" *New York Journal*, August 18, 1898, p. 3; Stephen Crane, "A Soldier's Burial That Made a Native Holiday," *New York Journal*, August 15, 1898, p. 2.

84. Wertheim and Sorrentino, *Correspondence of Stephen Crane*, 2:356.

85. Ibid., 306.

86. Crane mentions the $20 fee in a letter to his agent; Wertheim and Sorrentino, *Correspondence of Stephen Crane*, 381.

87. Stephen Crane, "Stephen Crane's Views of Havana," *New York Journal*, September 7, 1898, p. 7; Crane, "Stephen Crane in Havana," *New York Journal*, October 9, 1898, p. 27; Crane, "Stephen Crane on Havana," *New York Journal*, November 6, 1898, p. 26; Crane, "Mr. Crane, of Havana," *New York Journal*, November 9, 1898, p. 6.

88. Wertheim and Sorrentino, *Correspondence of Stephen Crane*, 2:491, 493.

89. The only critic to have analyzed "War Memories" at length is Marston

LaFrance, who places it among Crane's finest work: *A Reading of Stephen Crane* (Oxford, England: Oxford University Press, 1971), 25, 232–38.

90. Stephen Crane, "War Memories," *Wounds in the Rain* (New York: Frederick A. Stokes, 1900), 229, 248. Subsequent quotations, cited parenthetically, are taken from this text. I use the *Wounds in the Rain* version of "War Memories" because the version published in the *Anglo-Saxon Review* was heavily cut.

91. Wertheim and Sorrentino, *Crane Log*, 361.

92. Davis, *Cuban and Porto Rican Campaigns*, 360.

93. Ernest Hemingway, *Death in the Afternoon* (New York: Scribner's, 1932), 2. Hemingway's tribute to Crane is in *Green Hills of Africa* (New York: Scribner's, 1935), 22.

94. Ernest Hemingway, *A Farewell to Arms* (New York: Scribner's, 1929), 185.

95. Michael Herr, *Dispatches* (1977; New York: Vintage, 1991), 187.

96. Ibid., 260.

97. Philip Biedler, *American Literature and the Experience of Vietnam* (Athens: University of Georgia Press, 1982), 142.

98. John Carlos Rowe, "Eye-Witness: Documentary Styles in the Representation of Vietnam." *Cultural Critique* 3 (1986): 126–50.

99. Kaplan, "Black and Blue," 225–35.

100. Quoted by Melvin Schoberlin in "Flagon of Despair: Stephen Crane," an unpublished biography of Crane, Syracuse University Library.

101. See Ronald Weber, "Journalism, Writing, and American Literature," Occasional Paper no. 5, Gannett Center for Media Studies, New York, 1987.

6. Journalism and the Making of Modern American Literature: Theodore Dreiser and Ernest Hemingway

1. [Theodore Dreiser] "Literary Notes," *Ev'ry Month*, May 1896, p. 12, reprinted in Donald Pizer, ed., *A Selection of Uncollected Prose* (Detroit: Wayne State University Press, 1977), 58.

2. Dreiser's "Curious Shifts of the Poor" (1899) is modeled in part on Crane's "The Men in the Storm" (1894), and Dreiser's piece contains one direct, although brief, instance of plagiarism. See Ellen Moers's discussion of "Curious Shifts" and "Men in the Storm" in *Two Dreisers* (New York: Viking, 1969), 57–69.

3. Dreiser describes his use of the Gillette case in "I Find the Real American Tragedy," *Mystery Magazine*, February 1935, reprinted in *Uncollected Prose*, 291–99. The most extensive analysis of the Gillette case and *An American Tragedy* is found in Donald Pizer, *The Novels of Theodore Dreiser* (Minneapolis: University of Minnesota Press, 1976), 203–27.

4. Ernest Hemingway, *The Green Hills of Africa* (New York: Scribner's, 1935), 22.

5. For information on Hemingway's life to 1925 (the end point of my analysis) I have relied on Carlos Baker, *Ernest Hemingway: A Life Story* (New York: Scribner's, 1969); William Burrill, *Hemingway: The Toronto Years* (Toronto: Doubleday Canada, 1994); Peter Griffin, *Along with Youth: Hemingway, the Early Years* (New York: Oxford University Press, 1985), and *Less Than a Treason: Hemingway in Paris* (New York: Oxford University Press, 1990); Kenneth S. Lynn, *Hemingway* (New York: Simon & Schuster, 1987); and Michael Reynolds, *The Young Hemingway* (New York: Basil Blackwell, 1986), and *Hemingway: The Paris Years* (New York: Basil Blackwell, 1989).

6. Burrill, *Hemingway: The Toronto Years*, 2.

7. Theodore Dreiser, *Newspaper Days* (New York: Horace Liveright, 1931), 65. *Newspaper Days* was originally published in 1922 as *A Book About Myself.* Dreiser's original manuscript of *Newspaper Days* has been published by the University of Pennsylvania Press (1991), but throughout this chapter I have relied on the more widely available 1931 Liveright edition.

8. Charles A. Fenton, *The Apprenticeship of Ernest Hemingway* (New York: Farrar, Straus & Young, 1954), 31.

9. Alfred Kazin, "Introduction," *The Red Badge of Courage* (New York: Bantam, 1983), x.

10. For biographical information on Dreiser I have relied on Dreiser's *Newspaper Days* and *Dawn* (New York: Horace Liveright, 1931); Richard Lingeman, *Theodore Dreiser: At the Gates of the City, 1871–1907* (New York: Putnam's, 1986), and *Theodore Dreiser: An American Journey, 1908–1945* (New York: Putnam's, 1990); and W. A. Swanberg, *Dreiser* (New York: Bantam, 1966).

11. Dreiser, *Newspaper Days*, 4.

12. Ibid., 47, 63.

13. [Theodore Dreiser] "Cleveland and Gray the Ticket," *Chicago Globe*, June 21 1892, p. 1, reprinted in Theodore Dreiser, *Journalism*, vol. 1, ed. T. D. Nostwich (Philadelphia: University of Pennsylvania Press, 1988), 3–4. Dreiser writes about his coverage of the convention in *Newspaper Days*, 47–63.

14. [Theodore Dreiser] "Cheyenne, Haunt of Misery and Crime," *Chicago Globe*, July 24, 1892, p. 3, reprinted in Dreiser, *Journalism*, 1:4, 7.

15. [Theodore Dreiser] "Hospital Violet Day," *Pittsburg Dispatch*, May 12, 1894, p. 2, reprinted in Dreiser, *Journalism*, 1:288.

16. Shelley Fisher Fishkin, *From Fact to Fiction: Journalism and Imaginative Writing in America* (Baltimore: Johns Hopkins University Press, 1985), 99. See also the biographies by Lingeman and Swanberg; Pizer, *Novels of Theodore Dreiser*; and Nostwich, "Historical Commentary," in Dreiser, *Journalism*, 1:335–45.

17. Dreiser, "Lessons I Learned from an Old Man," *Your Life*, January 1938, reprinted in *Uncollected Prose*, 301. Subsequent quotations are cited parenthetically.

18. Robert H. Elias, ed., *Letters of Theodore Dreiser*, vol. 1 (Philadephia: University of Pennsylvania Press, 1959), 211. Dreiser made a similar statement in a 1911 interview; see *Uncollected Prose*, 185.

19. Dreiser, *Newspaper Days*, 140–41. See also 143–44, 147, 480, 487.

20. Dreiser, *Uncollected Prose*, 188.

21. Dreiser, *Newspaper Days*, 411; *Uncollected Prose*, 186.

22. Dreiser, *Uncollected Prose*, 186.

23. James L. West III, *A Sister Carrie Portfolio* (Charlottesville: University Press of Virginia, 1985), 47.

24. Jack Salzman, ed., *Theodore Dreiser: The Critical Reception* (New York: David Lewis, 1972), 17; see page 5 for a similar comment by another reviewer.

25. The Norton Critical Edition of *Sister Carrie* includes several articles from Chicago newspapers on Emma Dreiser and Hopkins: Theodore Dreiser, *Sister Carrie*, 2d ed. (New York: Norton, 1991), 388–93. All quotations from *Sister Carrie* are taken from this edition and are cited parenthetically.

26. "Did He Blow Out the Gas?" *New York World*, February 16, 1895, p. 3, reprinted in Dreiser, *Journalism*, 1:333.

27. Lingeman, *At the Gates of the City*, 241.

28. The University of Pennsylvania edition of *Sister Carrie* (Philadelphia, 1981) is based on the original manuscript. That edition's "Historical Notes," compared against the 1900 edition of the novel, provide a convenient guide to many of the proper names that were cut from the manuscript.

29. West, *Sister Carrie Portfolio*, 11–12. Dreiser describes his admiration for Ade in *Newspaper Days*, 1.

30. Salzman, *Critical Reception*, 13.

31. West, *Sister Carrie Portfolio*, 84.

32. The Norton Critical Edition of *Sister Carrie* reprints Dreiser's *Toledo Blade* articles as well as the relevant section from *Newspaper Days* (427–33).

33. Philip Fisher, *Hard Facts: Setting and Form in the American Novel* (New York: Oxford University Press, 1987), 175–78; Amy Kaplan, *The Social Construction of American Realism* (Chicago: University of Chicago Press, 1988), 151–60.

34. Theodore Dreiser, "Curious Shifts of the Poor," *Demorest's*, November 1899, pp. 22–26. The article is reprinted in the Norton Critical Edition of *Sister Carrie*, 415–23.

35. Moers, *Two Dreisers*, 3–14, 57–69.

36. West, *Sister Carrie Portfolio*, 26. Years later, as if to remind readers of his journalism's reliance on other journalism, Dreiser reprinted the "Curious Shifts" vignette based on Stephen Crane's article in his collection *The Color of a Great City* (New York: Boni & Liveright, 1923); this time he used Crane's title, "The Men in the Storm."

37. Robert Penn Warren, *Homage to Theodore Dreiser* (New York: Random House, 1971), 74.

38. Swanberg, *Dreiser*, 377.

39. Detailed summaries of the Chester Gillette case can be found in Pizer, *Novels of Theodore Dreiser*, 203–27; and Richard Lehan, *Theodore Dreiser: His*

World and His Novels (Carbondale: Southern Illinois University Press, 1969), 146–49.

40. Kathryn M. Plank, "Dreiser's Real American Tragedy," *Papers in Language and Literature* 27 (1991): 286.

41. My analysis of *An American Tragedy* builds on that of Thomas Strychacz, *Modernism, Mass Culture, and Professionalism* (New York: Cambridge University Press, 1993), 84–116.

42. Fishkin, *From Fact to Fiction*, 112–34; Pizer, *Novels of Theodore Dreiser*, 203–89; Plank, "Dreiser's Real American Tragedy." Strychacz's analysis of the Gillette case and *An American Tragedy* is an exception; see *Modernism, Mass Culture, and Professionalism*, 84–116.

43. Theodore Dreiser, *An American Tragedy* (1925; Cleveland: World Publishing, 1948), 868. Subsequent quotations are cited parenthetically.

44. Pizer, *Novels of Theodore Dreiser*, 227.

45. Fenton, *Apprenticeship*, 29.

46. Michael Emery and Edwin Emery, *The Press and America: An Interpretive History of the Mass Media*, 7th ed. (Englewood Cliffs, N.J.: Prentice Hall, 1992), 165–66.

47. Fenton, *Apprenticeship*, 31, 33.

48. "Back to His First Field," *Kansas City Times*, November 26, 1940, pp. 1–2, reprinted in Matthew J. Bruccoli, ed., *Conversations with Ernest Hemingway* (Jackson: University of Mississippi, 1986), 21.

49. Fenton quoted in Ronald Weber, *Hemingway's Art of Nonfiction* (New York: St. Martin's, 1990), 6.

50. Jackson J. Benson's influential essay "Ernest Hemingway as Short Story Writer" (in Jackson J. Benson, ed., *The Short Stories of Ernest Hemingway: Critical Essays* [Durham, N.C.: Duke University Press, 1975], 272–310) is representative of the many essays that have stressed the importance of Hemingway's newspaper journalism. Extended analyses of Hemingway's journalism include Fishkin, *From Fact to Fiction*, 135–64; J. F. Kobler, *Ernest Hemingway: Journalist and Artist* (Ann Arbor, Mich.: UMI Research Press, 1985); and Robert O. Stephens, *Hemingway's Nonfiction: The Public Voice* (Chapel Hill: University of North Carolina Press, 1968).

51. Ernest Hemingway, *Selected Letters, 1917–1961*, ed. Carlos Baker (New York: Scribner's, 1981), 62–63.

52. Arnold Samuelson, *With Hemingway: A Year in Key West and Cuba* (New York: Random House, 1984), 176–77.

53. Matthew J. Bruccoli, *Ernest Hemingway, Cub Reporter* (Pittsburgh: University of Pittsburgh Press, 1970).

54. Fenton, *Apprenticeship*, 35.

55. The assignment sheet is reproduced as the frontispiece of *Cub Reporter*.

56. "Dr. F. B. Tiffany Near Death," *Kansas City Star*, January 3, 1918, p. 1.

57. Griffin, *Along with Youth*, 44.

58. "Only Two Breweries Left," *Kansas City Star*, January 1, 1918, p. 1.

59. [Ernest Hemingway] "Six Men Become Tankers," *Kansas City Star*, April 17, 1918, p. 7, reprinted in *Cub Reporter*, 41–44.

60. [Ernest Hemingway] "At the End of the Ambulance Run," *Kansas City Star*, January 20, 1918, p. 7C, reprinted in *Cub Reporter*, 27–33.

61. Bruccoli, *Cub Reporter*, 27; Griffin, *Along with Youth*, 47.

62. Griffin includes several of these early unpublished short stories in *Along with Youth*.

63. Burrill, *Toronto Years*, 41.

64. Griffin, *Along with Youth*, 69.

65. Ernest Hemingway, "Taking a Chance for a Free Shave," *Toronto Star Weekly*, March 6, 1920, reprinted in Ernest Hemingway, *Dateline: Toronto*, ed. William White (New York: Scribner's, 1985), 6.

66. Ernest Hemingway, "Wild Night Music of Paris Makes Visitor Feel a Man of the World," *Toronto Star Weekly*, March 25, 1922, reprinted in Hemingway, *Dateline: Toronto*, 118.

67. [Ernest Hemingway] "Are You All Set for the Trout?," *Toronto Star Weekly*, April 10, 1920, reprinted in Hemingway, *Dateline: Toronto*, 16.

68. Ernest Hemingway, "There Are Great Fish in the Rhône Canal," *Toronto Daily Star*, June 10, 1922, reprinted in Hemingway, *Dateline: Toronto*, 169.

69. Gertrude Stein, *The Autobiography of Alice B. Toklas* (New York: Harcourt, Brace, 1933), 265.

70. In addition to "The Rhône Canal," other 1922 *Toronto Star* feature articles that display the mature Hemingway style include "Tuna Fishing in Spain," "Try Bobsledding If You Want Thrills," and "A Paris-to-Strasbourgh Flight," all reprinted in Hemingway, *Dateline: Toronto*.

71. Louis Henry Cohn, *A Bibliography of the Works of Ernest Hemingway* (New York: Random House, 1931), 112.

72. Fishkin, *From Fact to Fiction*, 148.

73. Ernest Hemingway, "King Business in Europe Isn't What It Used to Be," *Toronto Star Weekly*, September 15, 1923, reprinted in Hemingway, *Dateline: Toronto*, 295–300.

74. Fenton, *Apprenticeship*, 45.

75. Ernest Hemingway, *in our time* (Paris: Three Mountains Press, 1924), 17. Subsequent quotations are cited parenthetically.

76. Michael S. Reynolds, "Two Hemingway Sources for *in our time*," in Michael S. Reynolds, ed., *Critical Essays on Ernest Hemingway's In Our Time* (Boston: G. K. Hall, 1983), 34–35.

77. Fenton, *Apprenticeship*, 45.

78. E. R. Hagemann, "'Only Let the Story End as Soon as Possible': Time-and-History in Ernest Hemingway's *In Our Time*," in Reynolds, *Critical Essays*, 55, 59.

79. Reynolds, "Two Hemingway Sources," 31–33.

80. On the Greco-Turkish conflict of 1920–1922 see Richard Clogg, *A Short*

History of Modern Greece (Cambridge, England: Cambridge University Press, 1979), 112–20; and Jeffrey Meyers, "Hemingway's Second War: The Greco-Turkish Conflict, 1920–1922," *Modern Fiction Studies* 30 (1984): 25–36.

81. Ernest Hemingway, "A Silent, Ghastly Procession Wends Way from Thrace," *Toronto Daily Star*, October 18, 1922, reprinted in Hemingway, *Dateline: Toronto*, 232.

82. Fenton, *Apprenticeship*, 229–36.

83. The quotation is from Fishkin, *From Fact to Fiction*, who analyzes the Adrianople dispatch and the *in our time* chapter on pp. 150–51. Other critics who compare the two works include Keith Carabine, "Hemingway's *in our time*: An Appreciation," in Matthew J. Bruccoli and Richard Layman, eds., *Fitzgerald/Hemingway Annual 1979* (Detroit: Gale, 1980), 308–10; Phyllis Frus, *The Politics and Poetics of Journalistic Narrative* (New York: Cambridge University Press, 1994), 60–62; Kobler, *Hemingway: Journalist and Artist*, 9–16; Meyers, "Hemingway's Second War," 30–31; and Elizabeth Dewberry Vaughn, "'Truer Than Anything True': *In Our Time* and Journalism," *Hemingway Review* 11 (1992): 11–18.

84. Like "realism," "objectivity" is one of those words that mean nothing without quotes. Still, both are useful shorthand terms. Numerous writers have shown that journalistic objectivity is not actually an inherent property of texts but rather a journalistic practice and an ideological construction; see Michael Schudson, *Discovering the News: A Social History of American Newspapers* (New York: Basic Books, 1978), 121–59.

85. Hemingway, *Dateline: Toronto*, 232.

86. *Kansas City Star*, December 20, 1924, p. 6, reprinted in Robert O. Stephens, ed., *Ernest Hemingway: The Critical Reception* (New York: Burt Franklin, 1977), 3.

87. Lincoln Steffens, *The Autobiography of Lincoln Steffens* (New York: Harcourt, Brace, 1931), 834.

88. Burrill, *Toronto Years*, 139.

89. Baker, *Hemingway*, 151.

90. Fenton, *Apprenticeship*, 262

91. In addition to Weber's *Hemingway's Art of Nonfiction*, see his "Journalism, Writing, and American Literature," Occasional Paper No. 5, Gannett Center for Media Studies, New York, 1987.

92. D. H. Lawrence, *Studies in Classic American Literature* (1923; New York: Penguin, 1977), 8.

93. Fenton, *Apprenticeship*, 37–38.

94. Michael Robertson, "The Reporter as Novelist: The Case of William Kennedy," *Columbia Journalism Review*, January–February 1986, p. 49.

95. Tom Wolfe, *The New Journalism* (New York: Harper & Row, 1973), 3–52. Thomas B. Connery's "Introduction" to *A Sourcebook of American Literary Journalism* (Westport, Conn.: Greenwood, 1992) provides both a history of American literary journalism and a survey of critical discussion on the topic.

BIBLIOGRAPHIC NOTE

Whenever possible, I have used the original newspaper or magazine publication of Stephen Crane's journalism as my source. Fortunately, readers need not do the same. All of Crane's journalism has been collected in volumes 8 (*Tales, Sketches, and Reports*) and 9 (*Reports of War*) of *The Works of Stephen Crane*, ed. Fredson Bowers (Charlottesville: University Press of Virginia, 1973 and 1971).

Almost all the journalism is available in two collections edited by R. W. Stallman and E. R. Hagemann: *The New York City Sketches of Stephen Crane and Related Pieces* (New York: New York University Press, 1966); and *The War Dispatches of Stephen Crane* (New York: New York University Press, 1964).

Many works I discuss are reprinted in the widely available one-volume Library of America edition of Stephen Crane, *Prose and Poetry* (New York: Library of America, 1984).

INDEX